THE MARBLE THRESHING FLOOR

By the same Author

ORIENTATION AND DESCENT (POEMS)

(The Saville Press)

PHILIP SHERRARD

The Marble Threshing Floor

Studies in Modern Greek Poetry

Χάροντα, ἆς παλαίψουμε ἐσ μαρμαρένιο ἀλῶνι . . . .
GREEK FOLK-SONG

London : VALLENTINE, MITCHELL

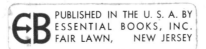
PUBLISHED IN THE U. S. A. BY
ESSENTIAL BOOKS, INC.
FAIR LAWN, NEW JERSEY

First published in 1956 by Vallentine, Mitchell & Co. Ltd.
37, Furnival Street, London, E.C.4

Set in 10 on 12 point Linotype Caledonia and machined in
Great Britain by Vallentine, Mitchell & Co. Ltd.

iv

Preface

THE Greek War of Independence broke out in 1821. Since that date, the vitality of Greece has manifested itself in many ways. But perhaps nothing has been so striking as the growth and fecundity of her intellectual life. And here pride of place goes to the poets and to poetry. From the turn of the eighteenth century, when the prospect of an independent Greece became more than an improbable dream, down to the present day, the voice of poetry has not been silent. With a fresh, unexplored language, and with the living stream of a demotic tradition on which to draw, poet has succeeded poet with an insistence that is astonishing. A great deal of this poetry is of course ephemeral, and no doubt deserves the forgetfulness which it receives. Yet, even so, much withstands the test of time. In any case, without a wealth and diversity of minor poets, a country is unlikely to produce major poets. Whether the five poets with whom I am concerned in this study are major or minor is a question that need not be answered here. They are, however, important poets. First of all, they are poets representative of Greece. The years over which they write are coterminous with the existence of their revived nation. The problems with which they wrestle, the imaginative patterns which their poetry reveals, are those that lie at the roots of the life of the Greek people. They are also those of the life of all people. In this study, I seek to analyse these problems and patterns. I am concerned, that is, with the ideas of the poetry, rather than with questions of style or biography, source or influence. At the same time, I am aware that ideas are not the same thing as poetry. Content in itself is not the measure of the value of a poem. There is danger that, through such analysis as I have attempted, the poetry is lost. Nevertheless, I believe, as I try to make clear in the text, that the method I have adopted is the appropriate one. I hope at least it may contribute towards an understanding of the poetry which is discussed.

Many have helped, directly or indirectly, in the writing of

this book. I cannot mention them all. But there are, first, Greek men of letters that I have been fortunate enough to know. Their friendship has meant a great deal. The works of two of them, the late Anghelos Sikelianos and Mr. George Seferis, are the subject of two of the studies which follow. Mr. George Katsimbalis, Mr. Zisimos Lorenzatos, Mr. Nikos Gatsos have in different ways put me in their debt. Then, what I owe to certain other writers, such as Plato or Ananda K. Coomaraswamy, will be obvious to all who know their works. Finally, I would like to thank Professor Romilly Jenkins for persevering support over several years. Needless to say, the inadequacies of the book are entirely my own responsibility.

PHILIP SHERRARD.

Athens, November, 1955.

Acknowledgments

Acknowledgments are due to Mr. George Seferis for permission to quote from his works ; to Mrs. Anna Sikelianos, Mr. Leander Palamas, and the Hogarth Press Limited, publishers of " The Poems of C. P. Cafavy," translated into English by John Mavrogordato, for permission to quote in the author's own translation from the works of Anghelos Sikelianos, Costis Palamas, and Constantine Cavafis respectively.

Contents

To
F.R.G.N.S.
and
S.M.S.

I. Dionysios Solomos

(1798-1857)

IN the space of a few years, the small island of Zante, one of
the Ionian group recently so ravaged by earthq'ake, produced
three notable poets: Ugo Foscolo, Andreis Kalvos, and,
youngest of the three and subject of this present study, Dionysios
Solomos. All three were born on Zante. All three left the island
early in life and travelled abroad. All three had as their first
language and wrote their first poems in Italian. One, Ugo Foscolo,
wrote in Italian only, and so is lost from the literature of Greece.
Kalvos and Foscolo were friends over a number of years.
Solomos, in spite of the fact that he lived for some time on the
same island, Corfu, as Kalvos, never, as far as is known, met
either of his fellow-countrymen and fellow-poets, although he
composed and spoke a long funeral oration on the death of
Foscolo.

Dionysios Solomos was born in 1798, twenty years after
Foscolo and six after Kalvos. His father's family had come
originally from Crete, and was now one of the aristocratic
families of Zante, wealthy enough to ensure the poet's economic
independence throughout his life. His mother was a woman from
the people. Solomos' parentage betokens his future poetry, that
fusion, as the poetry of Dante to which he was so greatly devoted,
of an aristocratic spirit with the simplicity and freshness of his
mother tongue, the demotic Greek language; and, although it
is a theme which lies outside the scope of this study, it is worth
while to remark in passing that Solomos' choice of the people's
language for his poetry was to have a significance for modern
Greek poetry comparable to that which a similar choice by
Dante had for Italian poetry. But to return: Solomos spent the
first ten years of his life on his native island. At the age of ten,
however, he was sent, as was customary for children of his rank,
to Italy for his education, first at Venice, then at Cremona, and

1

finally at the University of Padua. At the latter, he gained a law degree, given to him, as he said, out of kindness of heart by his professors. But whether or not he deserved reward as a student of law, there was already no doubt about his poetic gifts, evident as they were then only in Latin and in Italian. It was the quality of his first poetic exercises in these languages, for instance, that drew from his teacher the remark: " Greco, tu farai dimenticare il nostro Monti."[1]

In 1818, the twenty-year-old Solomos returned to Zante after an absence of ten years. There, on his native island, he was to pass the next ten years of his life, and there, mastering his mother tongue, and slowly discovering through contact with the living stream of the Greek demotic tradition and with the rich springs of the Cretan poetry of the sixteenth and seventeenth centuries, the sources of his own creative spirit, he wrote what may fittingly be called his early poetry. Apart from two long poems, " The Hymn to Liberty " and " Ode on the Death of Lord Byron," of which I do not propose to speak here, and one other long work, which I shall discuss, the great part of this early poetry is made up of a series of short lyrics. It must at once be confessed that these lyrics are not altogether encouraging. They are in the main devoted to singing, in a conventional and sentimental way, the praises of virgins, of virginity, and of those who die young and innocent. Among the first lines that he wrote in Greek, for instance, is a song addressed to a girl brought up in a convent:

> *My beautiful convent girl, I am here and I wait;*
> *Come to the grill to see how I am singing.*
> *For you my verse goes sweetly from my heart :*
> *May the wall let it pass and not be jealous.*
> *Try to flee if you can; come, so I may kiss you.*
> *Only with a kiss shall I put out my flame.*
> *My beautiful convent girl, come here, and think*
> *That I will not, my innocent one, deflower you.*

[47][2]

The theme is slightly varied in another early poem, "The Dream."

[1] Polylas, J.: Introduction to: Dionysios Solomos, The Complete Works, Vol. 1, ed. with notes, etc., by L. Politis, Athens, 1948, p. 11.

[2] All quotations from Solomos' poetry are from: Dionysios Solomos, The Complete Works, *op. cit.* The figure in brackets after quotations from

The poet dreams that one night he was with his beloved He asks the stars if ever they saw anything so beautiful:

> *Say if you ever saw*
> *On another such lovely hair,*
> *Such a hand, or such a foot,*
> *Such an angelic look.*

[51]

As he speaks to the stars, other women appear, adorned with the moon's light. They dance hand in hand round the dreamer and try to capture his heart. One may assume that these are ordinary common ladies. His beloved asks him how he likes them. He replies that they are very ugly. The poem continues with the dreamer embracing his beloved, whom he sees as a rose and whose every kiss is the planting of a new rose, and the whole thing ends:

> *This is the dream, beloved;*
> *Now it depends on you*
> *To turn it into truth*
> *And to remember me.*

[53]

In another of these early lyrics, " The Poisoned Girl " [139], Solomos comes to the defence of a young girl who has committed suicide. Rumour had it that the reason for her suicide was her disappointment in a love-affair in which she had been " dishonoured." In Solomos' poem, the girl comes before her Maker on the Day of Judgment, and calls upon Him to witness to her innocence. Finally, written a little later, but belonging to this group, is a poem in which these sentiments are expressed more directly and with more emphasis. The poem is called " To a Nun." It was written on the occasion of a young girl's entry into a convent. As she goes into the church, angels descend to see who approaches. On discovering that it is one who is about to take the veil and become the bride of Christ, they sing to

or references to individual poems or notes on individual poems, gives the number of the page of the above work on which the original Greek text will be found.

3

her, contrasting the world she is now entering with the storm
and turmoil of that she is leaving behind:

> *Sweet it is to meditate*
> *Paradise's beauty;*
> *Bitter is the terrible*
> *Whirlwind of the world;*
> *Only the echo comes here,*
> *The tempest does not come.*
>
> *Here does Christ descend*
> *Down to you in dreams;*
> *There arms shake*
> *And blood-stained thrones;*
> *Here is joy and triumph,*
> *There is wretchedness.*

[146]

The reason for quoting from these early lyrics, which in
themselves have little value, is that in them is beginning to
appear, in however fragile and sentimental a way, the outline
of a contrast between a state of goodness and innocence on the
one hand, and a world of evil and corruption on the other;
and this contrast is something which continues, with modifications, through all Solomos' work. In two other early pieces,
"The Woman of Zakynthos," a prose satire, and "Lambros,"
a Byronic melodrama, one aspect of this contrast, the sense of
evil and corruption in the world, and of the disgust that goes
with it, is more forcibly uttered. "The Woman of Zakynthos"
is the portrait of a woman who seems entirely vicious and evil,
the personification of all the vile and hideous aspects of human
nature. The poet describes her:

"Well, the body of the woman was small and misshapen,
and her chest almost always marked by the leeches which she
stuck on it to suck the phthisis; and lower down hung two
breasts like tobacco pouches. And this small body walked very
quickly and its joints appeared dislocated. Her face had the
shape of a shoe-last, and you could see, if you looked from the
bottom of the chin to the top of the head, on which was a round
twisted plait and, above, an enormous comb, that it was of
great length. And whoever tried to measure the woman with

4

a foot-rule would find a quarter of the body in the head. And her cheek broke out in eczema, which sometimes was liquid pus and sometimes was dried up and withered. And she opened every so often a big mouth to mock at others, and she showed her lower teeth, the front teeth, small and rotten, which met the upper teeth, which were very white and long. And although she was young, her temples and her forehead and her eyebrows and the snot of her nose were senile, always senile, but especially when she leant her head on her right fist, meditating her wickedness ; and this senile head was enlivened by two shining and jet-black eyes, and one of them squinted slightly. And they circled hither and thither, seeking evil. And they found it even where it did not exist ; and in her eyes flashed a certain something, which made you think that madness either had just left her or was on the point of possessing her. And that was the dwelling place of her wicked and sinful soul. And it revealed its wickedness both in speech and in silence. And when she spoke secretly in order to defile someone's reputation, her voice seemed like the rustling of the straw, trodden by the foot of the thief. And when she spoke aloud, her voice was like that which people use to mock at others. And in spite of that, when she was alone, she would go to the looking-glass, and, gazing, would laugh and weep, and she thought she was the most beautiful of all those in the Seven Isles. And her work was to separate husband from wife, and brother from sister, craftily, like Death. And when in sleep she saw the beautiful body of her sister, she awoke terrified. Envy, hatred, suspicion, falsehood, tugged continually at her bowels, in the same way as you see local urchins, ragged and dirty, ring the bells on the day of festival, driving everyone insane."[1]

Much ingenuity has been spent on trying to identify the female whom Solomos here describes ; she has been linked with actual historical characters in contemporary Zante, and even with the British rule of the Seven Isles. But such attempts at identification are not important, and it is enough to consider the Woman simply as a type of harridan, loose, evil-tongued, overbearing, the terror of her husband and her home. She is the equivalent of the French Margot and the English Meg,

[1] Solomos: The Woman of Zakynthos, ed. L. Politis, Athens, 1944, p. 44ff.

those mediæval viragos who, at their delight in evil, challenged even the most formidable power on earth, the Devil himself. The Elder Bruegel has given us a portrait of a similar woman in his " Dulle Griet."

This study in evil and corruption is further elaborated in "Lambros." Lambros seduced and deceived a fifteen-year-old girl, Maria. By her he had four children, all of whom he sent into an orphanage. Now Maria has lived for fifteen years unmarried in Lambros' house. The thought of her dishonour and of the unknown fate of her children weigh heavily on her ; her days are full of lament and her nights of black dream :

> It seems that I am voyaging
> In dream on the ocean's waste ;
> Alone with wave and wind
> I fight, you not being near me ;
> Nothing in my danger do I see
> But the sky wherever I look ;
> I gaze at the sky : " Help," I call,
> " Sailless, rudderless, out at sea I drift."
>
> And thus as with courage I call
> My three young lads spring up ;
> The boat's planks from their weight
> Creak as though they splinter ;
> Then inescapable death appears ;
> Huddled, together they whisper,
> And having in secret spoken
> Row on with broken oars.
>
> With bitter smile on her mouth
> My girl approaches me ;
> A shroud enfolds her body
> Blown out white by the wind ;
> But more pale is the hand
> She raises up before me,
> Which trembles, as the reed trembles,
> Revealing the cross in the palm.
>
> [161-162]

This cross Maria had made with a knife on the palm of her daughter's hand when Lambros had forced her to yield the child

6

up for him to take to the orphanage. At the same time she had put a necklet round the child's neck.

Meanwhile, Lambros has joined the Greek revolutionaries fighting the Turks, inspired by the justice of the Greek cause and by the desire to revenge the death of a holy monk, brother to Maria, whom Ali Pasha had burnt alive. In the army camp where Lambros is encouraging the men to battle, a young Turk appears, who warns the Greeks that the Turks are preparing an ambush for them. The young Turk then, struck by Lambros' kindness and moved by his protection, confides in him that she is really a girl who has left the Turks after witnessing the sacrifice of another girl, her friend ; she had watched the calm with which this girl, a Christian, had gone to her death, and she had then and there decided that she also would become a Christian. She now asks Lambros to baptise her. He, stirred by the girl's beauty and her sensitivity, falls in love with her, and eventually seduces her. He has never before experienced such passion with a woman. And it is only after the seduction that he notices on the girl's hand the cross which Maria had cut on the hand of her—and his—daughter, and round her throat the well-remembered necklet.

In the next scene, Lambros with his daughter, to whom he has confessed the whole ghastly story, is rowing on a lake one moonlit night. The daughter, sitting in the prow of the boat, unplaits her hair and lets it fall before her, so the rising moon does not behold her. Then, as Lambros is rowing, he suddenly hears a splash, and, turning, sees that his daughter has thrown herself into the lake. For a moment he hesitates: Shall he save her? Then he rows on as fast as he can for the shore of the lake, imagining that every impediment his oar meets is the body of his drowned daughter.

Guilt-stricken, Lambros now returns to his house. His appearance terrifies the already distraught Maria. At her insistence, he tells her what has happened. It is now the night of Easter Day. Lambros rushes into the church which that same morning had been the scene of rejoicing at the renewed miracle of the Resurrection and at the return of spring to earth. But for Lambros there is no Resurrection and no return of spring. The saints are as dumb and as motionless as tombs. Lambros' despair turns to defiance. Man, he cries, let fate do what she will, is his own God.

7

And he turns to leave the church. But at the first door from which he seeks to go out a voice gives him the Easter greeting: "Christ is risen." He turns to the second door. A similar voice greets him with the same words. At the third door the same. The three voices are those of his three young sons risen from the grave. They pursue Lambros through the church as he tries to flee them. They compel him to kiss their dead lips. Lambros' crimes have created his own Hell and now that Hell has risen up around him and has made him its prisoner. There is no escape except, as Lambros thinks, in death; and at dawn, when the visiting avengers return to the grave, he rushes from the church and throws himself into the same lake in which his daughter had drowned herself. And the poem concludes:

"And Lambros died with open mouth, not in the peace of God. But who will close his eyes? Where is Maria, the unfortunate Maria? She has been missing since dawn. She has been wandering over the fields by herself, and the sun's rays, which, rising, call on mortals to enjoy life, sparkle on all the still waters of the wilderness. Motionless was the centre of the lake, like the blue pupil of an eye untroubled by future cares. But at the lake's edge the scattered encircling trees were reflected faithfully in the eye. Forlorn Maria, when she had circled round about, approached the lake and seeing there the objects reflected, thought in her distraction that that was another world. She stopped short, and, raising her arms on high and smiling the smile of madness, she murmured: 'That surely will be a better world than this, and I will make ready to go thither. I shall see, maybe I shall see whether there no merciful hand reaches out to me. For on this earth I have walked so long frightened among strange people, as if I had appeared before them for the first time. Now I shall go yonder. Let me therefore adorn myself as best I can, lest new strangers there despise me.'

"So saying she stretched her thin fingers towards some wild grasses growing in the waste. Then she wove a wreath for her disconsolate head, she put round her throat the so lamented necklet,

And into the water, which she as a mirror sees,
She gazes again, and smiles, and downward falls."

[193-194]

8

This Ophelia-like death of Maria, the seduced demented girl, together with Solomos' early lyrics in praise and defence of maiden innocence and chastity and with his portrait of the obscene abandoned Woman of Zakynthos, give the impression that the poet is a kind of Hamlet-figure caught between dreams of virgin purity and disgust at that corruption of which the sexual passions seem to him the evidence, if not indeeed the root. On the one hand, there is the admonition to the innocent girl:

Get thee to a nunnery . . .

On the other hand, there is the embittered venom spat at the carnal woman:

Nay, but to live
In the rank sweat of an enseamed bed
Stew'd in corruption, honeying and making love
Over the nasty sty . . .

In a note to his "Ode on the Death of Lord Byron," Solomos, with considerable perspicacity, points out in how many ways Byron resembles Milton. In particular, "the antithesis (in 'Paradise Lost') between the first-formed beauties of Creation and the terrors of Hell made a great impression on the mind of Byron" [133]. One wonders whether it did not perhaps make a great impression also on the mind of Solomos, for, as we have seen, already in these early poems can be discerned the shadow of a myth that in many ways reflects that of Milton, not only in the antithesis it presents between the beauties of Paradise and the terrors of Hell, but also in its implied denigration of the sexual passions, of which woman is the provoker, as evil. Solomos was in addition saturated in the poetry of Dante, where, although the antithesis between Heaven and Hell is as strong as that in Milton's myth, the woman is not the temptress but is on the contrary a kind of redeemer, and it may be that the figure of Beatrice is the original of which Solomos' images of virgin purity are the somewhat etiolated copies. This contrast of the Beatrice-figure with the figure of the carnal temptress and instrument of human overthrow, the Miltonic Eve, may explain the dual aspect woman has in Solomos' early poetry. At all events, Solomos seems to have felt that underlying the appearance of things, forces of evil are at work which have the power to

9

B

destroy all that is noble in man's nature. Lambros, for example, is not a man without any redeeming features. He is able in a spirit of self-sacrifice and disinterested love to devote himself to and risk his life in the struggle for Greek freedom. And he is a man of action who can command respect and loyalty. But the blind destructive passions which flesh is heir to, drive him to inhuman and bestial crime. And, what is more, such is the damnable cunning of evil in this world, man may commit his worst offences altogether unwittingly: Lambros may have been responsible for his sin in seducing the young girl whose confidence he had won ; but it was hardly his fault that this young girl should have been his daughter. Solomos seems to have felt that in this "kingdom of Satan," man, if he is the doer of evil, is just as much the victim of evil. He is simply and hopelessly involved in a blind fate-driven world whose essential character is evil. And from this point of view, Maria also, that afflicted woman, is a portrait of the human soul caught up in the corrupt world of generation and death, and suffering the consequences of such entanglement. The young Solomos seems to have had some experience like that of the young Keats when he peered beneath the surface of nature and beheld her hidden workings:

> *But I saw*
> *Too far into the sea, where every maw*
> *The greater on the less feeds evermore.*
> *But I saw too distinct into the core*
> *Of an eternal fierce destruction,*
> *And so from happiness I far was gone . . .*[1]

Solomos too had seen this fierce destructive element and like Keats he was gone far from happiness.

But there is another note in these early poems which is more elusive. To describe it as an intimation of a mystical experience may be to beg the question, yet it is difficult to know what else to call it, especially in view of certain aspects of Solomos' later development. For now and again in these early poems occur lines which seem to refer to a kind of ecstasy, to a sudden suspension of distress and pain at the touch of an invisible hand. Sometimes this suspension of normal consciousness is indicated

---

[1] Keats: "Epistle to John Hamilton Reynolds." Oxford Edition of Standard Authors, O.U.P., 1951, p. 317.

10

by the awakening of a delicate wind. This is the case in the poem
" The Brother and Sister " and in the poem " The Mad Mother."
Both these poems are songs which the disconsolate Maria sings
in the longer poem " Lambros." In the first of these two poems,
a young boy goes out at evening to look for his sister whom he
has lost. He cannot find her anywhere. At length he reaches
a cemetery, and there, on a tomb, he sees the girl. She is dead.
The poet describes how, as she lay on the tomb, this sudden
wind rose:

Innocent butterfly,
In the burning heat
She seeks a breeze
To cool herself.

And there by chance
On a tomb she lay,
And suddenly blew
A sweet breeze.

She felt the breath
Which the air sent
And she did not know
Where she was, where.

[170]

The second song of Maria, " The Mad Mother," is about a
woman whose two children have been killed by lightning.
One night she comes to the cemetery where they are buried.
She circles round the wall of the cemetery in the darkness, groping
with her hands. Then she enters the moonlit bell-tower. The
black patches of night in the ravines seem to her like the torn
clothes of her dead children. In her distraction she tugs on the
bell-ropes. The sound of the bells clangs out over the surrounding
wilderness, while the mother weeps for her loss. Suddenly, at
the depths of her despair:

Suddenly a cooling
Breeze awakens ;
Whispering it comes
Laden with sweet
Scents of the dawn.

11

Into the mother's
Heart-depths it passes
Like the movements
Of imagination
That paint happiness. [182]

It is significant that the scene of both these episodes is the graveyard, for the graveyard is the traditional image of the place where body and soul fall apart, of the place at which the old life ends and the new life begins.

In " The Woman of Zakynthos," however, is a passage which describes an unmistakable visionary experience. The narrator of " The Woman of Zakynthos " is a monk, Dionysios (Solomos' own name). After describing, in a passage already quoted, the appearance of the Woman, he goes on to speak of the women of Missolonghi:

" It happened that in those days the Turks were besieging Missolonghi. Often all day and sometimes all night Zakynthos trembled from the great cannonade. And it was then that some women of Missolonghi went round begging for their husbands, for their children, for their brothers, who were fighting. At first they were ashamed to come out and they waited for the darkness in order to hold open their hands, because they were not used to it. And they had had servants and they had had goats on many a plain and cattle and numerous sheep. And consequently they were impatient and they looked often out of the window, to see when the sun would set, so that they could go out. But when the need became acute, they lost their shame, and went round all day. And when they were tired, they sat down on the shore and often they lifted their heads and listened, because they were frightened lest Missolonghi should fall. . . .

" And I followed the women of Missolonghi, who lay themselves down on the sea-shore; and I was behind a hedge and I watched. And each one produced whatever she had collected and they made a pile. And one of them, reaching out her hand and feeling the shore, cried: ' Sisters, hark if Missolonghi has ever shaken the earth as now. She triumphs perhaps, perhaps she falls.' And I began to go, when I saw behind the church an old woman, who had set up small candles in the grass, and she was burning incense, and the small candles shone

12

in the greenness and the incense went up. And she raised her bony hands, passing them through the incense and weeping. And opening and closing her toothless mouth she prayed. And I felt within me a great disturbance and I was carried away in spirit to Missolonghi. And I saw neither the castle, nor the camp, nor the lake, nor the sea, nor the earth I trod, nor the sky ; a pitch-black darkness covered the besieged and the besiegers and all their works and everything that there was. And I raised eyes and hands towards heaven in order to pray with all the fervour of my soul ; and I saw, lit up in the incessant flashing, a woman with a lyre in her hand, who stood in the air among the smoke. And I had just time to marvel at her dress, which was black like the blood of the hare, and her eyes . . . when she stopped, the woman, among the smoke, and she looked at the battle ; and the thousand sparks which flew into the sky touched her dress and went out. She spread her fingers on the lyre and I heard her chant :

> *At the dawn I took*
> *The road of the sun*
> *Hanging the just*
> *Lyre from the shoulder ;*
> *And from where it dawns*
> *Until where it sets . . .*

And scarcely had the goddess finished her words when she vanished, and our people shouted furiously because of the victory, and they and everything else disappeared from me, and my bowels again shook terribly, and it seemed that I had become deaf and blind. And soon I saw in front of me the old woman, who said to me : ' God be praised, Hermit, I thought that something had happened to you. I called you, I shook you, and you heard nothing and your eyes were fixed on the sky, while the earth leapt like bubbles in seething water. Now it is over, and the small candles and incense are exhausted. Would you say that our people have triumphed ? ' And I began to go, with Death in my heart ; and the old woman kissed my hand, and, kneeling down, she said : ' How frozen your hand is ! ' "[1]

" The Woman of Zakynthos " was probably written in 1827. In 1828 Solomos left Zante and went to live in Corfu. Looking

[1] Solomos : " The Woman of Zakynthos," *op. cit.*, p. 46 and p. 50ff.

13

at the work which he produced during those ten years on Zante after his return from Italy, one can begin to make out, beneath the effusion of his patriotic poems, beneath the sentimentality of his lyrics to young maidens and the Byronising of his "Lambros," the lineaments of a more solemn drama. Briefly, this drama seems to hinge on a contradiction that Solomos felt in life. On the one hand, he seems to have felt that human beings are the victims of a blind, evil, destructive force which drives them to commit acts of brutality and beastliness and sometimes corrupts their nature altogether. On the other hand, noble traits in human nature do sometimes reveal themselves and permit man or woman to triumph over the forces of corruption and to achieve a certain release by contact with some invisible power. Often this contact is only achieved at moments of great despair or of near madness, when the senses and human reason are deranged, unseated, and overthrown, and there is a kind of death. At such moments, man may feel relieved of the weight of mortality and even be granted insight into another world. The growing disgust for the "natural" world, and the definition of this disgust in such works as " The Woman of Zakynthos " and "Lambros," and at the same time, one must believe, a growing conviction that man's true life was not to be realised in this world, but in the attainment of a level of reality of which this world was the negation, seem to have compelled Solomos to make a change in his life and also a change in his work. His move to Corfu in 1828 is a fitting mark of both these changes.

As far as the change in his life was concerned, this move seems to have represented an advance to greater solitude and meditation. " It is delightful," he writes in 1830, " in the calm of one's little room to express that which the heart dictates. And only the idea of applause, when present with any force, is sufficient to disturb this delight, and very frequently urges the writer on to produce what is far from his best work. This delight must be pure."[1] And a year later he continues in the same strain : " One lives well only when one is alone. When I was a child I was always deeply impressed by the story of the lame god, whose mother hurled him down from heaven and he dwelt in the embraces of the sea ; there he worked, with no one to see him, and no sound to hear round about his cave but the murmur

[1] Cited by Jenkins, R.: Dionysius Solomos, C.U.P., 1940, pp. 129-130.

of the illimitable ocean."[1] But it is not so much the change in his life that concerns us, as the kind of work with which Solomos was to occupy himself in the coming years ; and it is about this that something must now be said.

In an introduction to an edition of Solomos' work published shortly after his death, Polylas, friend and biographer of the poet, writes: "His work in Art, as well as in conversation, was a spontaneous uninterrupted endeavour to extinguish his individuality in absolute truth "—giving effect, he adds, to the axiom of Heracleitos: "Although possessing a common Word, the majority live as though they have a wisdom of their own."[2] Side by side with this estimation, and supporting it, are several of Solomos' own remarks. While still a young man in Italy, he was present at some discussion during which Monti, the Italian poet and critic, is reported to have said: "One must not think so much, one must feel, one must feel." Solomos thereupon replied: "First the mind must conceive strongly and then the heart must feel warmly what the mind has conceived."[3] Again, in a note to his " Ode on the Death of Lord Byron " from which I have already quoted, Solomos writes: "The difficulty which an artist experiences (I speak of great artists) does not consist in showing imagination and passion, but in subordinating these two things, with time and with labour, to the intelligible meaning of Art" [133]. In another note, this time to his " Woman of Zakynthos," he writes: "E la forma sia l'abito del vero senso profondo d'ogni cosa."[4] Finally, in some notes that Solomos made in connection with the writing of what was to be his major poetic endeavour, he gives a more complete statement of his view of the poet's task and of the nature of poetry:

"Apply to the spiritual form the development of the plant, which begins with the seed and turns back to the seed, after it has been through, as stages of evolution, all natural forms, *i.e.*, root, stem, leaves, flowers, and fruit. Apply it and reflect deeply upon the nature of the subject and the form of art. See that this work is performed without interruption.

[1] *Ibid.*, p. 129.
[2] Polylas, J.: Introduction to: Dionysios Solomos, The Complete Works. *op. cit.*, p. 42.   [3] *Ibid.*, p. 12.
[4] " The Woman of Zakynthos," *op. cit.*, p. 87.

"A ripe and beautiful democracy of ideas, that will present substantially the Monarch invisible to the senses. Then it is a true poem. The Monarch, who is hidden to the senses and is known only by the spirit, within which it was born, is outside the area of Time ; but a democracy of ideas acts sensibly within the limits of Time.

"Reflect deeply and firmly (once and for all) upon the nature of the Idea before you realise the poem.

"Let the whole poem express the Intelligible Meaning as a self-existent world, graded mathematically, rich and deep. Only in this way is it possible to produce, with various and successive inventions, the biggest and most terrible effects. This has never been done well enough. Those who have tried to do it (like Euripides, and with him most of the moderns who are his children), have remained outside the Idea, and this is intolerable for anyone with intelligence.

"Grasp and concentrate a spiritual power, and divide it among various characters, men and women, in whom everything will correspond. Reflect well whether this will be romantic, or, if possible, classic, or a mixed but legitimate type. The highest example of the second type is Homer ; of the first Shakespeare ; of the third I do not know.

"Let the poem possess a bodiless soul, which emanates from God, and which is then embodied in the organs of time, of place, of nationality, of language, with different thoughts, feelings, inclinations, etc. (let a small bodily world be adequate to reveal it) ; finally, the soul returns to God" [207-209].

Some of these last notes, it has been remarked, reflect in many ways the ideas of various German philosophers, from Kant to Hegel, whose works Solomos is known to have studied after his move to Corfu.[1] This may well be so, but in case it should be thought that thereby the ideas are of less import, it should be pointed out not only that they are implicit in those earlier remarks of Solomos on the same theme which I have cited and

---

[1] See: Jenkins, *op. cit.*, pp. 165-170 ; Polylas, *op. cit.*, pp. 29-34 ; and for particular instances other than those cited in these two references, see such works as: Schiller, Fred., Essays Aesthetical and Philosophical, Bohn's Libraries, London, 1910, esp.: "On the Tragic Art," pp. 354-356 ; "On the Pathetic," pp. 142-143, 149 ; "On Grace and Dignity," pp. 173-178 ; "On the Necessary Limitations in the Use of Beauty of Form," pp. 225-226.

which were made before Solomos became acquainted with the German philosophers, but also that there is no connection between profundity and novelty, and as long as an artist has made an idea his own it does not matter whether it first occurred yesterday or before the dawn of history.

As a matter of fact, many of these ideas which Solomos held concerning his art do come, if not from before the dawn of history, at least from an early age, for they are implicit in the art forms of many cultures, above all of those based on principles enshrined and preserved in a living religious tradition and which may therefore be called traditional ; and as these ideas govern the whole of Solomos' later work, as well as much of the work of three of the other poets with which this study is concerned, to such an extent that no valid judgment of this work can be made without an adequate knowledge of what they are, it is necessary at this point to say something about them.

The development of artistic theory and practice from the end of the thirteenth century onwards seems, broadly speaking, to have passed through two main stages. The first stage covers the centuries between the so-called Renaissance and the end of the eighteenth century. During this stage, art was regarded as a rational process whereby the artist, through the observation and analysis of natural figures, works upward, idealising them, and achieving in the end a balanced and harmonious design. The artist begins with the natural object and ends with the abstraction, the formal design. The work of art is not " true to nature " in quite that literal way which it was later demanded that it should be, but it is true to the patterns which the mind, working by observation, experiment, and analysis, can discover in natural figures. After Masaccio, painting tends to begin with perspective, with the anatomical construction of nature. Florentine theorists like Cennino Cennini (fourteenth century) in his " Libro del' Arte," and L. B. Alberti (1404-1472), or Leonardo da Vinci in his " Treatise on Painting," elaborate a theory of vision that is basically scientific in the empirical and rational sense.[1] The attempt on the part of the artist to know the rational structure of things is regarded as an act of creation. Art tends

---

[1] See: Clark, K. M.: Leon Battista Alberti on Painting etc. Annual Italian Lecture of the British Academy, 1944. The authenticity of the " Treatise on Painting " has been questioned.

17

to become a science which begins with sensory observation and ends with the pleasing, harmonious, and abstract design that is the idealisation of the natural figures which the artist has observed in the first place. This conception of art may well be termed classic, for it is similar to that which appears towards the end of the fifth century B.C. in Greece and continues, with modifications, to be the guiding conception of the art of Hellenistic and Roman times.

Toward the end of the eighteenth century, however, this conception of art began to give place to another. According to this new conception, art was regarded as the expression of feeling, as the true voice of feeling, and its purpose to rouse in the spectator or reader similar feelings. " It was a tremendous discovery, how to excite emotions for their own sake."[1] Art became a sort of indulgence of the emotions. The process of creation still began with the artist's sensory reaction to natural figures, to nature, but now his purpose was less to discover the logical design in things and more to give voice to the feelings which they aroused, to the sentiments and associations which they stimulated. Art was self-expression, and by the self was understood the emotional self, which, if it thinks at all, thinks through and with the emotions. " I have said," writes Wordsworth, " that poetry is the spontaneous overflow of powerful feelings ; it takes its origin from emotion recollected in tranquillity."[2] This conception, according to which a work of art is a kind of regurgitation of purely private and emotional experience, may be called romantic, and it differs from the classic not in quality but only in degree. For in both conceptions, art begins with individual sensory reactions to natural forms and figures, and it is only in that while classic art aims to please and stimulate the individual mind, and romantic above all to please and stimulate individual feeling, that their ends may be said to differ. In either case, whether it is the artist or whether it is the spectator or reader we are considering, the process begins and ends with the individual.

But in that understanding of art which is not classic or

[1] Whitehead, A. N.: Religion in the Making—cited with approval by Herbert Read: Art and Society, 1937, p. 84.
[2] Wordsworth: Preface to 2nd ed. of " Lyrical Ballads." Poetical Works, Oxford Edition, ed. Hutchinson, 1920, p. 940.

18

romantic but is traditional in the sense that it is implicit in traditional cultures, the artistic process neither begins nor ends with
the individual. According to this understanding, art begins with
a supra-individual world that cannot be known by observation
or discursive reasoning but only by contemplation. This is the
world of spiritual realities, of archetypes and of archetypal
experience, and it is the task of the artist to embody this world
in his work. The artistic process begins, then, with the artist's
intuition of this world, his immediate experience of it, something
which is not possible until he has gone through an inner development corresponding to the Platonic initiation, in other words, a
kind of dying, that kind of dying to which the philosopher's life
is dedicated,[1] and which involves a going beyond the purely
individual state. By participation in the world of spiritual
realities, the artist will gain his knowledge of it, he will be able
to understand it so that his work will be an adequate " copy "
of it. Without such participation and understanding, the artist's
mimetic iconography will be at fault. For only to the extent
that a work of art correctly " imitates " its model can it be said
to fulfil its purpose, and such faithfulness can only be attained
when the artist himself has first seen, has first experienced the
model as it is. " Imitation " of a model involves a " likeness," but
not in that looking-glass sense that the naturalistic artist intends,
whose copies are not copies of what really is but only of what
appears to be. " Likeness " means an image akin and equal to
its model, in other words, a symbol. The art of which I am
speaking is therefore " imitative " not of what is presented by
our immediate and natural environment, whether visually or
otherwise accessible to observation, not of nature in the sense
now usually understood, but of " Mother Nature," Natura
naturans, Creatrix—that Nature to find which " all her forms
must be shattered."[2] And such " imitation " is achieved by the
use of symbols.

An adequate symbolism is one in which a certain level of
reality is evoked by a reality of another and corresponding level.
The latter is a symbol of the former. In the art I am now discussing, the reality to which the symbol corresponds is the

1 Plato : Phædo, 67 D.E.
2 Meister Eckhart, ed. Pfeiffer, trans. Evans, London, 1947, Vol. 1,
p. 259.

world of what Solomos called the Great Realities [210],[1] the primordial truths. The artist's purpose will then be so to arrange his work that its figures, its visibilia, are adequate symbols of these primordial truths and so capable of re-evoking a consciousness of them in the spectator or reader. This is the function of all religious myth, of whatever period, which, far from being invention, "a purely fictitious narrative,"[2] or something which man has outgrown, conceals behind it once and for always the great realities, the original phenomena of life: by means of the myth the spectator or reader may be brought into contact with these realities, may be brought into contact with that original life which they represent. Similarly, a work of art which is the imitation of a myth, whose visibilia are arranged by the artist in such a way that they are adequate symbols of the spiritual world—an achievement which pre-supposes the artist's participation in and experience of that world—such a work has as its purpose to free the reader or spectator from his habitual self, and, as in sacrificial rituals, to raise him to a like participation in and experience of the world in which the work itself was first conceived. Such an art amounts to a rite, and the purpose of a rite (as the word τελετή implies) is to sacrifice the old and bring into being a new and more perfect life. Thus in this traditional view of art, the artistic operation begins and ends not with the individual but with the supra-individual world of the Great Realities.

It follows from what has been said that if when we consider a work of art born under traditional conditions, we consider only its æsthetic surface and our own emotional reactions to it, or ask that it should be " true to nature " in the literal sense, then we miss its point altogether. A traditional work of art, in which the form of the work is " l'abito del vero senso profondo," has fixed ends and an ascertained means of operation and these depend upon a metaphysical reality which the artist has understood. Such a work of art is not meant merely to be enjoyed; it is a reminder, a summons to the spectator or reader to raise

---

[1] I am unable to discover whether Solomos borrowed this expression from any particular source, or whether he adopted it as an equivalent to such an expression as Schiller's " pure intelligences " (see: Schiller, *op. cit.*, " On Grace and Dignity," p. 180 ; " On the Sublime," p. 134). They would seem to correspond.

[2] See " Myth " in The Shorter Oxford English Dictionary, 1950.

20

his own consciousness to the level from which it derives. It makes demands upon the reader or spectator similar to those made upon the artist before he could begin his work. If, as I have said, he who seeks to "imitate" in his work the primordial and perpetual truths cannot do so unless he first of all lives them and experiences them, it is no less certain that he who would appreciate and understand such work—work, for instance, like Solomos' later poetry—can only do it subject to the same condition. It is this that accounts for the fatuity of so much art criticism and art history purporting to deal with work of this kind: so often those who undertake it have no knowledge or experience of the principles on which such work depends, and so take account only of its surface and of their own private and sentimental reactions to it and forget that it was created not to express or excite an emotion but to express and communicate a meaning, and that to consider it apart from its meaning is, quite literally, to reduce it to meaninglessness. Valid criticism where such work is concerned depends first of all upon the critic's capacity to understand what the artist intended to express, and this implies that he must conform his consciousness to that of the artist, that he must think with his thoughts and see with his eyes. Only then will he be in a position to judge whether the artist has been successful in his endeavour, whether, that is, he has succeeded in realising his intention in his work. He may then if he wishes, and as indeed it is very proper that he should, go on to criticise the intention itself, though in that case he will not be strictly speaking an art critic but a critic of values. But in any case, if his judgment of the work from whatever point of view is to have a more than merely subjective validity, he cannot avoid, any more than the artist himself can, raising himself above that condition where his purely individual likes and dislikes have the final word.

What, then, is this understanding which Solomos so persistently sought to communicate in his later work? We have already discerned the outlines of it in his earlier work, though because of the inadequacy of the expression it never becomes very convincing. We saw that this early work seems to point to a certain antithesis in life between an evil destructive force and a level of reality beyond the reach of such a force. We also saw that this destructive element seems to be identified with the natural world and with the passions, and that the poet seems to have regarded this world and life in it as evil. We saw finally that this other level of reality is realised at times of great distress, when the normal conditions of life are overthrown, and that this overthrow Solomos presents as a kind of death. In the passage which describes the vision in " The Woman of Zakynthos " and from which I cited, the other level of reality is revealed as a presence of deep darkness, a kind of superlunary power, and it is as such that it is again revealed in the first of Solomos' mature poems, " The Cretan " [197-206], written in 1834. The poem opens at the eighteenth section. The first seventeen sections are missing and were probably never written. As it now stands, the poem opens as a Cretan is escaping from Crete, after the Turkish conquest of the island. He is out on the open sea, in a small boat, and with him is his beloved, all he has been able to save from the disaster. There is a storm. Lightning flashes and it thunders. But suddenly the sea becomes quiet, a perfect mirror in which the stars are reflected. Some mysterious power constrains nature. The wind drops, and wound in the moonlight the dark presence rises, a dazzling darkness that fills creation with light. She—for this presence is for Solomos a feminine, a maternal power—stops before the Cretan and gazes at him. She reminds him of someone he has once known, of some Madonna painted in a church, of something that his loving mind has fashioned, some dream dreamt when taking his mother's milk, an ancient pre-conscious memory. In the tears he sheds at the sight of her, his eyes are confused and he cannot see her, only he feels her eyes deep within him, for she is one of the divine powers who " dwell where they see into the abyss and into the heart of man ; and I felt that she read my mind better than if I spoke sadly with my own lips " [201-202]. But now she vanishes, and in her place a still music sounds. " It was," the poet notes, " an inexpressible impression, which perhaps no one has known unless the first man, when he first drew breath, and the sky, the earth, and the sea, formed for him, still in all their perfection, rejoiced within his soul, until in the drunkenness of his mind and heart, sleep, image of death, seized him " [205, Note 44]. And he seeks in the poem to express this inexpressible, to communicate the living nature of this all but incommunicable experience:

> *No girl's voice it was from the green woods,*
> *Singing, as eve-star rises and the waters cloud,*
> *Her secret love to tree and budding flower;*
> *No Cretan nightingale, high on the wild rocks,*
> *Beside his nest, spilling the night-long over*
> *Far off plain and sea, his music till,*
> *Melting starlight, dawn breaks, and drops*
> *Roses from her hand in listening wonder;*
> *Nor shepherd's pipe it was, as once I heard*
> *Alone on Ida, when sorrow drew me thence,*
> *And, the sun mid-heaven, I saw*
> *Mountain, field, sea, smile in the brightness;*
> *Then did hope of freedom stir within my breast;*
> *Weeping, reaching out my hands, I cried:*
> *"O my country, my country soaked in blood"—*
> *Proud of her dark stone and of her barren grass.*
> *No, no sound, bird or voice, was like this sound—*
> *Perhaps nothing on earth is like it,*
> *Wordless, so delicate, without echo even.*
> *Whether from far or near it came I did not know,*
> *Only as May-time scents it filled the air,*
> *Utterly sweet, unspeakable . . .*
> *Love and death themselves have not such power.*
> *It seized upon my soul: sky, the sea and shore,*
> *The girl—nothing of these did I remember;*
> *It seized upon me, it made me even seek*
> *To leave my flesh behind, that I might follow it.*
> *Then at last it ceased, withdrawing from nature and my*
>   *soul,*
> *Which sighed and at once recalled my loved-one—*
>
>   [204-206]

Or, as Solomos put it in his note, " sleep, image of death, seized him," and he returned, as the initiate when the epiphany ends, back to his ordinary and habitual self, but only to find, as he reaches the shore with his beloved, that she is dead.

There is here, in this poem, an attempt to express an original experience of considerable complexity, and we shall do it scant justice if we try to explain away the supernatural element by calling it a sublimation of nature or a hallucinated vision. It is something more than this. The experience is not first of all a natural experience: nature is eclipsed while it endures, and the young girl, the natural creature, is found dead after it. It is interesting to compare the passage quoted from "The Cretan" with Emily Brontë's "He comes with western winds, with evening's wandering airs."[1] Before the visitation of Emily Brontë's "radiant Angel," a holy calm also descends, the struggle ceases, "mute music" fills the world:

> But first a hush of peace, a soundless calm descends;
> The struggle of distress and fierce impatience ends;
> Mute music soothes my breast—unuttered harmony
> That I could never dream till earth was lost to me.

> Then dawns the Invisible . . .

For Emily Brontë, as for Solomos, the experience is only achieved through the total quiescence of the natural world of the senses:

> My outward sense is gone, my inward essence feels . . .

And for Emily Brontë, as for Solomos, who seeks to leave his flesh behind that he might follow the wordless music, the return to the natural world is a return to darkness and death. It would seem that for Solomos, as for Emily Brontë, the world is a prison-house of wrath and it is only through great struggle involving the sacrifice of all that is natural that man can attain happiness; by shattering all nature's forms he experiences a supernatural Nature, what I called a Mother Nature, Creatrix, Natura naturans. Boehme describes an understanding similar to that which would seem to lie behind "The Cretan": "For man's happiness consists in this, that he has in him a true desire after God, for out of the desire springs forth the love; that is, when the desire receives the meekness of God into itself, then the desire immerses itself in the meekness, and becomes essential; and this is the heavenly or divine essentiality, or corporality: and therein the soul's spirit (which lay shut up in the anger, viz., in death) does again arise in the love of God; for the love tinctures

[1] Brontë, Emily: Selected Poems, ed. Henderson, London, 1942, pp. 115-116.

the death and darkness, that it is again capable of the divine sunshine."[1] The attainment of this happiness, in which, by a breaking through of all attachments to the world of time and place, "the love tinctures the death and darkness, that it is again capable of the divine sunshine," is the consummation of human life.

It was in what is perhaps his major poetic endeavour, "The Free Besieged," that Solomos tried to symbolise the drama of the human soul as she seeks to break through all the attachments and entanglements of the world of time and place and to realise her divine nature. I have already cited some of the notes which the poet made in connection with the writing of this poem and which indicate his intention clearly enough. He wanted to present this drama of the human soul in images of which each individual could, according to his or her capacity, partake, and which would thus serve as supports by means of which each individual could slowly raise his or her consciousness to that level at which the Great Realities, the Monarch invisible to the senses [207, 210], the divine nature, became the liberated and determining forces of his or her life. He therefore chose as the scene for his symbolic drama the now famous Missolonghi, and sought to unfold the drama in terms of that contemporary historical event which had made it famous, its besieging by the Turks and the final desperate attempt of the besieged to break out to freedom. Such a representation, fixed by the attention, would slowly induce in the reader a transforming process whereby he would become aware of the reality to which the symbolism corresponded and would thus be initiated into the way through which his own liberation from "darkness and death" might be attained. It would have the function, that is, of a myth or a ritual drama. That Solomos was well aware of this is, as I have said, clear from his notes. That too he was aware of that process by which the fixing of attention on a symbolic representation induces a corresponding inner transformation—a process which is after all the *raison d'être* and the condition of the efficacy of the myth or ritual drama, as of all meditative practice—that Solomos was aware of this is similarly clear from another note: "Chiudi nella tua anima la Grecia (o altra cosa). Ti sentirai

---

[1] Boehme, J.: The Signature of All Things, Everyman's Lib., p. 45.

c

fremer per entro ogni genere di grandezza e sarai felice."[1] In
" The Free Besieged" Solomos sought to create such a symbolic
representation—" la Grecia (o altra cosa) "—which " closed in the
soul" would conduct towards happiness. He sought to create that
" imitation " which would remind the reader of its original and
supersensual model. In the poem " Duty " (this was the title
he first gave to " The Free Besieged ") he writes:

" In the poem 'Duty' long must the terrible struggle among
misfortune and suffering last, for in this struggle is revealed,
immaculate and holy, the intellectual and moral Paradise."
Or again:

" Realise this Idea: all human ties—of father—of brother—
of wife—rooted in the earth, and with them the desire for glory:
—the earth seizes upon them, and in this way they are forced
to uncover in all its depth the holiness of their soul. At the base
of the representation always Greece and her future. From start
to finish they pass from suffering to suffering ; then ' the sea
ran,' and their soul floated in bitterness and they staggered like
drunkards. Then the enemy asks them to change their faith.
St. Augustine says that the Cross is the seat of true wisdom,
because all that Jesus taught in three years with the Gospel, he
recapitulated in three hours upon the Cross."
Or again:

" Arrange it so that the small Circle, in which the besieged
town moves, makes clear within its encompassment the greatest
interests of Greece, where the material state is concerned—worth
as much to those who seek to retain it as to those who seek to
capture it—and, where the moral state is concerned, the greatest
interests of Humanity. In this way the situation is linked to the
universal pattern. Look at Prometheus and in general at the
works of Aeschylus. Let the smallness of the place be obvious,
as well as the iron and unbroken circle that has enclosed it.
In this way, from the smallness of the place which battles with
huge contrary powers, will come forth the Great Realities "
[208 and 210].

In other words, the poem, through its presentation of
Missolonghi and the events which took place there, was to act as
a kind of mirror in which the reader might see reflected the

---

[1] Kairophylas: Solomos, Unedited Works, Athens, 1927, p. 6.

developing drama of man's inner life in its struggle for freedom through the realisation of its divine potentialities. At the same time, his contemplation of the poem, by inducing in him an awareness of that drama to which its symbolism corresponded, might reveal to the reader a knowledge of his own proper destiny and fulfilment.

Solomos was never able to complete " The Free Besieged." What he did complete remains in three sketches, written at different times and each representing a fresh attempt to realise in an adequate form his intention. The first sketch is only a short fragment which repeats the already quoted description of the monk's vision from the " Woman of Zakynthos." But from the second and third sketch it is possible to put together a fairly coherent picture of the drama's development.

The poem opens with an invocation to the Divine Nature, the Great Mother:

> *Mother, great-hearted in glory and in suffering,*
> *If always in the secret mystery live your children*
> *With thought, with dream, what joy have then the eyes,*
> *These eyes, to behold you in the desolate wood . . .*
>
> [238]

It is of course because her children do not live " always in the secret mystery," forget their true nature and get caught up in the flow of the world's storm, that life loses its meaning and it becomes necessary for the artist to remind them what it is. This he does through his art, which must give effectiveness to the truth: the artistic operation begins with inspiration, in the proper sense of the word, as " A supernatural influence which qualifies men to receive and communicate divine truth."[1] Thus the poet concludes his invocation with a question, asking whether he shall not receive that influence which will make it possible for him to communicate to his people a true knowledge of what they are and of the purpose of their life:

> *But am I, Lady, not to hear your voice, to give it*
> *At once to the Greek world ?*
>
> [238]

---

[1] Webster. "Inspiration" is a word often incorrectly used. One frequently comes across such phrases as: " He was inspired by such and such a place," or: " The source of his inspiration was such and such a passage."

27

The heavenly power replies to the poet and tells him to speak of the siege of Missolonghi. The whole action of the poem, from start to finish, unfolds as it were within the omnipresence of the Great Mother and receives its significance by participation in a drama that is above all her drama. For she, a divine power and the source of man's life, dwells, as Solomos puts it in " The Cretan," where she can see " into the abyss and into the heart of man " [202]. As for the heavenly Muse of Milton's invocation at the beginning of " Paradise Lost," Heaven hides nothing from her view nor the deep tract of Hell. To her are evident the most hidden things of the human soul. Her eye is at the root of man's mind [230]. Her anxiety and her tragic situation come therefore not from her doubt as to the resolution of the besieged, which she knows is fixed ; they come rather from her knowledge that the fierce destructive force, Fate, against which she is powerless, is in its stubborn fury relentless and unfeeling, and may well overwhelm her children before they attain that liberation in which her own unity and fulfilment consist. The drama, then, which we see on the human level, has its counterpart on, and derives its tension from, a supernatural drama, the conflict of Heaven and Hell for the possession of man's soul. But in this supernatural drama, man is far from being a mere spectator or accident, as he tends to be in Milton's poem of the same theme ; he is on the contrary the protagonist. For if on the one hand the consummation of human life is the attainment of happiness beyond the reach of " darkness and death," on the other hand, the Divine Nature itself, of which each individual partakes and which constitutes his true nature and his knowledge of what he really is—this Nature can never be at one with itself, must always be divided among countless independent and perishable beings, and will therefore suffer, until these beings, through struggle and sacrifice, deliver it from that " kingdom of Satan " of which, while they continue merely separate individual selves, both it and they are prisoners ; and whether this is achieved or not depends entirely upon their capacity to pursue the struggle against Fate through to the end. In other words, in Heaven's conflict with Hell, man is not simply the battlefield ; it is upon him that depends the triumph of Heaven, a triumph which indeed coincides with the realisation of his own true nature and of his happiness. It is against this background of understanding that the action of "The Free Besieged" receives its significance.

The poet now passes on to the scene of action, this small place against which battle huge contrary powers, the rabid furies of Fate, and where the few who remain living are faced with the choice of dying where they are or of trying to break through to freedom beyond the enclosing circle, an enterprise in which they also put themselves into the hands of death. The war has now ceased to be a burden to life, it has become life itself [240]. It does not stop girl from singing or child from playing; its very misery and hardship engender a heroism that surmounts the hardship and misery. The Greeks' flag, unfolding in the heroic air, is as a sun breaking from black cloud and bringing joy to the heart of man and the desire to perform great deeds [241].

But true greatness, the greatness which calls for sacrifice and which has man's inner freedom for its object, does not have to contend only with obvious material forces ; it has to contend also with those less visible but no less persistent ties which bind man to the life of the senses, to the conditioned world of impermanence and perishableness where he can so easily forget himself and others in fleeting sensual distraction. One of the most subtle of these ties is that which binds man to nature and to natural beauty. Solomos himself had a keen, a poignant sense of the beauty of the physical world. Polylas has recorded that often, when walking in the countryside, the poet would be seized by a kind of rapture, inexplicable to whoever was with him.[1] On another occasion, one spring evening, as Solomos stood watching the different colours of sea, mountain, and sky, he remarked: " Somewhere I say of these colours ' that they have no name but beauties infinite ' ; such we may say also are the many and varied powers of the soul."[2] He seems to have felt that nature was a sort of reflection of the soul's inner beauty, and that the contemplation of it woke a recollection of this inner beauty, with which, as a poet, he could then saturate his poetry, shedding upon it an abundance of borrowed loveliness. " Art," Solomos noted, " silently worships nature, which, in reward for this distant love, dances naked before her. These forms echo back in the mind of Art and she offers them to mankind."[3] But it is quite

---

[1] Polylas, *op. cit.*, p. 10.   [2] *Ibid.*, p. 32.
[3] *Ibid.*, note at foot of p. 32.

another matter if what is but a reflection of the soul's inner beauty is taken for the thing itself ; if nature, instead of being worshipped as a means through which man may approach supernatural beauty, is worshipped, after the fashion of romantic poets like Wordsworth, as an end in itself. Nature then becomes a hindrance and not a help to realisation, for by taking what, considered apart from its cause, is an illusion for something that is real in itself, man is in danger of reducing his own life to a sort of illusion. It is the tension between his own proper love and understanding of natural beauty and his awareness of the danger that this same natural beauty presents if wrongly worshipped, which gives the razor-edge tautness to the lyrical passages of Solomos' later poetry. Believing, as he did, that natural forms must be shattered before Nature herself is revealed —and we shall see this more clearly when we consider one of his later poems, " The Shark "—nature must in the first instance also be overcome as another of those forces that besiege man's soul. Thus, in " The Free Besieged," nature is presented as a temptation that will divert man from his heroic task. Spring, as well as the Turk, besieges Missolonghi:

" Life, which rises again with all its joys, bubbling over everywhere, young, passionate, outpoured into all being ; all life, from all nature, tries to overwhelm man's soul ; sea, earth, sky, mingled together, surface and depth mingled together, again besiege man's soul, surface and depth.

" Nature's beauty, which encircles them, makes the enemy even more impatient to capture the lovely place, and it makes the beseiged even more wretched at the thought of losing it " [216].

> Blond April dances with Eros, and nature knows
> Her best and richest hour. In the swelling
> Shade which closes coolness and fragrance, un-
> Heard of birdsong trembles. Clear lovely waters,
> Sweet waters, spill through scented caverns,
> Steal the scent, leave their coolness, and,
> Showing to the sun the treasures of their source,
> Hither and thither dash, and sing like nightingales.
> Life throbs through earth, through wave and sky.
> But over the clear, the dead-calm lake,

Dead-calm, clear to the depths, the butterfly
Who had perfumed her sleep within the wild lily
Was with a small unknown shadow playing.
Light-shadowed seer, what did you see this night?
Miraculous night, night with magic sown!
Without the earth, the sea and sky to breathe
Even as the bee close to the little flower,
The moon round something motionless, that
Shimmered on the lake, alone was pulsing;
And beautiful a young girl came out in her light.
[243ff.]

While this bewitching song of spring is heard—it is Polylas who supplies the commentary—threatening to wake in the besieged so much the love of life that their courage is enfeebled, one of the Greek captains blows a bugle, calling the others to council; and the stifled blast, coming from his weakened lungs, re-echoes in the enemy camp and provokes the Arabs to laughter and to a mocking blast of reply:

Loud laughter spreads through all the scattered camp,
And a mocking blast is thrown back to the skies.
Lungs loaded with joyful breath,
Fierce, strong, full-bodied,
Striking near and far, toss
The beautiful cloudless air.
Away the call streams, a falling star,
Loud, terrifying, flung against the fort.
[218ff.]

"Just as the Arab stops blowing, a many-voiced cry is heard in the enemy camp, and the first watchman, pale as death, tells the Greeks: 'The enemy fleet approaches.' The thick forest stood motionless on the waters, where they had hoped to see friendly ships. Then the enemy renewed the cry, and the new-comers echoed it back from their ships. Then ceaseless thunder made the air tremble for a long time and in this storm:

Like bubbles in boiling water leapt the black earth.

Until this moment, the Besieged have endured much struggle with some hope that a friendly fleet will come and perhaps cut the iron circle which besieges them. Now they have lost all hope, and the enemy promises to spare life if they change their faith. Their final resistance reveals them martyrs" [220].

"Reflect upon the balance of powers between men and women," Solomos had written in his final note to the poem, "Let the men experience all, and let them conquer all, with living awareness; let the women also conquer, but as women" [210]. He now speaks of the women:

"I was frightened sometimes lest they should lose heart and I watched them continually, for their strength is not as big as their other gifts. This evening, while they had the windows open for coolness, one of them, the youngest, went to shut them; but another said to her: 'No, my child, let the smell of food come in. We must get used to it: a big thing is patience; God gave it us, and it contains treasures. We must have patience even if all the scents of earth, sky, and sea come in.' So saying, she opened the windows again, and the many scents flooded in and filled the room. And the first said: 'Even the wind fights against us'" [225].

Then a girl, sick through sorrow at the death of her young man in the fighting, speaks in delirium to the women who are around her and who console her. She talks of the Angel who in dreams has offered her his wings:

> *Angel, in dream only do you give to me your wings?*
> *By Him who shaped you, this lonely vessel needs them ...*
> [246ff.]

Then she remembers words which the women have spoken to her while she has lain sick; and finally she sees her young man, transfigured, dance in the day of triumph:

> *And I heard you say : "Child, sweet is your voice."*
> *Sing as the nightingale, my breast, before the sword cuts*
>   *you.*
> *Dear good women of this my desolate night,*
> *Let me die with you, let me be the first!*
> *Flowers behind the ear deck the dancer's crooked cap,*
> *His eyes show longing for the upper world,*
> *Lovely in his face the light, and full of wonder.*
> [247]

" One of the women takes refuge in the thought of death as
the only salvation with the joy that the bird feels which sees a
paradise of shade and welcomes it with rushing wings, songless,
at the moment when it is exhausted from a long journey in the
flame of the summer sun " [248].

It is now the last night. The Besieged have decided to make
a bid to break through the encircling enemy, or, as is most likely,
to die in the attempt. They gather in the church to pray. Incense
rises. All is silent. Not even a dog barks. It is as if life had stopped.
In this last moment, now that the decision to face death has been
reached and they are as it were stripped naked, no longer
attached to any material form or fortune, hope or desire, the
heroes feel strangely united, and, in themselves, murmur:

> Words fit for eternity, which only just contains them.
> Their thoughts show in eye and in the face;
> Great tidings rise within them.
> Love, immortal longing, shakes their heart . . .
> As something disembodied is the soul, free and sweet;
> Smiling, they raise their battle ravaged faces.
>
> [228]

The women, too, destroy their last attachments to their familiar
life:

> And children I see, and women, about
> The fire they have kindled, and, sad, have fed
> With loved household things, modest beds,
> Still, unsighing, tearless;
> And sparks fall on their hair and torn clothes.
>
> [249]

Only after, when they make a final prayer together, do the
women become frightened a little and weep. This is the last
external power with which the fighters have to contend, and
which, as all the others, they conquer.

Then, as the dawn breaks and the wheel comes full circle,
the Martyrs—for so their actions reveal them [220]—make their
sortie, to issue free, either with their brothers beyond the circle
of the besiegers, or with death. For in this final moment of self-
sacrifice, the division between life and death is transcended, the
limitations of the mortal world vanish, and man becomes

possessed of a new and liberated existence. Only when all has been surrendered; only when all which bound man to mortal life and when all which he has borrowed from the world of time and place has been given up, and when he faces his own nothingness and death without fear or hope—only then his soul's spirit, his true nature, which lay shut up in the anger and in death, is revealed; only then does the love tincture the death and darkness, so that it is again capable of divine sunshine; and only then does man become, through a paradox which lies at the heart of existence itself, absolutely and indomitably free, rooted in some centre where the destructive force, the rabid furies of Fate, are powerless to reach:

> From depth to depth he fell until there was no other:
> Thence he issued invincible . . .   [209]

Solomos, in his effort to communicate that understanding of which all his later poetry is the outcome, never again attempted anything so ambitious as "The Free Besieged." But he did not cease to meditate his problem, which was always one and the same: how to create an adequate symbolisation of the struggle of Heaven and Hell in which man, the protagonist against the relentless violence of the world's flow, emerges, even at the moment of self-annihilation and death, triumphant. As Dante said with reference to the Commedia, Solomos might have said with reference to all his later poetry: "the whole work was undertaken not for a speculative but a practical end. . . . The purpose of the whole is to remove those who are living in this life from the state of wretchedness and to lead them to a state of blessedness."[1] He seems to have felt that this life, the natural life, and the very existence of the natural world, were, as the product and sphere of Fate, incompatible with man's true happiness, and that such "happiness" as man achieved in them was the result of his own forgetfulness and selfishness. Solomos stands at the opposite pole to the Wordsworth who could write:

> How exquisitely the individual Mind
> . . . . to the external World
> Is fitted :—and how exquisitely, too—
> Theme this but little heard of among Men—
> The external World is fitted to the Mind.[2]

---

[1] Dante, Ep. ad Can. Grand., 15. 16.   [2] Wordsworth, Preface to the 1814 Edition of "The Excursion," op. cit., p. 755.

Such complacent adaptability could only, from Solomos' point of view, be the consequence of spiritual death. For, to Solomos, the external world, far from fitting the "individual Mind," was man's most bitter and irreconcilable enemy. The world in its natural state is a kind of Hell, life in it is death, and only within, by a break through into another state of existence, can "the pure world with its lilies flower" [262]. In the only poem he wrote after "The Free Besieged" that came anywhere near to receiving a definite form, "The Shark" [251ff.], Solomos sought to bring together his recognition of the world of nature as the sphere of Fate and his sense that the moment of self-annihilation is the moment of self-realisation into a single and sudden clash, so that the resolution of the conflicting opposites might appear the impossible miracle it is.

The actual occasion for the poem was the killing by a shark of a young English soldier while he was swimming in a bay off Corfu. The day after his death, what was left of his body was washed up on to the shore of the island. The poem opens with what one might call a "Prologue in Heaven": Hell surrounds man on all sides, but has no power over him except when he is far off from the Paradise of which his nature partakes. The young soldier is then presented: he is in the full bloom of youth and beauty; he is the crown and perfection, the outcome and end of the natural loveliness about him; he is the embodiment and highest expression of the ravishing world which greets him as he comes down to bathe and which seems to have flowered solely for his delight and happiness, as if in recognition of his sovereign presence. In him the partial beauty of flower, sky, sea, rock, and birdsong is fully achieved and consummated. Like a classical statue of a god, he is the harmonious perfection of the universe around him, the idealisation of nature, blessed by every natural grace. But as this human creature on whom nature has lavished all her care and all her gifts enters the water, the force of fierce destruction which she hides beneath her dazzling surface strikes him: the shark, the "tiger of the sea," rises from the depths and in a few seconds rips all that physical perfection to shreds. Solomos, in a note [358] which refers to the poem, expresses his intention: " In him were rifle and sword, in him the strength of assembled regiments. The struggle was short, but unrelenting and immense the courage. This ceased only with life, and the irrational monstrous force did not know what world of grandeur it had destroyed. If secret worlds had opened around in order to shower crowns upon him, they would have found him indifferent, like the thought whose operation no one will ever know. Immaculate and holy is often the inspiration of man. A Paradise of happiness must have filled his great-hearted breath before it ceased. At the moment at which he felt like lightning his arm shattered ":

Light flashed and the young man knew himself.

[255]

As in "The Free Besieged," the opposites of life and death are fused and transcended: death is life, the moment of self-annihilation the moment of self-realisation ; as man frees himself from the embrace of the world of the five senses, from the mortal world, he awakes to a true knowledge of himself and experiences the touch of divinity, for then the gate of Paradise, which remains closed to all who have not overcome the sphere of Fate, is opened, and Nature, all her forms broken, stands at last revealed.

These, then, are the main works in which Solomos sought to give expression to his understanding of life. From a formal point of view, they are easy to criticise. To begin with, not one of them is more than a collection of fragments. Then, often, the form seems ill-chosen. Was Solomos, for instance, in writing "The Free Besieged" trying to write a drama? In which case, the insufficiency of his protagonists, of his dialogue, and, more important, his inability to subordinate the various parts of the poem to a continuous and developing line of action, condemn it straight away. Or was he trying to write an epic? Then, there is no successive narrative, only a series of static incidents not linked in any organic way. On this line of analysis, one is bound to confess that Solomos' poetry possesses one or two beautiful lyric passages, one or two lines of concentrated insight and meaning—"At the root of the child's mind is the eye of the Mother of God " or " Light flashed and the young man knew himself," for instance—, but that it possesses little more ; and that as an attempt to hold up before the reader a pattern of the inner purpose that he should confer upon his own life, it is too tattered a fabric to permit of serious judgment.

36

Or one can criticise the understanding itself. This I shall not attempt to do fully here, and will only indicate what seems to me its main weakness. Solomos seems to have thought that man's life reaches its ultimate end when all functions of body and mind are suspended, and realisation takes place in one single moment of the present in which a state of eternity-in-one-moment is attained, a state of absolute transcendence at the still centre of the turning world. It is an attitude that recognises a duality in life, a duality in reality. On the one hand there is the world of the spirit, which is good, and on the other hand there is the world of the flesh, which is evil. Such an attitude not only ignores the bonds that link these two aspects of reality, but also, and as a consequence, threatens the very heart of life itself.

But when one has said all that, and a lot more besides, one is still faced with the deep power which Solomos' poetry does nevertheless contain. It is not simply that a rare and complex vision of man's part in the great universal drama is, however spasmodically, allied to a concentrated simplicity of expression, to a language in which music and imagery are wrought to a degree of perfection seldom attained—and which disappears of course entirely in translation. It is that the few fragments themselves—a passage here, a line there, another passage, a few words, a note in the margin, a blank space—all without any realised external coherence, are yet held together by an internal unity which becomes, as one contemplates the poetry, suddenly visible and convincing, just as the spiritual power which lies behind the form of some ancient temple of which perhaps but a few columns remain standing, will reveal itself to whoever has the creative capacity to look penetratingly and deep. A poetry like that of Solomos, which seeks to be the faithful servant of the Great Realities, does not ask merely to be enjoyed ; it summons to an understanding ; it makes demands upon the reader equal to those made upon the poet himself, no less than that he should endeavour " to extinguish his individuality in absolute truth." And, where Solomos' poetry itself is concerned, its broken fragments testify both to the strictness of that endeavour and to the beauty of the truth which the poet sought to express.

II. Costis Palamas
(1859-1943)

AFTER the formal and hieratic atmosphere of Solomos'
later poetry, where little scope is left for the indulgence
of individual feeling, for the confession of private grief
or of private exultation, the early poetry of Costis Palamas seems
to belong to another world. Palamas was born at Patras two
years after the death of Solomos. His father was a judge, and
in fact belonged to a family already distinguished by more than
one educator of note. At the age of seven, however, the young
Palamas lost both his parents, and he passed into the care of
an uncle at Missolonghi, a man obviously of powerful character
and one that Palamas was later to describe in terms which, as
we shall see, might very well have applied to himself: " The
teacher, as everyone called him, the student of Greece, the
theologian, the philosopher, the mystic, the hesychast, the artist
of word, and the expounder of the Word, sealed with the seal of
a mysterious joy, the strange, secretive, appointed interpreter
of prophecies. . . ."[1] In 1875, Palamas left Missolonghi for Athens,
where he was to pass the rest of his life, the greater part of it,
from 1897 until his retirement in 1928, as General Secretary to
the University of Athens.

Palamas' first years at Athens, during which he grew to
maturity and which, from the point of view of his poetry, may
be called his formative years, coincided with the breaking of
the full tide of romanticism over the Greek literary scene. We
have already noted some of the characteristics of romantic art.
The poet tends to regard himself as someone of powerful
feelings, and his art as the expression and communication more
of these feelings than of the intuition of any supra-individual
reality. Quite how far Palamas looked upon himself as working

[1] Cited by Demaras, The History of Mod. Greek Literature, Vol. 11,
Athens, 1949, p. 117.

according to this romantic image of the poet is best indicated by some of his own remarks. "Ego-pathic" he calls himself at one point.[1] Or, again, poets are "hearts that suffer, that is, men who idealise passion, and give life to the soulless."[2] Whatever impression touches the poet's heart is a fit subject for his verse.[3] The beginning of the poet's creative process "is not to think, to energise, to discover, but to feel, to suffer, and to accept."[4] We would seem to be far from Solomos' "The difficulty which an artist experiences . . . does not consist in showing imagination and passion, but in subordinating these two things, with time and with labour, to the intelligible meaning of Art." If, as Palamas put it,[5] Solomos was of those who prepare first their poetic and then their poetry, Palamas himself seems to have thought his own poetry should be the spontaneous overflow of emotional or psychological excitement.

But this ego-pathic poet, of whose trials, hopes, fears, humiliations, pettiness, self-pity, self-disgust, self-torture, love, exultation, and, finally, deliverance, Palamas' poetry is the expression, is by no means only a romantic. He is, on the contrary, an acute and tragic sufferer whose conscience would seem to be tormented by problems belonging to a religious, or, more specifically, to a Christian rather than to a romantic world. Something in him longs for a life of which he is now deprived, for some lost paradise. At the same time something prevents him from ever realising this life or regaining this paradise: "It is something like sin, and like a fall, like a descent, like exile, loss of some paradise that he would think his life was destined to dwell in originally, a displacing on to a now barren and joyless earth. A secret affliction devours him. Remorse. Something which prevents him from ever treading firmly. A terrible powerlessness."[6] It is not a passing mood, not something that he imagines: "It is an idea fixed, rooted, with all the tension of reality, in the thought and in the art of the poet."[7] "It is the desire for the Christian and

1 Palamas, "Altars," 1st Series, Athens, 1915, p. 11.
2 Palamas, Foot-Roads, Vol. 1, Athens, 1928, p. 106.
3 Palamas, "Five-Syllable Lines, etc," Athens, 1925, Prologue, p. 3.
4 Ibid., p. 6.
5 See Demaras, op. cit., Vol. 2, p. 115.
6 Palamas, Poetic, Vol. 1, Athens, p. 130ff.
7 Ibid.

Buddhist confession of sin."[1] "From what I suffer," he writes, "may sometime be learnt. Why and how I suffer thus will not I think be learnt by anyone."[2] "No one sees what I suffer, I alone see it" [Altars, 91]. Even as a child he has never known innocent peace [L.I., 8].[3] He was born with love, not with innocence ; the idyll of childhood was never his.[4] From his first years something horrible and speechless has bound him to an unknown shadow, has cut him off from life:

> *Life's black widower am I,*
> *Life's mighty impotent!*
> [L.I., 32]

Far off is the feast of joy in which he longs to share ; the road that leads to it is bad and passes through "swamps and rushes," he cannot travel it [L.I., 33]. On the bank of the river, in the waste land, he gazes, paralysed and sick, across to the further side, where all is green and flourishing, and where beings like demi-gods walk beneath the ancient trees [L.I., 72]. Some scornful power or divine mirth has thrown him prisoner into this world and holds him fast, in a grip of iron:

> *An all-mocking power, or some heavenly mirth*
> *Has nailed unmercifully your hands, has nailed your will,*
> *Coward, you, dotard, sluggard, smitten down with grief.*
> [L.I., 89]

He is held captive by an unrelenting Fate, but whether his fault is sickness or crime he does not know [Altars, 93]. Beneath frozen hands a fear grasps him in the "expectation of some punishment, I do not know, I do not say, of what just payment for what ancient sin" [Altars, 104]. Within him, age-old miseries, age-old lusts, the crimes of unknown ancestors live again [L.I., 80]. The spawn of lunacy runs in his blood, that also visitation for some ancestral and now forgotten crime [L.I., 37]. The flesh is rank, the spirit fled, existence a sickness and a horror

---

[1] *Ibid.*, p. 67.
[2] Foot-Roads, *op. cit.*, p. 78.
[3] "Life Immovable," Vol. 4 of the Poetical Works of Costis Palamas, Athens, 1952. The figure in brackets refers to the page number of this work.
[4] Foot-Roads, *op. cit.*, p. 71.

D

against which he has no strength to battle. In other words this forsaken creature is the victim of a morality that has persuaded him that mortal life is the product of some ghastly original sin, that the whole human condition is one of unrelieved evil. Spirit and flesh, soul and body, are involved in bitter warfare. Caught in their antagonism, the poet feels himself a hideous sinner; he feels a disgust for his own degraded state which amounts to a kind of perverted idolatry, a self-contempt which amounts to self-immolation; he is like the monk of his own poem:

> *Sinner and monk on Athos' holy mound*
> *Me daily Satan burns and Hell devours :*
> *A traveller forever lost and drowned,*
> *A damned soul that sighs away the hours.*
> *Without, the isles in sapphire seas are bound,*
> *And Daphnis-Heaven upon Earth-Chloe showers*
> *His genial radiance : shoots spring from the ground*
> *And swarming creatures suck the sap that pours*
> *From her warm breast. Olympus, Pelion,*
> *The island peaks, the headlands every one,*
> *Kassandra's magic lake, each thing appears*
> *In bridal dress. But I? Ah, I do nought*
> *But cry " Have mercy, Lord" and wash with tears*
> *The painted Christ that Panselenus wrought.*
>
> [L.I., 10][1]

But the poet has a more poignant anguish even than the monk of Athos. He feels the full bitterness of his disgrace, the full ignominy of his existence, all the pangs of Hell and the Devil's spite, but he lacks that one thing which gives hope and courage to the Christian monk: he lacks his faith, he does not believe in the God to whom the monk prays; he has eaten of the tree of knowledge and the seed of the denial, rejection, has rooted itself in his soul: "the caterpillar of unbelief and the nails of doubt" torment and riddle him [C. & S., 20].[2]

Yet in spite of his unbelief and his doubt, the poet still has dreams of and a deep nostalgia for a lost eclipsed life of beauty

---

[1] Trans. by Jenkins, R., and cited on p. 26 of: " Palamas," An Inaugural Lecture Delivered at King's College, London, on 30th January, 1947.
[2] Palamas, " City and Solitude," Athens, 1912.

and wonder, for a kind of idyllic paradise beyond the walls of his prison. Indeed, it is precisely because he has these dreams and this nostalgia that his present state troubles him so painfully. Without them, he could perhaps live, if not nobly, at least in the content of the unaware, of those so sunk in the mire of existence and of their own petty interests that they have lost even the sense that they lack anything or that anything else is possible. He cannot indulge in such oblivion. Strange visions visit him, remind him of his loss: visions of a more than natural beauty whose reflections gleam in the natural world and contrast so vividly, as they did for the monk of Athos, with the black night of his own condition. This beauty seems to him like rays from stars whose light left them long before there were eyes on this planet to receive it and which themselves are now dead; the last reminder of a lost golden age of gods, of " the people of relics " who, although their estate was centuries ago destroyed, still live and reign on the soil of Attica and shed over the Attic landscape a lustre that struggles with the thick inner darkness:

> *Of the sacred olive here the temples and the fields.*
> *Among the crowd that sluggishly stirs here as on the white*
> *flower a caterpillar, the people of relics lives and reigns,*
> *a thousand-souled; spirit and soil gleam: I feel it; with*
> *darkness within me does it struggle* [L.I., 8].

It is the life of the sun contrasted with that of the moon. It is the sun who is father of the divine beauty, of " the woman who has the firm breasts, milk-full " [L.I., 35], the heavenly Aphrodite that all nature yearns towards and that fills the prisoner's soul with dreams of some life which he has lived far back in another time:

> *Who knows? There might I have lived young and*
> *beautiful, for my clouded mind has some urge for far*
> *journeys, and still something relic-like it holds of a*
> *struggle, of a struggle of noble men in distant, vanished*
> *years, sometimes for the wild olive crown, sometimes for*
> *divine limbs. And some words I have preserved, pearls in*
> *an unsuspected box, some words of light and music*
> [Altars, 93-94].

But, as I said, this distant recollection of a vanished life stimulates rather than assuages the poet's anguish; it is by the spasmodic gleams of light that now and then penetrate through the bars of the prison window that he is able to see the full horror and disgust of his present abysmal state; it is they that stir his remorse, produce an inner tension and a degree of suffering that make it imperative that somewhere, somehow, he should find release from his pathetic situation:

> *In despite of the suffering poet, in despite of the female dream-tormented, moon-struck, spell-bound, vision-haunted creature, in despite of the wretched unproved one that is myself, I want to escape from myself, I want to go towards whoever and whatever outside myself exists and is the world* [Altars, 63].

And in his desire for that release he turns to woman.

Woman, or, rather, the female, plays a central rôle in Palamas' world:

> *And a spring-head is woman, and from her come You, sin, and deliverance, resurrection, and death.*
> [King's Flute, 46]

It is woman who wakes that passion in the poet's life, the passion of his flesh that so torments him. She is the priestess of passion, mistress of caress [Altars, 98]. She is the cause of downfall, it is her sweet blood that makes man forget himself and lose what little good there is in him in the slough of corruption, where the worm gnaws [L.I., 80]. In her nakedness flashes the beauty of unseen worlds, idea and flesh meet in a single dazzling presence:

> *O you, who have no name, and your flesh is only the idea of flesh, statue you are not, image you are, breath, that breathes and will become a woman, and you are a mysterious lamp with light that always trembles and always seems to stand above the earth, light that neither rises to enter the heavens nor that like a star's decline slowly begins to fade, your light's a sentinel and seems to attend upon some soul that has fallen captive into clay, for you are an uncapturable soul, a wanderer of the sky* [Altars, 110].

44

Yet at the same time she is the very core, the very crown of
elemental life, something born of the blind conjunction of wind,
seas, sun, and earth. In her flesh runs blood red like the rose and
hot as fire ; she is nursed at the breast of an enchantress
[L.I., 204], the wings of nereids hide beneath her armpits [Altars,
80], to the gulls she is as a wave, to the waters as the moon's
ray, at once mistress of the loom, the daimon's companion, sinner
and Hell's bride [L.I., 204]. Great she is, but not with the wisdom
of the learned, with the hero's strength or the prophet's voice:
her mind, spider-spun, has its own woman's wisdom, but it is
her heart that is her strength [Altars, 62], and her beauty that
is her greatness [L.I., 205]. Her erotic passion is its own justification and glory, something far superior to the judgment of
the world's tepid moralists [Altars, 94ff], however destructive
and self-seeking it may be. Palamas' most complete portrait of
her is in his description of the Byzantine Empress, Augusta
Theophano, mother of the Emperor Basil the Bulgar Slayer:

> *Behold her, Augusta Theophano ! Pleiades and Furia !*
> *A stick she holds, a slender stick, and on the stick's top*
> *motionless the three-leaved lotus, golden. And it is the*
> *lotus that you do not eat, a witch's herb it is, whose sight*
> *destroys you, whose touch dissolves, and, whoever you*
> *are, ascetic or pleasure-lover, you forget all : life, strength,*
> *youth, and if you are honourable, honour, and if you are*
> *a king, the throne ; and if a hoarder you become a beggar*
> *and a homeless-one, a child for her love, a murderer for*
> *her kiss. . . . Like the sky's bow the grapes of her breast*
> *glow, and the languid woman-given prince and the*
> *undefeated conqueror alike suck them and shudder to the*
> *bone ; and, angelic sentinel of a heavenly gate, a musical*
> *smile glows on her shapely lips. . . . Behold her, Augusta*
> *Theophano ! She smiles sweetly and lets fall murder and*
> *ruin, as the dawn drops from her rosy hands the pearls*
> *of freshness. Inspirer of youth, cheater of age, she bends*
> *the unbending, lowers down the stars ; in her form her*
> *beauty is like the golden sickle, like the spider her thought,*
> *opium her love. You, mania and sphinx, flesh, dragoness,*
> *Aphrodite* [King's Flute, 39-40].

It is towards this woman, then, this creature in whom flesh and idea fuse, for whom soul is body and body soul, that the guilt-smitten, passion-swept dreamer turns for some release from the tension of his dual self that seeks to tear him asunder. Or, rather, he does not turn towards her, it is she who appears before him, and seeming to be the very embodiment of that lost world of beauty towards which he aspires, seeming to unite in one what is so tragically divided in him, his whole condition compels him to fall at her feet. She accepts his worship, opens to him her embrace, gives him the warmth of her love. And truly his wound seems healed, he seems once more a whole person ; the Lamia of his distress becomes a sad sweet ghost, and his new-found happiness finds expression in the music he plays for her delight [L.I., 73].

But of course it is not so simple. The very unity of idea and flesh, soul and body, in the woman, far from healing their division in him, only exacerbates it. For in this woman he sees that ideal, that long lost beauty of which he dreams, gleams of which still pentrate fitfully into the gloom of his prison and rouse his longing for release—in this woman he sees that beauty embodied ; it is this that draws him towards her, for this she appears such a paradise. In her love, in embrace with her, he attains to union with that beauty. But now comes his fit again. For he only attains to such union, only realises that beauty, in moments of sexual passion, in, that is, becoming ever further entangled in the bonds of that flesh which a rigid dualistic ethic has taught him to regard as evil, as the very stuff of the devil, and from which it is his chief desire to escape. At the same time, her presence, her beauty, makes more keen than ever his sense of that lost ideal beauty ; she is as it were the mother of some tenderness that until her coming had lain unborn in his mind, sister of a simple love hidden until then in the depths of his heart [L.I., 73-74]. Thus she rouses in him his longing for an ideal beauty to a fever-pitch, but when, in union with her, he seeks to satisfy this longing, he does it only by plunging back into that world of the flesh and the devil which is, from the point of view of the ethic to which his whole consciousness subscribes, the negation and denial of all that is good and beautiful. She frees him from his passion by allowing it to externalise itself, to find outlet in her, but he pays for that momentary relief with

the knowledge that he has committed something like mortal sin
for which he must undergo the punishment of the damned.

It is difficult when brought up in a world in which an ethic
such as this no longer has the same force, to imagine the enormity
of the terror that its transgression could induce. It was not simply
that the sinner had consented to the promptings of what he
regarded as his corrupt nature, to the lower instincts, to that
which is gross and beastlike. It was also that he had closed up
in himself access to his higher nature ; he had made impossible
communion with all that is pure and holy, with the divine itself.
James Joyce, in his " Portrait of the Artist as a Young Man,"
describes the state of someone when, following his " sin " with
woman, a conscience persuaded from childhood to regard that
ethic as God's law, begins to work :

" The next day brought death and judgment, stirring his soul
slowly from its listless despair. The faint glimmer of fear became
a terror of spirit as the hoarse voice of the preacher blew death
into his soul. He suffered its agony. He felt the death chill touch
the extremities and creep onward towards the heart, the film of
death veiling the eyes, the bright centres of the brain extinguished
one by one like lamps, the last sweat oozing upon the skin, the
powerlessness of the dying limbs, the speech thickening and
wandering and failing, the heart throbbing faintly and more
faintly, all but vanquished, the breath, the poor breath, the poor
helpless human spirit, sobbing and sighing, gurgling and rattling
in the throat. No help ! No help ! He—he himself—his body to
which he had yielded was dying. Into the grave with it. Nail
it down into a wooden box, the corpse. Carry it out of the house
on the shoulders of hirelings. Thrust it out of men's sight into
a long hole in the ground, into the grave, to rot, to feed the
mass of its creeping worms and to be devoured by scuttling
plump-bellied rats."[1]

It must have been something like this that Palamas, who
could count among his ancestors, it is worth noting a Byzantine
saint, Gregory Palamas—it must have been something like this
that he also experienced after his " sin " with women, something
like this that made him regard woman if sometimes as " the

1 Joyce, James, Portrait of the Artist as a Young Man, Traveller's
Library, London, 1942, pp. 126-127.

angel in the house," at other times as the destroyer, the traitress, the vessel of iniquity:

> But woman is the destroyer, who is
> inexplicable and matchless and strange,
> and her thought riddle, and a tomb
> her beauty however it may dazzle,
> and she is the traitress.

[C. & S., 127]

And from one point of view, a large part of Palamas' poetry is, as we shall see, the expression of his endeavour to redeem his conscience, his very life—and, it might be added, the conscience and life of others involved in the same way—from the world in which that flesh-denying, instinct-denying ethic ruled with such persuasion.

The whole troubled, dislocated condition of the poet's life that I have been seeking to outline, received its first complete expression in Palamas' work in " The Palm-Tree " [L.I., 91-102]. "Within a garden," runs the introductory note, " in the shadow of a palm-tree, some blue flowers, here a deep blue, there a more open blue, speak. A poet (who is now dead) passes and gives shape to their words." The flowers are as the human victims: something unknown has brought them into life, perhaps some cursed Fate, perhaps some good-intentioned mind. For no reason at all that they know of, for no purpose that they know of, they grow in the palm-tree's shade—the shade of death or of life? Rain after summer drought refreshes the garden around them, giving life and joy to everything, making each bird dream it is a nightingale, making the rain-drops like small shots of pearl drip down from the overshadowing, star-concealing boughs of the palm-tree to the flowers beneath. But what to everything else is like divine grace, for them is a wound, a sickness, a burning. For it gives them life, and, with life, life's restless questionings, its seemingly unanswerable problems. As man grows in the valley of life—or is it the valley of death?—they grow in the palm-tree's shade, but what the palm-tree is, what its why or wherefore, is concealed from them. They simply feel imprisoned, while, as for the monk of Athos, all outside appears in bridal dress. They feel caught between two worlds, on the one hand a world of harmony and beauty, on the other hand

COSTIS PALAMAS

the world of death. Everything else in the garden, worm, bee, butterfly, the other flowers, lives its one hour of life carefree, in blind unconscious delight. They cannot. They are set apart by the possession of that one quality, both diabolic and divine, which nothing else in the natural world shares with them: thought. They are loaded with the burden of consciousness. And if this consciousness is divine because through it they seem to be in touch with some higher world, it is diabolic because it allows them to realise the full extent of their imprisonment. They are aware of their tragic situation [L.I., 91-94].

We pass now to the second phase in the development of the human drama I have sought to outline, the appearance of woman. The flowers see the palm-tree rise up before them into the sun's light, naked, covering the garden of which it is the mistress with a dream-woven veil. What rhythm governs her divine body! Nothing is so beautiful, not the young cypress swaying in the breeze, not the cool spring that sings like the poet and nourishes like the mother, not the dawn or the sunset. The day-spring of another world shines on her topmost branches. She is indeed the embodiment of a more than natural beauty, of that ideal beauty of which the imprisoned flowers sometimes have intimations: angelic phantom in the hermit's hut, mouth of harmony in the night of silence, thought when it first flashes in the broad sky of the artist, or even before, when a virginal and uncaptured dream, it has not yet found lodging and become word, music, marble, or colour—nothing equals her image, her idea, as it falls and is reflected in the mind's mirror. Does a transparent, a deathless blood run within her, or sap unable to wake her from a soundless, sightless sleep in the lovely intoxication of an unstained life? Is her crown something false, or her hair, the boughs, which when the wind strikes them become a lyre that proclaims the symphony of everything and her own beauty? The boughs, her hair, are wings that tremble, that will raise her toward some higher creation for which, like the human soul, she longs. Is she the last remaining witness to some vanished age, or the first intimation of a life to come? Sometimes it seems that she struggles to give birth to an immortal spirit captive within her, sometimes she is like the last column of an ancient Greek temple [L.I., 95-97].

But now, just as before the enraptured poet the woman, whose

49

soul was body and body idea and who seemed to hold out the promise of some impossible release, becomes, for reasons we have seen, suddenly a deceiver, a destroyer, so the palm-tree, now symbol of this woman-idea, or Muse-Idea as Palamas elsewhere [L.I., 138] puts it, suddenly shows another aspect. Her branches, that, in the time of enchantment, had seemed radiant hair or wings, now seem spears ready to strike. The flowers, with their sleepless consciousness, see her dance at night with all the sinister vicious brood of the dark world: she is a vampire, a blood-sucker; within her flesh a devouring worm has nested; her trunk, her lovely body, is hollowed out and rotten within; vultures feast on her, snakes crawl from her roots to her top-most height. In other words, "the next day brought death and judgment"; after their lyric ecstasy before the palm-tree's female form, the flowers suffer that terror of spirit, that revulsion of the body, which for the poet, looked in his stony ethic, follows in the wake of the carnal love of woman [L.I., 98-99].

The drama of "The Palm-Tree" has developed to the point at which we left our discussion of the poet's drama. But now comes the turn, the swift awakening that breaks the spell of that stony ethic and takes us beyond the point of deadlock, into a new phase of the drama. For now, at this point of death and judgment, when all seems evil, and the very beauty in which alone life has any significance, tainted to the roots, ugly and foul-smelling; when, in total disillusion, the remorse-laden soul experiences the extremes of abandonment and despair: at this point, like a sudden dawn, comes a new realisation, a new insight: is it not precisely the ugliness, the unclean, the evil, the very rottenness that lies at the core of things—is it not this that nourishes the beauty in which life finds fulfilment? Does not the sweetness issue from the decay? Are not the two aspects of life, which a perverse ethic has compelled us to see as antagonistic, as irreconcilable, really the two sides of one and the same thing, the one depending on the other? And does not the purpose of life consist, not in trying to force it to submit to our mind-made ideas of right and wrong, but in living it, in the actual experiencing of it, as it is, with all its passion? And is not our happiness achieved simply in living out our condition as it has been given to us, until the same hand that brought us into the world, takes us out of it again, and life, in its overflowing abundance, brings forth new forms, new manifestations, to take our place? From minute to breathing minute life flows on, all that is now has been before and will be again, all is an endless circle, an everlasting return. To accept this, to say "yes" to it all, to accept the destruction as part of creation, the decay as a condition of a new flowering: in this is wisdom. Our life is on earth; we hear its heartbeat, signal of births to come, of songs not yet uttered; secret unexpected passions weep within it, seeking release, world-destroying fire crackles. Let us live this life of earth, this life of flow, of passage from birth to death and new birth; let us live it without complaint, with joy, receptive to all its manifestations. For from its lowest, its ugliest forms, rise up the forms of beauty, rises up the palm-tree that reaches into another world, the dream reality, the world of ideas, the Olympian world, which again sheds its light back on to the mind's mirror and so fills it with beauty and harmony. Thus are the two aspects, the lower and the higher, which had seemed so opposite, through this process of sublimation, reconciled; and the terrible anguish at the soul's divided state soothed in a new acceptance that embraces both [L.I., 99-102].

We can see now how it is that woman plays such a central part in Palamas' world. It was she who woke the poet's passion in the first place; it was she who dragged him down into the mire of sin, so that he could only look upon his life with loathing and repulsion. Yet it was she also who woke in him a sense of beauty and happiness beyond the torment and the strife, a nostalgia for a lost paradise. And it was through his carnal love for her that the division in his soul, product of his dualistic attitude to life, his sense of life's present horror and of his own degradation on the one hand, and his sense of a once-known world of beauty and harmony on the other, had developed to such a point that it led to the brink of lunacy and complete overthrow. But at the moment that the poet experienced the extremes of suffering, sickness, physical and mental anguish, torment of mind and body, total eclipse and abasement, a kind of death—at that moment the new realisation was given; the two poles of life between which he had been stretched as on a rack and torn asunder, were seen to be not dread irreconcilable opposites, but complementaries, the one issuing from the other and giving birth to the other, the darkness to the light, the

ugliness to the beauty, the discord to the harmony, the light
and the beauty and the harmony in their turn being the fulfilment
in which all finds release and happiness. And this exchange is
not something that happens on two different levels of reality
which never meet, or which are separated by an interval of
time ; it happens here, now, in the experience of every moment,
in the passionate throb of life spilling over itself in endless
abundance, in the living instant, in its Dionysian dance from
minute to minute, through forms which are always changing yet
always the same, always dying yet always being born, constancy
in movement, sameness in never-ceasing recurrence. And it is
because woman is as it were the priestess who initiates the poet
into all those stages of development, first separating him from
life only to bring him back, after a passage through Hell and
Death, to union with life in an altogether richer way, that the
poet can write as he does in the lines already quoted :

> And a spring-head is woman, and from her come
> You, sin, and deliverance, resurrection, and death.

The poet is now in a position to replace his formerly negative,
life-denying attitude by a positive attitude of affirmation, a
creative attitude. The ugliness, the gross and bestial aspects of
life, which before he had regarded with loathing and revulsion,
must be accepted and embraced, for from them rises the very
beauty which is life's fulfilment. Palamas sees this understanding
reflected in an old fable, a reversed version of the familiar
Beauty and the Beast. There was once a beautiful girl who
through some terrible fate had become a dragoness, the sister
of Death. In that state of ugliness and bestiality she was doomed
to remain until someone came and with love kissed her, where-
upon her virginal beauty and freshness would be restored. And
she lived on in the hope that perhaps some day someone would
come to give her, in spite of her beastlike appearance, her
frightful ugliness, the kiss of release. But no one came. Only at
last a young hero, someone who had tasted death and had learnt
the secrets of the lower world, had learnt, that is, like the poet,
that from the ugly and the bestial rise the beauty and the
harmony, and with this knowledge had learnt to love with a
divine love " the vomitings of the dark and of disaster "—this hero

loved the ugly beast, and set off to give her the kiss that would bring her back to the sun and to joy. And the poet concludes:

> *And should you fall and should the terror of your startled horse throw you, rider, over the precipice, the moment that the hideous beast opens its flaccid lips to drink your kiss . . . you will have time to see, falling from the precipice, falling for ever into the embrace of death on the now unenchanted journey that has, unlike the first, no coming back—falling from the precipice you will have time to see something like rebirth on the face of the beast!*
> [Altars, 31]

And so it is with all the seemingly repulsive, the seemingly ugly and bestial aspects of life: if only they are accepted, if only they are confessed and embraced with love, they will then, through miraculous metamorphosis, reveal the beauty which, rejected and denied, remains for ever frustrate in them:

> *Whatever you have within you, good, suffering, sin, some affliction of the soul, some sickness of the flesh, confess it. Into the light! All the beautiful things of earth, to be more beautiful, and the world's ugly things, to be stirred by the breath of loveliness, seek a priest to confess them, seek a love to kiss them.* [Altars, 54]

In the same way, those moments of passion, which before had given birth to such feelings of shame and self-disgust, can now be seen as those moments in which life fulfils itself, in which the ugliness becomes beauty, body and soul marry in ecstatic fusion. And these moments are not only moments of fulfilment; they are also the moments in which life renews itself. For this reason they are worth more than all the laboriously built-up systems of philosophy, all the study of history, all the fact-piling and information-distributing of learned scholars, for all these things are the consequences of reflection and research into life that is past and dead, and they only involve other people in life that is past and dead; they dry up the soul and the body, they close up the pores through which life can be experienced at all, they result in cobweb-spinning and impotence. For life is only now, in the immediate experience of it, in its passionate flow from minute to minute, in its beating pulse:

*Blood, that boils and beats, flames and overflows, fire
or freshness, in man or flower—you, blood, allotted, shared
most wisely by the faultless artist, Life! What pyramids,
what immortalities can excel the greatness of the flashing
moment which rises, becomes a rose, becomes Helen, and
dies?* [L.I., 117]

A sick race, are all the grammarians, philosophers, scholars, full
of high-sounding titles and empty heads, mere weavers of words
and singers of stupidity. Death is beautiful from what it has in it
inexplicable, unlimited, deathless, great, and these people, instead
of enjoying the lily that flowers above the tomb, instead of giving
attention to the world that passes, yet is the same and yet
changes—all these learned gentlemen prod among the bones in
the tomb and seek to nourish their pitiful lives on the relics of
death. And what they discover, grovelling there among the
things of death, they think has something to do with truth. And
all their labour and study, their writings and deliberations, are
nothing beside the despised, the unwritten evening song of the
shepherd as he comes down the mountain-side, giving a final
moment of joy to the day that sinks [King's Flute, 137-138]. And
the poet greets that passion which flowers in the moment and
dies in the moment, whose value he has learnt to understand
from those women who, whether they know it or not, are its
guardians and its votaries:

*But, Passion, welcome to you, from wherever and
however you come, Passion, one holy moment, passion,
sacred drunkenness when you burn upon the altar, and on
the altar itself when you burn the same torch to the world's
twins, love in death, death in love, and even when you
come with the wolf's hunger, even then, however and
from wherever you come, welcome! Because of this I from
this hour unhesitating bring you to the altar that my magic
art has built to offer sacrifice to your shades, women, to
you, children of life, to you, idea's nereids, grey ghosts,
to you, to you, blue shadows; and to my women-
worshipping altar because of this I bring unsupplicated
you, women of the street, flock of lust and slavery, red
shades, who without knowing it gamble with passion, and
are like stones, like nakedness, and your heart, the world's*

54

enmity and scorn, is as the empty discarded broken vases whose only use is in the hands of guttersnipes to gather dirty water from the streams. But I bring you to the altar I have built, and I stand reverently before you, for I am your lover, because the moment when you gave to me relief and gratification, with all the ugliness and shame, gratification and relief the same both in the swamps and in the rugged places, is life from my life, blood from my own blood. [Altars, 109]

Not any longer is he held captive in the soul's darkness, in hell's torment, in the monk's bitter agony: fire has leapt up from that ascetic ash [L.I., 131], he is free from the life-devouring shadow, ghoul of a perverse morality, to which in youth some terrible dumb influence had bound him; he becomes the singer of the burning sun-filled moment, of the Dionysian ecstasy; he is himself the satyr to whose music all dances in beauty and nakedness, and whose rapid passage from living moment to moment may be worth more than all the static immortalities of art [L.I., 4].

All is naked round us,
All is naked here,
Sky and field and mountain,
Unrestrained the day.
Crystal is the world, open
Its deepest palaces:
Eyes, take your fill of light,
Of rhythm, guitars, your fill.

Here the trees are scattered
Unharmonising stains,
Pure wine is creation,
Nakedness rules here.
Here is dream the shadow,
Here the tender mouth
Of night breaks into still
A white untainted smile.

Shamelessly, bare-breasted,
All is here possessed:
The dry rock is a star,

55

The body burning fire.
Your heavenly nakedness,
O Attica thrice-blessed,
Distributes rubies here,
Silver and pearl and gold . . .

Distant whatever unfit,
Clothed and concealed,
The crippled and the ugly,
Unpurified and strange.
Upright all; uncovered, clean,
Earth, air, bodies, breasts!
Nakedness too is truth,
And beauty nakedness.

"—In the sun-glad nakedness
Of the Athenian day
If you should imagine
Something beastlike unclothed,
Something like a leafless
No shade conferring tree,
An unchiselled marble,
A body, slender, lean,

Something bare, uncovered,
In the open space
Which but two eyes of flame
Show to be alive;
Something which from the satyrs
Descends, and is wild,
And its voice is silver,
Do not flee: it is I,

The Satyr. Like the olive-tree
I am rooted here,
And with my pipe's refrain
I make the breezes faint.
I play and see! there mate,
Worship and are worshipped,
I play and see! there dance
Man, element, beast."

56

This same flow of life from minute to minute, through forms which are always changing yet always the same, always dying yet always being born, the eternal recurrence, the never-ceasing cycle of events and phenomena through time, the " pirouetting dance " as Palamas calls it [King's Flute, 156], is not the law which governs nature only; it is the law which governs all history:

> *The eternal circling-round of May and January*
> *Governs History, as it governs too the lilies . . .*

he writes in one poem [L.I., 115]. Nothing endures; the glories of nations pass like summers, like youth [Altars, 143]. All rises from the great ocean of time and passes back again into it. There is neither going forward nor going back. In everything is the return of everything. The world, and man in the world, at once the butt of everything and the pride, are both obedient to the all-governing law; hearts and stones submit to it; it may have one appearance here, another there, but everywhere it is the binder and the looser, ruler and crucifier. Autumn, spring, winter, summer are brought in in due season and in due season give place successively. One hand compels all, a great over-mastering Fate whose bride is the course of time, is history; and so linked together are they, this Fate, the Great Creator and the Great Destroyer, and history, that no one can comprehend:

> *There where the two walk closely embraced together*
> *Which one leads the other, which of the other is cause.*
> [King's Flute, 155-156]

Above everything Fate stands. For even if immortals are above mortals, she is above both. Fate, as the ancient Greek tragedians knew, is the final arbiter of life [King's Flute, 99].

Yet this is no cause for despair. On the contrary. If everything is the expression of Fate, if everything is brought into life and swept out of it again by the same indomitable and supreme power, everything then is of value, everything has its part to play in the whole of creation, nothing must be denied, all belongs to the great stream of life of which we too are a fraction. The only crime is to deny this stream, is to seek to impose man-made and artificial moralities upon it, splitting it up into sections, some good, some bad—the good to be encouraged, the bad to be

57

E

suppressed—for in this way life itself is crippled, wounded at the roots, frustrated. And this is what the enlightened man, the creative artist who has risen above the false moralities of the feeble-minded and the half-asleep, and who understands that from the ugliness may rise beauty, from discord harmony, light from darkness—it is this denying of life, in whatever form, which he will not do, for he knows what others, confused and ignorant, often forget, that it is from these very aspects of life which are so often condemned and suppressed that man draws those energies which make it possible for him to create higher and more beautiful forms of life:

> *Of nothing am I ashamed, nothing do I silence, nothing do I despise, for all with purpose, alike the world's priceless things and what the world rejects, are by the law established, determined by fate, and you cannot alter them, neither say them nay ; everything of man is holy, everything deserves sympathy, and the sins and failures of my trivial life, and what uncontaminated it has, are holy; my sickness is song, and prayer, temptation, strength, and weakness are germs that create, passions that energise* [Altars, 109].

And it is in the same spirit that Palamas addresses the future poets of Greece, telling them not to be frightened of or to turn away from life, even in its most destructive aspects, for it is only from life that they can draw the sustenance on which their art depends:

> *And if bad years come, and if the times are enraged, and all the birds are fled terrified, and the trees serve for nothing but fortifications, do not fear the havoc. Fire! Axe! Go, unseed it, lay the garden waste, root it up, and build a stronghold on it, and enter in, to struggle, to wound, for the new birth for which we all wait, which begins to come, and which is lost, broken in the turning of the cycles. It is enough if it reveals to you an idea, dictates to you an idea, a supreme idea, which will be above everything* [Altars, 19-20].

These last two lines bring us to what was of outstanding

importance for Palamas, his conception of the artist and of his art. This too arises from and is a counterpart to that understanding of life of which I have been speaking. The artist, the true artist, that is, is someone who has risen above the antinomies into which the ignorant, the feeble-minded, the vindictive, divide life. He has risen above them through that inward drama whose course we have followed. He has passed through all the stages of self-abasement and despair, through even a kind of death, and he has risen up again with his new creative insight. He sees now, as others do not, that the so-called antagonisms and opposites in life are really complementaries. It is from the lower elements, from all that seems bestial and ugly, that beauty can rise, and the world of ideas, the Olympian world, be born. He must accept, he must respect, he must embrace all manifestations of earth's life so that each one can give birth in his imagination to its own particular idea, its logos, in which consists its release and its true identity. These ideas, or logoi, born thus in the artist's imagination, he now, through his art, embodies in concrete form, in word, stone, music or whatever material it is, and in the contemplation of his works of art thus wrought, all those manifestations of earth's life which provided the original stimulus for the creative act, find now their fulfilment. It is a process analogous to that indicated in the phrase of Solomos which I have already cited: " Art silently worships nature, which, in reward for this distant love, dances naked before her. These forms echo back in the mind of Art and she offers them to mankind." For Palamas, however, it is not simply to mankind that Art offers them back ; it is to everything: " The ancient, the new, marbles, trees, what has gone, what remains, seek a reconciliation in a single embrace " [L.I., 182]. It is this embrace that the artist can give and the artist alone ; he only can " redeem the time," confer on it the idea which is at once above it and at the same time saves it from nonentity and meaninglessness. Hence the supreme importance of art for Palamas: it was, quite literally, the consummation of life, life's deliverance. For this world of ideas, this Olympian world, which is the province of art, is above time, out of the ceaseless flow of things. There, all that occurs in the flow, all life's passion-ridden moments, all the fury and the mire, all the hungry longings and the hungry savageries, the ugliness and complexity, is transmuted into a state of changeless beauty, eternal harmony, free from strife, uncontaminated, pure, at rest. And this act of transmutation can only, as was said, be performed by the artist, the inspired bard, the Orpheus of the new Golden Age.

To this drama, whose development I have sought to trace, in which human life passes from a state of frustration and slavery to a state of creative freedom, Palamas gave full expression in three poems to which he gave the collective title " The Great Visions." As has been pointed out,[1] to give these poems an external form, a framework within which the various parts might be held together, Palamas adapted for his own use certain features of Orphic myth and ritual. In the same way and for the same purpose he adapted features of Orphic cosmogonies, particularly that of Empedocles, with its vision of the world of the four elements acted upon by the influences of Love and Strife: at the beginning of things, the elements, under the rule of Love, are in fusion: then, as Strife encroaches on Love, they are gradually brought into a state of separation, until, at the worst point, when Strife has total sway, all is chaos and dissolution ; and then this state is again followed by a period when Love encroaches on Strife, the elements are again brought gradually together, until the world " as it was in the beginning " of unity and cohesion is once more achieved. It would be wrong, however, to imagine that Palamas' use of these features of Orphism necessarily implied his subscription to Orphic theology, or that they were for him much more than a simple objective pattern through which he could give formal coherence to his own particular vision. As we have seen, and as we shall see more clearly later, the kind of religious beliefs that lie behind Orphism, do not, at this " sceptic " stage in Palamas' life, play any significant part in his vision.

The first of the three poems of " The Great Visions " is " Ascraios " [L.I., 161-182]. The hero of this poem, the Ascraian —the " plot " of much of the poem is taken from Hesiod's Succession of Ages described in " Works and Days ": hence the hero's title—is, like the hero of Palamas' Beauty and the Beast legend, one who has tasted death and has learnt the secrets of

[1] Jenkins, Palamas, *op. cit.*, p. 5ff.

the lower world; he has, that is, achieved the insight that has freed him from the world of opposites and antinomies within which most people are caught and by which they are prevented from any fruitful creative life. He now comes back from Hades to tell of the stages through which he had to pass before that insight was given to him, and to hand on to the new Orpheus, the poet himself, his divine gift. In fact, under the mask of the Ascraian we have not much difficulty in recognising Palamas himself, and the final lines of the poem, which speak of the hero handing on his lyre to the new poet, make it clear that this we are meant to do: Palamas there takes off the mask, to indicate that, having passed through the drama which the poem describes, he is now fit to fill the rôle of prophet of the new age which in the later poems of the trilogy he assumes. Thus the poet begins with a description of the age in which he was born, the present age, an age of strife and misery:

On the firstborn soil the jackals of nakedness
howl among the joyless lives of my fathers . . . [L.I., 162].

But he is distinguished from the rest of men by his poetic gifts: the nine Muses have appeared to him, he has eaten the fruit of the laurel and has come to know the works of God and man, things past, present, and to come. He has had visions of the Ages of Man. First, there was the Golden Age, the age in which love and harmony rules, where men were equal with the gods, the just governed, lust and violence did not exist, earth yielded her fruits without labour, there was no suffering or growing old, or murder. All lived in beauty under the sun, and there was no death: from earth to Olympus all passed as one might cross a light bridge from one green bank of a river to the other green bank, though here, in the ideal world, the world of earth was not forgotten. In other words, this Golden Age is one in which everyone lives the artist's fulfilled vision, where nothing is denied, but all is accepted, embraced, and so gives birth to that world of beauty in which it is transfigured.

But now begins the period of separation and dissolution; barriers begin to intrude between the world of ideas, the Olympian world, and the natural world. No longer now does man live beneath the sun, he lives beneath the moon: it is the Silver Age, and those who live in it are neither dead nor alive but dwell in a sort of penumbral state of limbo. They reject the inspired singer who offers to show them the way back to the paradisaical age they have lost; they are the generation of the godless. But their rejection of the prophet's voice brings a further fall: a burning cloud passes over them and buries them. And from that time the rejected singer, exiled by his fellow-men (an exile which indicates their exile from life more than his), has in solitude sought to recover the vanished state:

> But from then I close within myself and alone I search
> the ruins of a sick and an accursed world [L.I., 167].

Thus through man's stubborn self-will and stupidity, the influence of Strife gains on that of Love, the Age of Silver passes and gives place to the more warlike and destructive Age of Bronze. Force, enmity, violence drink the wine of blood. And here the singer's soul, servant of the caressing rhythm, is drawn still further into the world of wrath, he feels the hardness enter his heart, he is still further separated both from his fellow-men and from the age of love and beauty, the longing for which still burns within him.

But the discord increases, and the Age of Heroes comes, the last which still preserves some contact with the Golden Age; only it too is doomed to pass, destroyed in those catastrophies like the fall of Troy or Thebes which it itself has brought about, and in its place comes the Age of Iron, that in which the singer was born, the present age. Now the world of beauty, the Olympian world, is quite eclipsed; ugliness, vice, brutality, have total sway, life is sunk in the mire and the filth. It is a state like that described at the opening of the poem; and it is while in this state, cut off from life and oppressed by inner and outer sickness, that the singer sees rise before him the woman of his dreams, the superb Pandora.

Pandora is an embodiment of all those aspects of woman which we have already seen Palamas describe. In her, beauty and flesh fuse in a sudden dazzling blaze of whiteness. Like flowers is her hair, the sun's rays upon her are caresses, the winds kisses; she is lovely beyond all things, and she seems a last living token of the golden world, promise of release from that agonising division of his soul which so torments the fallen mortal creature. In spite of all creation's warning, he draws towards her, gives himself to her embrace, knows her nakedness, only to discover what vicious hag-like brood her beauty hides. In other words, he reaches that condition of despair which follows the Palamas' "sin with woman" episode; he touches the extremes of internal tension, his whole being is split apart on the relentless knowledge that he can only find relief for his pent-up passion by committing what amounts to mortal sin, by plunging back into the world of the flesh and the devil which to his moral convictions is the total negation of the beauty towards which he aspires. All seems evil, all hope of happiness an illusion, life tainted and sick to the roots. It is a moment of overthrow, of death, of descent into the bowels of the earth, into the black kingdom of the underworld, into Hades.

But at this moment of death and descent to Hades, in a sudden flash the new insight is given. In "Ascraios," this realisation, or, rather, the inner power of the heart which confers this realisation at the moment of despair and near madness, is symbolised by Persephone; it is she who gives the singer release from his terrible bondage, allowing him to see that the misguided morality in whose thrall he had been held, lacerating the body in the name of the soul, is nothing but an attitude of mind and vanishes on the instant if the mind but shift its ground: one can get beyond the world of opposites and contradictions that so confounds one. There is, Palamas seems to say, a moment which, like Blake's grain of sand in Lambeth that Satan's watch-fiends cannot find, escapes from all mental and moral categories, that "flashing moment which rises, becomes a rose, becomes Helen, and dies." In the experience of this moment, where idea and object fuse, when heart and soul burn with the harsh gem-like flame of a sudden perception that transcends all dualism— in the experience of this moment consists life's only happiness and peace:

> *Swift the dawn, and more swift than her,*
> *within her, heart of the dawn itself,*
> *there is a moment that catches fire and dies,*
> *and eye can scarcely grasp it.*
> *It is the blessed moment of the dew-drop*
> *which as a spotless crown the lily wears,*
> *and the regal sun rejoices in it,*

fills it with light, and does not swallow it.
I am as the dew, the sun of the swift and blessed moment :
peace, partner of love, in my soul you dwell,
within me have you taken root, and you do not pass.

[L.I., 179]

The poet now has a more adequate insight into life and its purposes. He understands, as Orpheus did, that it is his task to reveal the true nature, the true logos, or everything, of bird, beast, flower, tree, man—that true nature which is so often hidden under a cover of ugliness, ignorance, confusion, even from its possessor ; to reveal it so that this moment, when idea and object fuse in a single transfigured identity, can always be taking place. He, the poet, with his new insight which has been born of his harrowing experience, will now know this inner nature of everything, the idea of everything, and to this knowledge he must with his artistic skill give rhythmic, harmonious expression, so that in his art everything will recognise its own particular idea, and in that recognition will exchange its natural state of strife and disarray for a new state of love and concord. It was this transmutation which Orpheus had been able to accomplish, and this is what is meant when it is said that he had power to move rocks and trees and that the animals came and knelt before him : he through his music revealed to them what they really were, he conferred on them that embrace in which all seek to be reconciled, listening to him their hate was changed to love, their strife to harmony. Now the new Orpheus in his turn must accomplish it. Thus will the two worlds, the higher and the lower, the Olympian world and the world of earth, which in the present age have fallen so disastrously apart, be brought into contact again ; the breach will be healed, nature will nourish the ideas, the ideas illuminate and refine all that is gross and dark, and the Golden Age will return.

It is for this reason that the poet addresses Persephone as the reconciler of the two worlds, of the upper world and the lower world, for she is the power that will inspire his art through which that union is brought about ; and he gives thanks to her for the new love which allows him to recognise all creation as a creature that suffers, awaiting its deliverance in the new world of beauty which it is his duty to reveal to it ; which has made it possible

64

for him to accept everything, reject nothing, and to give heart and craft to bring creation from a state of misery to one of happiness. For if he with his prophetic insight is now above everything, yet he is now also the forgiver of everything ; if he is a stranger to the world, he is not the denier of it. And the poet, conscious of his great task of reconciling in every living thing the two worlds, the world of ideas and the natural world, which through his own suffering have been brought together in himself, returns from his journey to the kingdom of death back once more to earth.

The second poem of the trilogy, " The Great Visions," is " The Chains " [L.I., 183-193]. This, the shortest of the three, in part recapitulates with a different emphasis what was expressed in " Ascraios " and prepares the way for the third and by far the longest poem of the trilogy, " The Dodecalogue of the Gypsy," of which indeed it had once been the poet's intention to make it a part. The drama is now not given a legendary setting, as in " Ascraios," which perhaps softens its impact ; it is set in a prison, image of the present age in which man lives. Into this prison the poet himself is dragged, isolated, however, from the other inmates who, less awake, perhaps do not notice that the prison is a prison, or at least that there is any alternative to it, and who therefore escape the torment which the poet, possessor still of some consciousness of a lost world of happiness, suffers as a consequence of his knowledge :

> *Among the separated*
> *I am set apart ;*
> *among the prison's chosen,*
> *I am the jailor's*
> *chosen-one . . .*
>
> [L.I., 184]

Into the prison-house of the world under its present dispensation the poet is, then, dragged. It is an Arab who drags him, symbol of that demonic power that separates him from life [L.I., 31]. The poet pleads his innocence, asks what crime he has committed that he should be thus condemned. The jailor does not know : he is simply the servant of Fate, the great Law, the Judge, and it is Fate that determines, that condemns, without giving reasons. All creation is bound in the same chains, all breathes the air of the prison, which is itself both solid and fragile, real and illusory. It seems at one moment like Satan fallen from Heaven to the pit of Hell, standing upright motionless, bound by the curse of God. Who knows for what great crime it is the payment? Within its circles all the lusts of night dwell, it is like a tomb. Sorrow drips down its walls, bats gyrate aimlessly, all stand dumb, wounded, and the chains alone give tongue, an accursed sound. Yet the poet's own chains make a separate music, a music which does not mingle with, which resists, the sound of the other chains, and which is like the beginning of something new, of a new life.

But the Arab compels the poet on, down narrow black corridors, sunless. By the glimmer of three candles which he lights, those of mercy, help, love, he beholds the other prisoners, and he offers them what little consolation that he, sick child of the sun, misformed image of freedom, can still dispense. At last he sees before him a patch of earth, and above him a glimpse of the sky ; and he finds a little corn, and he scatters it, and it grows, and his patch of earth becomes a garden, and the light spreads shade, and a stream runs, and he hears one morning a lark sing somewhere in the sky, and unwittingly he raises his arms upward to pray. It is then that the Arab shows him, high in the wall, a small hole, a skylight, and the poet, up a rough, thorny ladder, that tears his hands, begins to climb toward it, chained as he is. And at last he reaches it, and looks out, and there opens before him a vision of a land of beauty and love and innocence, sun-drenched, liberated, a vision again of the Golden Age. And the poet, as if he himself were there, free among the free, forgets the Arab, and the chains, and he feels the iron become wings. And prophet, painter, artist, he tells to his fellow-men enslaved in the darkness beneath him, what he sees, and his words become a song, and his chains a guitar, and his music begins slowly to transform all that is below and to raise it up towards the vision of happiness.

So we come to the third poem of the trilogy, " The Dode-calogue of the Gypsy," possibly the most important work that Palamas wrote and described by himself as " the poem which integrates all his ideas."[1] Now the drama which we have been

---

[1] Palamas, Poetic, *op. cit.*, p. 67.

following of the poet's development from a state of isolation, frustration, aimlessness, to a state of creative purpose and responsibility not only as an individual but in relationship to society as a whole—now this drama is set in an historical context which makes it possible for the poet to give a more definite form to that vision of a new age which he envisages, of which he claims to be the prophet, and which up to now has been left too undefined to be convincing. Although the poet does not restrict himself to the arbitrary and artificial bounds of chronological succession, the main action of the poem is concentrated in the years round, both before and after, the fall of Constantinople to the Turks. In this way, from the start the poet links his hero's, the Gypsy's, individual development with an objective development through which we can grasp his attitude to European, and particularly to Greek, civilisation, and thus can discern the values of which he hopes the new age—the new age of Greece—will be the realisation.

The fall of Constantinople marked, as far as Greece was concerned, the end of a world, of the Byzantine world and the values which went with it ; it also marked, or, at least, coincided with, the beginning of a new world, that of the Renaissance and post-Renaissance West, with its new set of values. The growing consciousness of the Gypsy is thus linked with the emergence of this new set of values. In addition, all those elements out of which the new world of the West was to grow —Christianity, ancient Greek culture from the point of view of ideas, and, from, so to speak, a biological point of view, the various people of Europe—met in one way or another at Constantinople. Finally, the Constantinople of the " Dodecalogue " is not the splendid city at the height of her greatness ; she is, on the contrary, the city at the time of inner dissolution, waiting only for her end to come ; in fact, her death is the very condition of the new birth, of the new flowering of civilisation: the old state must be destroyed before the new can be created. Thus, through her Palamas can represent that " law " which determines not only individual but also historical development ; he can illustrate the positive aspect of destruction as opposed to its negative aspect which is so often emphasised: destruction, and evil itself, without ceasing thereby to be less the cause of misery and affliction, yet give birth to creation and to the good ; the

67

destroyer is at the same time the creator. It is Palamas' insistence on this point of view that explains not only his legend of the Tearless One, which forms Canto XI of the "Dodecalogue," but why in the second of his two major works, "The King's Flute," written soon after the "Dodecalogue" and which I have already cited, the hero is the Byzantine emperor, Basil the Bulgar Slayer, a personification of war itself, of that force of destruction which is at the same time the force of creation: War the father of all. Palamas himself wrote[1] that the "Dodecalogue" was the propylæum which leads into "The King's Flute," and it is the emphasis on the positive, if tragic, aspects of destruction in contra-distinction to the conventional emphasis on its purely negative aspects, which links the two works.

Before the city of Constantinople, then, in which is concentrated this multiple significance and round which are now gathering all the various peoples of East and West in the hope of taking her, the gypsies, in the first canto of the poem, also gather. But they, unlike the other barbarians, have no warlike intentions; they are the wanderers, the people outside the great marches of civilisation, treaders of the open road—in fact, it is as if they have lost all road, and all purpose, and have no memory, no hope, no country either behind or before them. Among them is the hero of the poem, the Gypsy:

> And I among the tempest
> and the tumult of the world,
> untaught by any father,
> unknown by any mother,
> by no caress enslaved,
> stood like the topmost branch
> of an unpruned ageless tree,
> of a barren, deep-shaded tree.
>
> [D. of G., 45][2]

He rides upon a mule, image of his nature and of his fate. We are now at the beginning of the Palamas drama, in a state of separation from life and society, from creative purpose and harmony, in a state of anarchy and strife. But as the Ascraian

[1] Foot-Roads, *op. cit.*, p. 13.
[2] "The Dodecalogue of the Gypsy," Vol. 5 of the Poetical Works of Costis Palamas, Athens, 1950.

and the poet in "The Chains," something distinguishes the Gypsy. Even among his own people, themselves separated from the rest of men, he is separated. Something he knows which sets him apart, above the world's welter, a dim consciousness of another, lost state, which he had once possessed and which he must find again if ever he is to live fully and creatively; a memory of the Golden Age:

> And it was like a golden indissolvable
> dream of a wakeless sleep
> which never had touched the earth,
> whose source is elsewhere, far away . . .

[D. of G., 49]

And it is this knowledge, this memory, that distinguishes him; he has the divine discontent of those who understand that their present state is a kind of parody of the life they ought to be living, which they have once lived, and which they must do all in their power to recover. It is this understanding which is the starting point of, and the impulsion behind, that search for a lost state of creative freedom, the stages of which are recorded in the remaining eleven cantos of the poem.

The Gypsy now, with the opening of the second canto, turns towards his own soul for instruction, and as from the depths of a well his own voice comes back to him. It tells him that, in spite of his great gifts, all he does is like the playings of sunlight on cloud, insubstantial, aimless, closed within the narrow circle of his own self-centred world, and having no content through which it can become significant to mankind. He must learn first to master his own will, his own likes and dislikes; he must engage in some occupation which serves society and not merely his own vanity; he must overcome his ego-pathic world which keeps him separate from the commonality of man. He becomes, therefore, in obedience to his inner voice, by turn a coppersmith, a piper, and a builder, not out of economic need or from habit, as others might, but from a conscious desire to give his life some meaning and fulfilment, to find some activity that at once provides outlet for his creative gifts and is at the same time useful to society.

But in all the three occupations that he attempts, the Gypsy fails to achieve this reconciliation for which he seeks. As a coppersmith, he accepts orders and tries to turn out useful and practical goods, but some mysterious power seizes him and he only manages to produce what is "purposeless, useless, odd" [D. of G., 57]. The truth, although he does not yet realise it, is that his gifts are such that they can find that practical outlet for which he searches only in a creative society, in one, that is, in which, to return to the terms of Empedocles, the influence of Love is gaining upon that of Strife and a new age of harmony approaches ; while at the moment he is trying to serve a practical purpose in a society in disintegration, one that is moving towards total dissolution and collapse, and one, therefore, in which all his endeavour is from the outset doomed to failure. So, too, when he stops being a coppersmith and becomes a piper: he satisfies himself playing his tunes, gives himself peace, but round him all is violence and passion, and he achieves nothing in relation to the rest of society. And in a moment of complete isolation, far from the hurly-burly of the world, he looks as into a lake into the depths of his own soul. All is quiet and he waits to be revealed the great unrevealed secret of creation. But it is a false peace which the Gypsy has ; it is the result of a narcosis under the lulling influence of his own piping ; it is not the peace which comes from inner conquest of the self, from an integration with a higher level of consciousness. Thus, just when the secret might have been revealed, the Gypsy, in a spasm of denial that rises from his sense of his unworthiness, breaks the holy calm, disturbs the lake's surface, and when he looks again into the now ruffled waters, he sees his true image reflected, ugly, rabid, distorted, product of his narcissistic, auto-erotic indulgence. And in disgust he flings the pipe away, and becomes a builder. He sets to work in a palace that is being built, he lends a hand in everything, every corner of the building knows him. But again his creative powers are frustrated: it is not he who has conceived the building, who has given birth to it ; he is merely the slave of someone else's conception, a conception utterly at odds with his own ideal vision. Thus in building it his gifts are prostituted, denied, unfulfilled. He is forced back again into isolation, into the distress of his own self.

The Gypsy has sought release from his tormented condition in useful social activity. He has failed to find it. He turns now, in the third canto, to seek it in love, in the merging of his own identity in another and opposite identity in whom he feels embodied all his ideals and his dreams. The third canto is the Gypsy's song to his beloved, a gypsy-girl, the "enchantress of the stars" and image, as Pandora, of all women seen through the burning, blinded, and transfiguring eyes of a passionate and romantic love. He asks that she teach him how to tame all physical and metaphysical disquiet, that she teach him all the secrets of the ideal world of beauty of which her body is the incarnation. Thus enriched, with her he will forge the new race of faultless children, a higher race, where each individual will fulfil the Nietzschean ideal of being both artist and ruler; and this not through a gradual and biological evolutionary process, but at once, in one daring leap of the soul. So the Gypsy, in his Dionysian intoxication, sings. But no sooner does he seek to realise this love, no sooner does he give himself to the girl in bodily embrace, than his exaltation turns to disillusion, he learns only the "slavery of the flesh" [D. of G., 72], and from the heights of expectation he drops to those depths of despair and emptiness whose features have already been described.

The Gypsy has now reached the nadir of isolation and inner tension and depression. His every attempt to escape from himself has only thrown him back more absolutely upon himself. He has tried to find release in working in a useful way for society; he has tried to find it in love. In both he has failed, and the life for which he searches remains as far from him as ever. His despair changes to nihilism, his passion to mockery and sarcasm, he proclaims himself the prophet of the great Nothing, of pure denial. And, his search for the moment abandoned and having reverted to a gypsy state, outside history, he watches pass before him the gods and ideals of past and present civilisations as one by one they go down. The next three cantos record the death of the values, of the supports and traditions of the old world, as they are seen through the eyes of the Gypsy. He himself does nothing to bring about their downfall. Although in the prologue to the poem [D. of G., 21], the poet notes: "My hero is by turn a destroyer and a creator," during this great disintegration and destruction of the old world out of which the new world is to rise, the Gypsy does not play any active part. Thus, when he speaks of the death of the ancient gods [Canto IV], he does so only to contrast his own indifference and nihilism, product of his

disillusion, with the religious superstition of man in society. It is
the same with the passing of the culture of ancient Greece
[Canto V], of which Byzantium had been the treasury: he
watches it go down without lament; it has lived its life, it is now
dead, and never again can it be restored: what is important is
life now, the purely physical moment—if he happens to find an
old papyrus, some ancient manuscript, he will burn it to enjoy
its warmth; and he will light his fire indifferently among
whatever ruins he happens to come across, whether of palace
or of monastery, of school or church [D. of G., 95]. In the same
spirit [Canto VI], he stands by as the Christians vindicate and
the polytheists lament the burning of the book of Gemistus
Pletho, who in the fifteenth century had sought to revive the
Platonic and neo-Platonic tradition in the face of the extreme
asceticism, other-worldliness, and monotheism of mediæval
Christianity: both, Christians and polytheists, are idol-
worshippers, whether they know it or not; all myths, all gods,
are simply creations of man and differ only as the disposition of
man differs from one age to another, from one place to another;
they do not correspond to any abiding reality; both, Christians
and polytheists, are equally mistaken in their wish to preserve and
to continue a tradition which is past; both should look to the
living moment of history, as the mountain-rebels of Greece preparing their revolution against the Turks. And in the next canto,
Canto VIII, which describes the great spring festival of the
gypsies, the Gypsy proclaims with all his vehemence the anarchic
life of the Gypsy race as opposed to the settled life of society:

> We are the immortal uncivilised;
> and cities are dwellings of the unclean,
> and cities are bulwarks of cowards . . .
> [D. of G., 123]

During all these last cantos, the Gypsy has, as I said, been
speaking as one totally disillusioned with life, a denier of all
values, of all "higher purpose," one for whom all life except the
purely biological day-to-day life is a pretence and an artificiality,
and for whom all search for any permanent substructure of ideas
or principles for the world of the senses is misguided folly. The
first three cantos of the "Dodecalogue" described the stages

through which the Gypsy's " old " self passed as it was brought
down to this state of disintegration and nihilism. The cantos
which followed described the stages through which the old
world, the old Byzantine world, passed as it was brought towards
its state of disintegration and collapse. Thus the individual and
the historical development has now reached a common point:
both the " old " self of the Gypsy, and the old world of Byzantium,
await their fall, so that the new world, both in an individual and
a historical sense, can come into existence, though, as we shall
see, then the individual and the historical will be at one, the
Gypsy himself working to bring about on the historical plane
what he has now realised on an individual plane. But this is to
anticipate. At the stage the poem has reached, both individual
and society must pass through one of those periods of death
which is a condition of rebirth; and of this death, of both
individual and society, the fall of Constantinople, symbol and
historical event, is the climax. And at this turning point of the
poem, the prophet in the midst of the condemned City cries
aloud that inescapable process of descent and death through
which the old, corrupt, accursed state must pass before it is
overthrown and the new delivered life of creative freedom can
once more begin:

> And your Soul, accursed City,
> will not find rest;
> the ladder of evil it will
> step by step descend,
> and wherever it goes, wherever it stops,
> into a worse body will it enter . . .

> Until the god of love
> has mercy on you,
> and a dawn breaks,
> and deliverance summons you,
> O Soul tormented by crime!
> And you will hear the deliverer's voice,
> you will shed the dress of evil,
> and again controlled and light
> you will move like the grass, like the bird,
> like the breast of woman, like the wave,

73

F

and not having beneath another step
to fall lower
down the ladder of evil,—
for the ascent again to which he summons you
you will feel there blossom on you
the wings,
your great original wings!

[D. of G., 146 & 148]

What this death and new awakening signified for Palamas I have already discussed. Here I need only add a few words to make it more clear in this context. For reasons it would be out of place to discuss here, the intellectual teaching of Christianity had, in mediæval Byzantium as in the mediæval West, become confused with a moral teaching that tended to deprive the natural world of its quality of an original divine creation, and at the same time to encourage the notion of a world of the spirit that had no contact with the natural world. It had thus split creation in two. On the one hand, there was the pure transcendental world, and, on the other, the fallen, corrupt, and abominable world of the flesh and the devil, the world of nature, which had no part in or contact with the processes and purposes of the spirit. As a consequence of this moral teaching, man too had been divided against himself; in so far as he was part of nature and had natural passions, he was sinful, and both were felt to be inimical to the spiritual life.

In these moral antinomies both the old world of Byzantium and the " old " self of the Gypsy had been caught. As far as the Gypsy was concerned, the effect of this morality had been to induce in him a feeling that he was separated from life and from any creative purpose, and the first part of the " Dodecalogue " had described the stages through which he had been led in order to heal his schizophrenia. This is not to say that the Gypsy was consciously aware of the cause of his malaise: he was simply a victim of it, someone born into a world where such a moral teaching was the order of the day, and a typical product of a society to which its strictures applied. But, unlike the majority of his fellows, who lived in tepid consent to this state of affairs, he, although just as much as anyone else consciously persuaded to the truth of this morality, yet had gifts and visions which could only be realised in a world where it did not apply, in a world of a different order. This was the root of his deep unrest, and this was why to whatever he turned he was bound to meet disappointment and frustration. It was in his erotic experience with woman that the split between his conscious ethic—that the world of nature and the ideal world are irreconcilable opposites —and his unconscious longing for a state in which his ethic was destroyed and in which consequently his gifts and his visions might be realised—it was in his erotic experience with woman that this split had developed to such a point that it produced in the Gypsy a feeling of utter fatuity and nihilism, of the worthlessness of all values and ideals ; his life had become empty, drained of meaning, poisoned to the roots, rotten, death-like. He had reached the bottom of the ladder [D. of G., 150].

But at that suicidal, self-annihilating moment, a new realisation is given to the Gypsy, marked in the poem [Canto IX] by his finding a violin : these moral antinomies and the attitude to life which results from subscription to them, are not really true ; they are the product of a false and vindictive teaching. The ideal world is not something irreconcilably separated from the natural world ; it grows out of it, is part of it, its fulfilment but not its denial. Everything in the natural world must be accepted and embraced. The earth itself is divine. It only waits for the bard who with his inspired insight can see into the heart of things and discerning there their essential beauty will by his art work it into forms through which it can be recognised and proclaimed. In other words, the artist must be the one who creates the ideal world, the Olympian world of harmony, love, and beauty through which the discord, strife, and ugliness that were a consequence of the life-denying ethic are overcome and transformed. The new dispensation will be based not on the opposition of the two worlds, that of ideas and that of nature, but on their reciprocity, their mutual support and inter-dependence, their essential oneness. The idea of a metaphysical world existing outside and beyond the natural world is quite simply illusion, for it is out of the earth itself that grows, through the artist's transmuting genius, the world of beauty, harmony, love. This is the understanding which has been struggling for realisation in the Gypsy's soul, and which he has now realised. At once all fits into place ; he is no longer divided against himself ;

and the nature of his mission, that in which his creative gifts find outlet that not only employs them to the full but is also of service to mankind and society, is now clear: he must through his art help to bring into existence the world of beauty, harmony, and love, of which his new understanding and his new knowledge of himself has allowed him to realise both the need and the possibility. And as his realisation on the individual plane has coincided with the fall on the historical plane of the old dispensation and its false values, the way is now open before him to set about his task:

> *Strike, my bow, and build,*
> *the world is made through me,*
> *within my own two hands.*
> *O birth, birth!*
> *Violin, you alone exist,*
> *and one is the voice, and your sound it is,*
> *and one is the creator, and I am he,*
> *and the miracle-performing word,*
> *that word is music!*
> [D. of G., 153-154]

And, Orpheus of the rising age, he begins to play, not to the adults, relics of the old world, who shudder at the revelation of his music, but to the children, future inhabitants of the new.

The last three cantos of the "Dodecalogue" describe, not the realisation of the new world, but its taking a more definite shape in the consciousness of the Gypsy. Thus, in Canto X, those values which his old state had led him to deny, he now with his creative music resurrects. Country and state under the growing influence of harmony are no longer negative; they become positive. The gods, the divine ideas, that is, which dwell in nature, and which under the old ethic, that denied to the world the quality of divinity, had been driven underground, had become demons, vampires, creatures of the night, now must be affirmed, must be drawn back again into the sunlight. And love itself, transformed now into a love of an ideal beauty and no longer prisoner of the flesh, becomes the source of creative inspiration. Canto XI foreshadows, under the cover of legend, the new type of man, whose character has already been

indicated[1] and of whom Palamas was to give an epic delineation
in his portrait of the Emperor Basil the Bulgar Slayer in " The
King's Flute." Finally, in Canto XII, the Gypsy withdraws into
the embrace of nature that he may learn, as Orpheus had, the
inner mysteries of the world. For he has passed through
the same trials as Orpheus and therefore is ready to receive the
same reward: the lyric joy born of his new pantheistic faith.[2]
The trees speak of Orpheus' initiation:

> And from root to topmost bough
> sweetly in our embrace
> from out of our deep heart
> all the blood he drank.
> And he learnt the lessons of earth,
> and the ancient sorrow died;
> creator of the second Olympus
> he became, and minister.
>
> [D. of G., 194]

But the Olympus which the Gypsy will create will not be
that of Orpheus. It will be the third Olympus. The first Olympus,
the polytheist Olympus, had been characterised by the separation, the autonomising and atomising into distinct hypostases
of the physical and spiritual powers of life. In the second
Olympus, that of Orpheus, these hypostases had been brought
together and unified, seen as the various expressions of a single
underlying reality. But that Olympus had also fallen and had
given place to Christianity with its conceptions of an ideal
world set apart from the natural world: earth was again left
orphaned. The third Olympus will re-establish the unity of the
world of ideas and that of nature, only now with a difference.
Now earth, nature, will not be seen as the expression of an
underlying metaphysical reality, as Orpheus had seen it; on the
contrary, the world of ideas will be born from earth itself, from
nature will come Truth:

> And cast away the dreams,
> bend, place the ear to Nature,
> divinatory is the rose,
> Sibyl the cypress-tree!
>
> [D. of G., 195]

[1] See p. 68, above.   [2] Palamas, Poetic, op. cit., p. 69.

But this Truth is not to be anything in which the heart cares to believe ; its final judge is to be the mind :

> *If the miracle is the heart,*
> *the eye of the heart is the mind.*

[D. of G., 196]

The third Olympus will be a scientific world, not assuredly Huxley's Brave New World, for it will be based on a pantheistic worship which recognises the divinity of nature, but one in which the critical temper of the humane mind watches over and corrects the errors, the confusions, the bewilderments, into which man is ever liable to fall.

Such then, in outline, is " The Dodecalogue of the Gypsy," Palamas' central and most comprehensive work. In an analysis such as this, it is impossible to do justice to the poem ; all that it has been possible to do is to distinguish the main features of the understanding of life that seems to lie behind it, to try to see what it was that Palamas sought to express. The question now arises : is it a valuable understanding ? Is what Palamas sought to express of much import ? Or does the poem really dissolve into several fine lyrical fragments—quite impossible to reproduce in translation—held together by a " myth " whose meaning, not being important, is best forgotten ? We can of course discount Palamas' belief that the scientific attitude is capable of discerning truth, and he himself later rejected it.[1] This, however, is not a serious point, for that belief is a sort of addendum tacked on to the main body of his vision, and can be subtracted without in any substantial way disturbing it. No, if we wish to make a serious criticism, we must make it of the very vision, or understanding of life, itself. That something is amiss, and that Palamas was aware of it, we may at once suspect from a reading of a " Last Word " of the " Dodecalogue," a short personal confession with which, after the " Twelve Words " of the Gypsy, Palamas closes the poem. Palamas obviously meant this to go with the other twelve cantos ; he did not, that is, put it in for amusement, but intended to convey something important through it. And " Last Word " is a confession of despair, frustration, and bitterness as black as anything Palamas wrote. What made Palamas

---

[1] See: Sikelianos, A., Costis Palamas, Athens, 1943, p. 25.

include it in the poem ? What is there lacking in his understanding, that its expression should have left him not with happiness but with despair ?

I have discussed this understanding fully enough not to have to make more than a brief recapitulation of it here. The great effort of Palamas' creative life was to redeem the world of nature from the negative, not to say evil, character with which it had been attributed ; was to affirm life, the passionate throb of life spilling over itself in inexhaustible abundance, the living instant, the Dionysian dance from minute to minute. It was to communicate a recognition that all life is positive and has some part to play, even its most ugly and destructive aspects ; all is worth out attention, our compassion, our reverence. The only crime is to deny life, to split it up in obedience to a man-made ethic and to try to suppress all that part of it which does not harmonise with some imagined good, with whatever intellectual prejudice has led one to believe is " spiritual." Everything that lives is holy. The divine is in nature herself. Man's task, the creative artist's task, is to reveal that divinity which nature hides in herself ; it is to release through his art the world of ideas which grows from her roots and in which, thus released, she finds fulfilment and beauty. This is the artist's great function, to transform the low into the high, and to reveal the world of ideas in which nature can behold her own intrinsic beauty. This is the positive and valuable aspect of Palamas' vision, and where it stands opposite to that of someone like Solomos, who, as we saw, tended to emphasise only the negative and evil aspects of the natural world and its destructive forces. Indeed, in this respect, Palamas and Solomos stand at opposite poles of a very similar dualism, the one asserting what the other tended to negate. For it is when one comes to ask what is the world of ideas for Palamas, that one can discern some flaw which may account for his distress and suffering.

Because what in fact is it ? It is not a self-existing reality, a world of ideas in the Platonic sense ; it is not something which, however involved with the natural world, can yet exist apart from that world, beyond all phenomenal manifestation. On the contrary, it is itself entirely contingent and relative to the natural world, a sort of æsthetic throw-off of the natural world as foam is a throw-off of the sea's waves. It depends upon the natural

79

world, not the natural world upon it. In "The Chains," it will be remembered, the guitar of the poet who seeks to reveal, to those imprisoned in the darkness and iron of a completely determined life, the boundless limits of an ideal subjective world,[1] is still the heavy chain which binds him without hope of release to that same life of darkness and iron in which everyone else is trapped. The ultimate consummation of the natural world and of life can, then, be no more than that which is achieved in transforming them into æsthetic beauty, into an æsthetic experience which has no roots in any abiding reality. The world for the Palamas of the "Dodecalogue" was a world with no real principles above the categories of time and place. It was because of this that when it became a question of finding "supports" for the new age he envisaged, he found them in the secular values of the post-Renaissance West. He lacked that quality, perhaps best indicated by the term "faith," which would have made it possible for him not only to affirm, as he did, the positive character of natural life, but also to relate that life to a level of reality in which its fulfilment was not subject to the chances and turmoil of time and place; to relate the multiplicity and diversity of the world which he so strongly proclaimed to an inner and unifying centre of understanding in such a way that its ultimate character is seen to be beyond the sphere of destruction and necessity. As it is, nothing really is changed of "the painful, high, disabled and tragic reality" of man, who, "bound with the golden chain of verse, lives incapable of grasping any solid creations, and advances embracing only phantasies."[2] For over both the natural world and the world of ideas as Palamas envisaged them, stands a higher, a more dread, an impersonal and ruthless power, Fate. In the end, everything, not only nature, but also man's noblest sacrifice, his deepest affirmation, his beauty and his love, are the mere playthings of Fate. The last word of Palamas' vision as the "Dodecalogue" expresses it, is, as the poet knew in placing the "Last Word" at the end of it, one of irresolvable tragedy.

Was it the last word also in Palamas' own life? This is not simply a question of impertinent curiosity, for, if it was not, we must make an adjustment to our final estimation of the under-

[1] Palamas, Poetic, *op. cit.*, p. 138.
[2] Palamas, Foot-Roads, *op. cit.*, p. 179.

standing of life he wished to communicate. I think it was not. Among Palamas' later poems, written many years after "The Dodecalogue of the Gypsy," is an Orphic Hymn.[1] In it the poet, as once behind the mask of the Gypsy, so now behind another mask, speaks:

> A kingdom, a peace, and both supreme, I have.
> When I tread the earth, flowers break forth upon it,
> And when I gaze upon You, Sky, stars break forth. I am all,
> And wherever I am, everywhere. And uncreated what I
>   can create.
> Man ? No : God am I.
>
> When my end shall come on earth, elsewhere shall it have
>   beginning.
> No deep grave shall bury me, neither shall fire dissolve me.
> A white peak will welcome me in the glory of the blessed,
> In music, I the undying sound. They wait for it.
> Man ? No : God am I.
>
> And the gods of air, of meadows, and of the seas,
> Of peaks, ideas and forms, of beasts and everything,
> The superhuman, however man's own making they may
>   seem,
> I shall draw near to them, shall see, shall share their
>   boundless vision,
> As it becomes an equal.

---

[1] Cited by Sikelianos, Costis Palamas, *op. cit.*, pp. 56-57.

81

III. Constantine Cavafis
(1863-1933)

THE last decades of the nineteenth century, during which the Alexandrian poet Constantine Cavafis grew to maturity, were, as far as certain literary circles are concerned, decades of a peculiar temper. It was then that æstheticism came into fashion, and decadence. There was, in these circles, a craving for sensation, a fastidious search for exotic refinement, a cultivation of art as something removed as far as possible from the common affairs of men, and from nature. Gautier praised Baudelaire's " Fleurs du Mal " as creations from which nature was entirely absent,[1] and could say that " there is nothing truly beautiful but that which can serve no purpose ; all that is useful is ugly."[2] The hero of Huysman's " A Rebours " lived in a tropical room shut off from the outer air ; he avoided all natural, external experience and cherished solitude and what was unnatural because what was not nature was art and art was the only thing that made life worth while. Pater, catching the style, and blending it with a native pre-Raphaelitism, wrote commending in poetry " a strange complex of conditions where as in some medicated air, exotic flowers of sentiment expand, among people of a remote and unaccustomed beauty, somnambulist, frail, androgynous, the light almost shining through them."[3] And Swinburne issued his prolix challenge to a sense denying ethic:

> Wilt thou yet take all, Galilean ? but these thou shalt not take :
> The laurel, the palms and the pæan, the breasts of the nymph in the brake.[4]

[1] See p. 117 of: Gaunt, William: The Æsthetic Adventure, London, 1945.
[2] Quoted by Richardson, D.: Saintsbury and Art for Art's Sake in England, PMLA LXIX, 1944, p. 245.
[3] Quoted by Gaunt, William, op. cit., p. 56.
[4] Swinburne: Collected Poetical Works, London, 1924, Vol. I, p. 68: " Hymn to Proserpine."

Art was thought to be a kind of sensation, evoked by and having for its end the expression and re-evocation of sensations. The love of art was equated with a love of fine sensations and works of art came to be looked upon as little more than a superior and sophisticated form of aphrodisiac.

Cavafis' early poems, those, let us say, which he wrote before 1901, in the main reflect at second-hand this fashionable romantic exoticism and decadence of the late nineteenth-century literary world. Behind them one can discern the compound but etiolated shadow of Gautier, of Henri Murger, of Baudelaire, Wilde and Pater, affected, æsthetic, feminine, haunted by the sense of corruption, by the canker in the rose, and reverent before the studied artificiality of Art:

> I do not want genuine narcissi, neither do lilies
> gratify me, nor the genuine rose.
> They decorate ordinary and common gardens. Their flesh
> accords me bitter weariness and sorrow—
> I am bored by their perishable beauty.
>
> Give me artificial flowers—the glories of glass and metal.[1]

There is the scornful indifference to nature:

> It does not bother me if winter
> outside spreads mist, cloud, and coldness.
> Within me there is spring, is authentic joy.
> Laughter is all a golden ray,
> there is no other garden like love,
> the warmth of song melts all the snows.[2]

The inward mood affects everything:

> When you are sad May resembles December,
> more cold are tears than the cold of snow.[3]

The sensitive soul is above the pollution of the crowd, he does not allow himself to be soiled by the common and vulgar world:

[1] Quoted by Perides, M.: Life and Work of Constantine Cavafis, Athens, 1948, p. 159.
[2] Cited on p. 10 of Ta Nea Grammata, Jan., 1936.
[3] Quoted by Perides, op. cit., p. 140.

Whether I am happy or wretched I do not examine.
But one thing with joy I always put into my mind
that in the great addition—their addition that I hate—
which has so many numbers, I am not there
one of the many units. In the total sum
I have not been counted. And this joy suffices me.[1]

With this studied, self-satisfied superiority and aloofness there
is also the refined melancholy of the dandy and of the sophist,
of the æsthete for whom the sensation of the passing moment is
the only things of value which life has to offer and who is overcome by the oppressive sadness of things:

The happy profane nature.
Earth is a temple of sorrow.
Unknown how many tears dawn sheds,
the pale evenings lament,
and the elect soul sings mournfully.

I hear sighs in the breezes.
I see complaints in the lily.
I feel the rose's sorrowful life ;
meadows are full of a mysterious sadness
and sobs sound in the thick wood.

Men honour the happy
and false poets hymn them.
But the gates of nature are closed
to those harsh ones who laugh indifferently,
laugh strangers in the unhappy country.[2]

The trouble with all these early poems so far quoted is that
they are too vague, generalised, and mushy to be convincing.
They convey an amorphous sentimentality rather than any sincere
and precisely realised experience. In the absence of anything
significant to express, the poet is indulging in a vapid romanticism
of a fashionable type, and so it is not surprising that really
nothing is communicated to us, that we are not given any insight
which adds to or alters the way we look at things.

1 *Ibid.*, p. 158.
2 *Ibid.*, p. 143.

Nevertheless, it is the note of refined melancholy that dominates even the best of Cavafis' early poems, those in which some slight intimation of real quality begins to sound. It is not the melancholy of Keats:

> *Seen of none save him whose strenuous tongue*
> *Can burst Joy's grape against his palate fine.*[1]

It is not the melancholy that follows in the wake of joy tasted, but the melancholy that comes from thinking on joys which never have and never will be tasted, which are doomed to remain for ever unrealised—it is this melancholy that Cavafis feels:

> *Like the beautiful bodies of the dead who have not grown*
> *   old*
> *and are shut away, with tears, in the splendid tomb,*
> *with roses at the head and at the feet jasmin :*
> *so seem the desires that have passed*
> *without fulfilling themselves, without the chance of a*
> *   single*
> *night of voluptuousness, or of one brilliant morning.*
> [7][2]

There is an echo of Gray here:

> *Full many a gem, of purest ray serene,*
> *   The dark unfathomed caves of ocean bear,*
> *Full many a flower is born to blush unseen,*
> *   And waste its sweetness on the desert air.*

But for Cavafis the regret is not so much for those whom history has destroyed wantonly, without any apparent rhyme or reason, before they have had time to develop, or even for those who because of circumstance have been wasted. He laments rather those moments of pleasure which have been lost through weakness and indecision, through fear of the consequences or because it seemed there would be another opportunity:

> *In the back part of a noisy café*
> *an old man sits bent at the table,*
> *a newspaper before him, companionless.*

[1] Keats: "Ode to Melancholy"; Oxford Ed. of Standard Authors, 1950, p. 248.
[2] C. P. Cavafis: Poems, Athens, 1948, from which all quotations from Cavafis' work are taken unless otherwise stated. The figure in brackets gives the page number of this work.

And in the despite of miserable old age
he thinks how little he enjoyed the years
when he had strength, and purpose, and beauty.

He knows that he has aged greatly ; he feels it, sees it.
Yet none the less the time that he was young appears
Like yesterday. What a short span, what a short span !

And he reflects how Prudence has deceived him,
and how he always trusted—what stupidity !—
the liar who said : " Tomorrow. You have much time."

He recalls impulses that he controlled, and what
joy he has sacrificed. Each opportunity
lost now mocks his foolish mind.

. . . But with so much thought and recollection
the old man has become dizzy. And he sleeps
leaning across the table of the café.

[11]

In another early poem, " The City," the theme of failure and
of frustration is enlarged and at the same time made more
direct. Instead of describing the waste in terms of an old man
recalling his past and regretting his stupidity in not seizing the
pleasure of the moment whenever it was offered, the poet now
seems to carry on an internal dialogue with himself. One part
of himself tempts him to flee from this town where his life has
been ruined, by holding out before him the romantic possibility
of finding somewhere else to live where he can begin over again
and perhaps after all make a success of things ; renews, in other
words, the cry which fills so much of the " poésie des départs "
of the latter half of the nineteenth century:

La chair est triste, hélas ! et j'ai lu tous les livres.
Fuir ! là-bas fuir ! Je sens que les oiseaux sont ivres . . .[1]

The other part of himself knows that there is nowhere he can
go, that he himself is the city from which his romanticism tempts

[1] Mallarmé: Brise Marine.

him to flee: he himself is the condition that he describes, and from himself there is no escape, nowhere to flee to:

> *You said : " I shall go to another land, shall go to another*
> *   sea.*
> *I shall find another town that is better than this one.*
> *All I endeavour here is for disappointment done,*
> *and my heart—like a dead body—within me is entombed.*
> *Until when is my mind to this marasmus doomed ?*
> *Wherever I turn my eyes, if I look no matter where,*
> *the black ruins of my life I see, here,*
> *where so many years I have spent, ruined, wasted utterly.*
>
> *" New places you will not find, you will not find another*
> *   sea.*
> *The city will follow you. The same streets will hold*
> *your footsteps, in the same districts you will grow old,*
> *in these very houses will you become grey.*
> *Always you will reach this city. Do not hope to go away—*
> *For you there is no ship, no road is there.*
> *As you have destroyed your life here*
> *in this small corner, so everywhere have you wrecked it*
> *   utterly."*
>   [32]

This is a step forward. It is now no longer the old man who is the subject of this city of folly, error, vice, regret, and huge boredom: it is You—Hypocrite lecteur—mon semblable—mon frère ![1] And however much you may dream of other lands and of other climes, you are condemned, you cannot escape, you must resign yourself to it, it is your destiny. You are yourself the centre of the scene you describe, you are the subject of its decay, all its waste and rottenness is but a reflection of your own condition. And in another one of these early poems, Cavafis seems to imply that there comes a moment in life when you, inhabitant of this city which is so to speak your shadow, have the power to choose, to accept it or to reject it; if you accept it, if you make the refusal to go some other way, you will be for ever crippled; yet you will not repent, you will have been true

---

[1] Baudelaire: " Au Lecteur " from " Fleurs du Mal."

to what you are, you will have had the courage to live a life which, however appalling, it was your destiny to live, even if only to reveal the full horror of its degradation:

> *To some men there comes a day*
> *when they must deliver the great Yes or*
> *the great No. He is revealed immediately who has*
> *ready within him the Yes, and, pronouncing it, forward*
> *he goes towards honour and towards his certainty.*
> *The denier does not repent. If he were asked again,*
> *no, he would repeat. And yet it cripples him,*
> *that no—the true no—for his whole life.*
>
> [14]

In other words, if for a moment we may, in spite of the *non sequitur* which is perhaps involved, read from the poetry back to Cavafis' own life and identify the " you " of " The City " and the denier with the poet himself, it seems that the borrowed æstheticism of the early poems is giving place to a more positive attitude ; the poet is beginning to integrate himself with a world and with a pattern which he was at first only imitating. What began as an affectation is becoming a personal destiny, is becoming the poet's own life. He has chosen and reconciled himself to his City, his æsthetic City, as it was his lot that he should. His task now as a poet is to explore in all its aspects that City which, at the price of immolation, he has chosen ; which, having chosen, he has become. It is to reveal all the consequences of such a choice as a surgeon might cut through the outer flesh to reveal some distempered part in the human organism, with the difference that it is on himself that the poet must perform the operation. It is to make a myth of that City which is his own condition. It was to the creation of this myth that the greater part of Cavafis' mature poetry was devoted.

Part of the weakness of those early poems at which we have glanced is due to the fact that Cavafis has written them without possessing any real background, without having integrated himself with and made his own a landscape with wider terms of reference than that provided by the rootless " fin de siècle " æstheticism whose moods and attitudes he was borrowing. It is always one of the major tasks of a poet to provide himself with a landscape of figures through which he is able to express his particular vision. When society moves within a framework whose figures—symbols and images—are common to the great mass of the people, this task is relatively simple, for then the poet can express himself through these common figures, communicating the particularity of his vision by slight shifts of emphasis or of relationship. All traditional societies move within such a framework. It was thus, for instance, that the ancient Greek tragedians were able to write works which were both profound and popular, for, belonging to such an integrated society, they were able to draw upon a heritage of myth and local rite familiar to all through long use, and yet transformed by their individual genius. One has only to compare the treatment of, say, the character of Orestes by the Greek tragedians to perceive how various can be the shifts even of a single figure, and to understand of what great advantage it is to a poet to possess such a figure in whom the least change of emphasis or relationship will at once be recognised by the audience: it allows the poet to express subtle shades of distinction in his vision by slight alteration in the action of his hero when compared with the action of the same hero in the work of other poets ; by—if Orestes is the figure in question—setting his treatment of Orestes against the background of other treatments of the same hero which he knows are present in the mind of his audience. Christianity provided another such framework of myth and ritual through which the artist could communicate his vision. One would, for instance, be able to discover a great deal of the intellectual history—and is there any other history in the real sense of the word?—of Byzantium from a study of the different treatment of the Christ-figure in the icons of various epochs ; or a similar study would give one an insight into the change of intellectual climate which took place between the world of Byzantium and the world of the Italian Renaissance that otherwise it would be difficult to obtain.

It is when there is no such common framework to society that the poet's task is more difficult. Traditional values, traditional terms of reference break down, the poet no longer shares any immediate and recognised means of communication with the people, and, forced back upon himself, his poetry tends to become increasingly private and "esoteric." The kind of poetry written during periods of dissolution tends to be what is called romantic poetry ; tends, that is, to be the expression of individual emotion rather than expression controlled by the discipline of consciously held values and purposes. The poet begins to see himself as someone set apart from society, or even set over against society, a lonely figure, a pariah, or an outcast, or even perhaps a criminal, forced into the wilderness by society's disintegration and loss of quality. If he has a positive relationship to society, it is generally that of a revolutionary: he desires to overthrow the order whose values no longer correspond to his own and to inaugurate a more creative phase of life. One can trace the course of one such romantic period through the nineteenth century, beginning with the ardent revolutionary idealism of a Shelley and ending with the recluse "pure" poetry of a Mallarmé. And how far, for instance, is the "social" poetry of Pope—the poetry, that is, of someone who has a status in society and knows to whom he speaks and with what values he speaks—how far is this poetry from that Art for Art's sake poetry under whose influence Cavafis began to write?

For Cavafis began to write in a period when the process of dissolution was well under way, when all those tendencies latent in social break-down and which at first seem full of energy and excitement, have run their course and are exhausted and when new and perhaps unwelcome syntheses begin to appear on the horizon. The old values are discredited, the revolutionary ardour which led to their overthrow has turned to disillusion, and the poet finds himself adrift in a nondescript and formless society to which he feels himself superior and for which he assumes little or no responsibility: it can go to whatever hell it chooses in whatever way it likes. Thus isolated on the one hand from a community, and on the other unable to find in life any purpose which transcends his own individuality, the poet tends to find value only in the immediate gratification of the senses, in the stimulation of æsthetic beauty, in pursuits which concern the life of sensation only. I say "poet" here, not because the rest of society is any better off, but because, on the contrary, the poet is pursuing consciously, as a way of life, what the rest of society does unconsciously, generally under the cover of high-sounding ideals, and on a level of vulgarity that deprives life of even that semblance of elegance which the cultured æsthete is able to confer on it.

It was in such a situation as this I have described that Cavafis found himself. Yet where could he discover a counterpart to the world in which he was living? Through what could he express his experience of it? How could he avoid falling back on the already debased language and imagery of an effete romanticism?—the language and imagery we find in his early poetry. Cavafis had no relationship with the indigenous Greek tradition, that tradition on which Solomos, Palamas, Sikelianos, and Seferis, for instance, were able to draw with such fruitful results; to pretend that he had would merely have meant the substitution of one alien background for another alien background. In addition, the Greek demotic language was a young, fresh language, admirably suited to a nation in the process of birth and to poets whose vision was orientated dominantly towards the future and was fundamentally heroic and optimistic, whatever the degree of tragedy it foresaw between the present and the future which it envisaged; and such a language could hardly have been a fit vehicle for Cavafis, who, a colonial Greek, was little concerned with the emergence of a new Greece, and whose pessimistic vision foresaw a future of conquest, corruption, and death from which relief could only be found in present æsthetic pleasure, in a stoic reserve, or in the contemplation of a past that was already beyond recall.

Quite how Cavafis lighted on that landscape through which his vision could be given coherence it is impossible to say. It often seems that poets as it were conjure up precisely those elements which they require for their poetry in a way that is inexplicable to others, as if this too was a part of their genius. In Cavafis' case, it may have been that in the modern Alexandria in which he lived there were enough visible remains of, and associations with, an older Alexandria towards which his mind was turning to stimulate his curiosity and to suggest that act of recreation which his poetry was more and more to become. It may have been that in the mixed races and the confusion of tongues, in the Christian churches and the ruined temples, in the bustle of the port and in the bargaining of merchants in bazaar and market of his contemporary environment, there was enough to awake in Cavafis the latent memory of ancient crowds and vanished ceremonies, of pagan priest and Roman soldier, of bizarre corruption and daring vice, of that whole City in which Cavafis could see as in a mirror the faithful reflection of a human condition to which his own life corresponded. At all events, behind the dull, constricting provinciality of present-day Alexandria, with whose *bourgeois* sense of values and moral philistinism Cavafis had slight sympathy, he began to discern the lineaments of an Alexandria which promised to be far more congenial to his temperament and one through whose figures he might express himself with greater assurance and freedom.

The Alexandria which Cavafis began to see as his City was the great hellenistic Alexandria, the capital of the Ptolemies, whose ground-plan had been traced out by Alexander himself between Lake Mareotis and the Mediterranean Sea. Under the protection and patronage of its rulers, the Ptolemies, chief city of a flourishing kingdom and a rich terrain, standing at a vital point between East and West and master thus of all the commerce of Europe with the East, Alexandria quickly became the most splendid and wealthy city of the known world. Greeks, Jews, Egyptians—each had their own quarter in the city; other foreigners, from all parts of the Middle East, flocked to it. Under the first two Ptolemies, a huge library had been built, housing, it is said, some four-hundred-thousand volumes: Callimachus was among its chief librarians, and later his pupil-turned-enemy Apollonius of Rhodes. At the same time also a Museum had been built where literary men were kept at public cost, while out at Serapeum, where another library had been built, men worshipped the divine Serapis, God of the dead and of the underworld and God also of the sun. The Alexandria to which Cavafis turned was in fact the crown and focus of that whole hellenistic world which included also such famed cities as Antioch and Jerusalem, Seleukeia and Ephesus, and numbered kingdoms like those of Syria, of Media, of Commagene, and of Macedonia itself, from which, with the conquests of Alexander the Great, all had begun. It was a curious, chequered world, knit only perhaps by the common Greek language. "Then he was that best of things," Cavafis was to write, "a Hellene: mankind has no quality more precious" [131]. And in a mock-serious poem he celebrates that expedition which gave the word Hellene the status it had in that world of which Alexandria was the centre :

> And from the amazing all-Greek expedition,
> the victorious, the brilliant,
> the much talked of, the glorified
> as no other has ever been glorified,
> the incomparable, emerged ourselves :
> the great new hellenic world.
>
> Ourselves : the Alexandrians, the Antiochians,
> the Seleukeians, and the countless
> other Greeks of Egypt and of Syria,
> and those in Media, and in Persia, and all the rest.
> With the far reaching dominations,
> with the various influence of prudent assimilation,
> and the Common Greek Tongue
> which we carried into Bactria, to the Indians.
>
> [189]

It was in this world of Alexandria, then, that Cavafis found a landscape through which he could express himself. Out of it he was to build a myth that could give coherence and form to a personal and yet at the same time perennial human condition. For it is a mistake to think that Cavafis used the past as an escape from the present or from the problems by which he was tortured. On the contrary, he used it so as to approach more closely to the present, which is the only way a poet can use it. The poet annihilates the history of the academic historian by making the past contemporary. This does not mean that he brings it up to date by interpreting it in the light of the latest fashionable theory or by using it as a case-book from which to illustrate the validity of an intellectual prejudice or a political creed. It means that he seizes upon certain episodes and incidents in the past, certain moments in time, which he again brings to life because in them he finds embodied types of an ever-present human drama ; and these episodes and incidents, these selected moments, have the advantage of being once and for ever fixed, whereas events of the present are often too fluid, their implications are too obscure, to permit their adaptation by the poet in quite the same way. In other words, the re-creation of a certain period of

94

the past by the poet—and this may be an imaginary past as well as an historical past—provides a point of view from which the present may be looked at, its actions mirrored ; it provides an image in which the present may see itself. In either case, it is the present that matters. As soon as the poet loses his sense of the present, of actual experience, and uses what should be his means of expression as an end in itself, he stops being a poet and becomes something else, a grammarian or poetaster, " literary " in the donnish sense, however much skill and learning his verse contains. This was in fact what happened in the case of several of Cavafis' " ancestors," writers like Herondas or, more particularly, Callimachus, and it is because of this that their verse has little significance except for the scholar concerned more with trends, sources, and influences than with poetry. Of course, the present must not be taken to coincide with the politician's or sociologist's view of the present, nor must one fall into the mistake of trying to identify what particular contemporary incident lies behind or has provoked a poem whose setting is in the past. To have a sense of the past is above all to have a sense of living human beings and of human life. To make history live in the way here implied one must first of all have actual experience. And Cavafis, because he had this sense of the present, of an actual human condition, is able in his poetry to make the past live. It is this if anything which justifies his claim to be an historian—" A hundred and twenty-five voices cry within me that I might have been an historian," he said[1]—for he certainly could not, as far as one can judge, have been an historian in any other sense.

We are now in a position to see what kind of myth Cavafis was to create out of his Alexandrian hellenistic past. We have already seen that his early poetry reflected at second hand the prevailing æstheticism of the late nineteenth century, with its refined hedonism, its value of the pleasure of the moment, its dislike of dogma and orthodoxy, its search for the exotic and the abnormal, its feminine feeling for beauty, its hostility towards the unknown and the supernatural, its fear of death and its worship of Art as the only thing deserving the respect of civilised man. But Cavafis until now had not been able to integrate this

[1] Cited on p. 121 of Perides, *op. cit.*

æstheticism with any background of his own. It had been but an attitude, a daring pose in the face of the strait-laced mercantile society in which he moved. With his discovery of the old Alexandria, however, a new perspective was added to his poetry. The past belonged and was accessible to everyone. By his use of the past, Cavafis could step outside the narrow world of romantic decadence and become universal—use, that is, episodes and figures from the common stock of European history and known consequently, or, if not known, at least discoverable with a little labour, by everybody. Of course, Cavafis' use of these episodes and figures would be coloured and modified by his whole personal temperament and outlook, just as the figure of Orestes was coloured and modified by the personal temperaments and outlooks of the Athenian dramatists. Indeed, it would be through his own selection and angle of approach that the particularity of his own view of life would make itself felt. We must now consider this view of life as it is presented to us through Cavafis' myth of the City of Alexandria and of the world of which it was the centre.

The first thing about this hellenistic world whose features Cavafis is to examine is of course its whole-hearted dedication to the life of sensation, its downright hedonism. I have already indicated how it is that in a period of dissolution when all values are discredited and life emptied of all metaphysical content, all that is left is the immediate gratification of the senses, and in the following poem Cavafis recounts in bored, ironic, blasé accents the attitude of one superficially disillusioned with every ideal and " higher purpose " and consequently having nothing left to value but such gratification and indulgence, for which, indeed and fortunately, he is admirably equipped:

> Two years he remained a pupil of Ammonius Sakkas;
> but he was bored both by the philosophy and by Sakkas.

> Afterwards he went into politics.
> But he gave them up. The Prefect was an idiot,
> and his entourage solemn and serious-looking blockheads:
> their Greek disgusting, the barbarians.

His curiosity was attracted
a little by the Church : to be baptised
and to pass as a Christian. But quickly
he changed his mind. He would quarrel doubtless
with his parents, ostentatious pagans ;
and they would stop—a frightful thing—
at once their very generous allowances.

He ought however to do something. He became the
*   frequenter*
of the corrupted houses of Alexandria,
of every secret haunt of debauchery.

Fortune had been kind to him in this :
she had given him a face handsome in the extreme.
And he enjoyed the divine gift.

At least for ten years yet
would his beauty last. Afterwards—
perhaps he will go again to Sakkas.
And if in the meantime the old man has died,
he will go to another philosopher or sophist :
there is always someone suitable to be found.

Or in the end possibly he will return
even to politics—laudably remembering
the traditions of the family,
duty towards the country, and other suchlike pomposities.
                                                    [126]

Or there is the young Jew who sometimes tries to renounce the
City and return to the " ways of his fathers":

Painter and poet, runner and discus thrower,
beautiful as Endymion, Ianthes son of Antonius.
From a family beloved of the synagogue.

" My most valuable days are those
when I give up the search for sensation,
when I abandon the beautiful and the harsh hellenism,
with its sovereign attachment to
the perfectly built, the white and perishable limbs.
And I become the person whom I should like
always to remain : of the Hebrews, of the Holy Hebrews,
*   the son."*

Very fervent his declaration. " Always
to remain of the Hebrews, of the Holy Hebrews—."

Yet not at all like that did he remain.
The Cult of Pleasure and the Art of Alexandria
as their devoted child possessed him.
[102]

At the centre of this Cult of Pleasure and Art of Alexandria
is the worship of the beauty of the male body. Æstheticism, no
doubt because it stimulates the sentimental and passive side of
man's nature, that feminine side which "senses" things and
reacts to them, seems generally speaking to go hand in hand
with homosexuality. It need of course hardly be pointed out
that the homosexuality of Cavafis' world has little to do with an
ascetic athleticism or with a warlike virility after the Spartan
fashion. It has little in common with that of Tyrtæus with its
exaltation of well-disciplined strong soldier-citizens, or with that
of Stephan Georg who praised the body as the Godlike norm
of human life. The worship of the male body where Cavafis'
world was concerned was rather on account of the pleasure it
could give, for the pleasing associations and sensations it evoked,
than for any purpose connected with the State or with any
quasi-religious ideal. And, according to one of Cavafis'
characters, there is "an erotic tension" [104], "an especial
voluptuousness" [133] in a homosexual relationship which the
normal relationship does not contain. Cavafis' erotic poems
generally describe incidents in the lives of such lovers. The
following poem, "Two Young Men, 23 and 24 years old," is
typical of many he wrote:

From half past ten he was at the café;
and he expected him to come shortly.
Midnight went by—and still he expected him.
Half past one went; the café
had emptied almost completely.
He grew bored with reading the papers
mechanically. Out of his last three shillings
one alone remained : such a time had he waited
he had spent the others on coffees and cognac.
He had smoked all his cigarettes.

98

Such a waiting exhausted him. Because
already alone for hours as he had been, there had begun
to possess him disagreeable thoughts
of his depraved life.

But when he saw his friend approach—at once
the tiredness, the boredom, the thoughts, went.

His friend had brought him unexpected news.
He had won at the casino sixty pounds.

Their beautiful faces, their splendid youth,
the sensitive love that existed between them,
was refreshed, was revived, was strengthened
by the sixty pounds of the casino.

And all joy and vigour, feeling and beauty,
they went—not to the houses of their respectable families
(where, however, they were not any longer wanted):
to a well-known, and very particular
house of debauchery they went, and they demanded
a bedroom, and expensive drinks, and they drank again.

And when the expensive drinks were finished,
and when already it was almost four,
to love they gave themselves, happy.

[158]

Sometimes, as in the next poem, " A Young Poet, in his 24th Year,"
he describes some psychological aspect of this love:

Work in what way you can now, mind.—
A partial enjoyment destroys him.
He is in an exhausted condition.
He kisses the face, the beloved face, each morning,
his hands are upon his most splendid body.
Never has he loved with such an enormous
passion. But the beautiful fulfilment of love
is absent; is absent the fulfilment
that must come from both of them with wished-for
intensity.

(They are not, both of them, equally given to abnormal
   love.
Only he is possessed entirely.)

And he destroys himself, and is altogether exhausted.
And also he is out of work, and that makes matters worse.
A few small sums of money
with difficulty he borrows (almost
he begs them sometimes) and he scarcely supports himself.
He kisses the worshipped lips, upon
the splendid body—which now however he feels
acquiesces only—he excites himself.
And afterwards he drinks and smokes, drinks and smokes;
and he drags himself daily to the cafés,
drags with boredom the wasting of his body.—
Work in what way you can now, mind.

[161]

Or on another occasion he speaks of the pleasure of some
association to which the sight of a handsome body gives rise:

From the fight at the tavern they brought in wounded
Remo, our friend, yesterday at about midnight.
Through the windows that we left wide open,
the moon lit up his beautiful body on the bed.
We are a mixture here : Syrians, Greeks, Armenians, Medes.
So also is Remo. But yesterday when the moon
lit up his lovely face
our mind went to the Platonic Charmides.

[76]

And in another poem he describes such a figure of ideal beauty
passing through the streets of one of those " pleasure-loving,
absolutely æsthetic" hellenistic cities, this time Seleukeia, on
his way to some enjoyment. The poem is called, " One of their
Gods":

When one of them passed through the market-place
of Seleukeia, at about the hour of dusk,
like a tall youth of perfect beauty,
with the joy of the inviolate in his eyes,
with his black perfumed hair,

100

the passers-by regarded him,
and the one asked the other if he knew him,
and if he was a Greek from Syria, or a stranger. But some
who with greater care observed,
understood and moved to one side ;
and while he was lost beneath the colonnade,
among the shadows and the lights of evening,
going towards the quarter that lives
only at night, with orgies and debauchery,
with every kind of drunkenness and lasciviousness,
they wondered which of them it could be,
and for what suspicious enjoyment
he had come down into the streets of Seleukeia
from the Venerated, Most-Honoured Mansions.

[77]

Here then is the first part of Cavafis' myth, this picture of a pleasure-delighting, beauty-haunted world of wit and sophistication, proud of its fine æsthetic sense and artistic skill, supercillious towards and sceptic of high-sounding ideals and other worldly faiths, tolerant, lazy, refined, bored, and capable only of reverence before the æsthetic perfection and sensual possibilities of the male body. But this is by no means the whole story. If the voice of the cultivated hedonist in a sentimental mood or a mood of self-esteem was the only one which Cavafis possessed, he would not be the significant poet he is. But so far the myth has been only partially inked in. The æsthetic world, being a world divorced from any principle, is a world of disorder, uncertainty, and despair. It is a doomed world. It is subject to attacks, against which it is powerless, both from without and within. From without, it is subject first of all to attack from any temporal power possessed with the sense of an historical mission or simply possessed with the desire for domination and conquest. Such a power Cavafis indicated when he speaks of the Romans. Rome, as an efficient State and military machine, and as a type of all efficient State and military machines, is hostile to practically all the values of that cultivated æsthetic humanism of which Cavafis' hellenistic world is the portrait. From the historical point of view, Rome's great military power overthrew those small kingdoms upon whose existence the superficial poise of hellenistic life depended, and such a life, lacking any true stability, must always be in dread of such temporal calamities. The following poem, "Darius," in which the barb is aimed not in fact at the Romans but at one of the hellenising monarchs, Mithridates Dionysus Eupator, king of the Pontus and, according to Cicero, the greatest of all kings after Alexander, a large part of whose reign was occupied with struggle against the Romans, reveals this permanent sense of insecurity and impotence:

The poet Fernazes is composing
the important part of his epic poem:
how Darius, son of Hystaspes,
received the kingdom of the Persians. (From him
descends our glorious king,
Mithridates Dionysus Eupator.) But here
philosophy is needed: he has to analyse
the feelings that Darius would have had;
perhaps arrogance and intoxication; but no—rather,
as it were, understanding of the vanity of greatness.
Deeply the poet ponders the matter.

But his servant interrupts him who comes in
running, and he announces very important news.
The war with the Romans has begun.
Most of our army has crossed the borders.

The poet is dumbfounded. What a disaster!
How now for our glorious king,
Mithridates Dionysus Eupator,
to concern himself with Greek poems!
In the middle of a war—imagine, Greek poems!

Fernazes frets. How unfortunate!
Just when he was certain with his "Darius"
to distinguish himself and to confound
once and for all his envious critics.
What a postponement, what a postponement to his plans.

And if it was only a postponement—good once again.
But let us see whether we have security
in Amisos. It is not a particularly well-defended town.

The Romans are the most frightful enemies.
Are we, the Cappadocians, able to compete
with them ? Can it be possible ?
Are we to measure ourselves with the legions?
Great gods, protectors of Asia, help us.

But between all his agitation and the disaster
the poetic notion with persistence comes and goes—
the most probable is, certainly, arrogance and intoxication ;
arrogance and intoxication would Darius have had.

[116]

But the Romans in Cavafis' myth do more than merely reveal the instability of a life based on no deep foundations. Let us look for a moment at the following three poems. The first is entitled " The Battle of Magnesia." The Battle of Magnesia in 190 B.C. was one of the crucial battles in the Roman conquest of the Middle East. It was then that the two Scipios defeated Antiochus the Great. In the following poem, Cavafis pictures the ageing Philip V of Macedonia, who himself had suffered defeat at Roman hands, after he has received the news of the Roman victory at Magnesia, a victory which ensured the Roman domination of the hellenistic world and the end of the way of life that it stood for:

Lost is his ancient vehemence, his prowess lost.
Chiefly for his tired, for his ailing almost,

body now is his solicitude. And the rest
of his life he will pass carefree. This at least

is Philip's intention. Dice he plays tonight. He has
a hankering to amuse himself. Put many roses

on to the table. What and if at Magnesia
Antiochus is ruined. There has fallen, they say, a

total destruction upon the whole of the excellent force.
They may have exaggerated ; they make some error of
    course.

God grant. For although hostile, they are of the same race.
But one " God grant " is enough. Perhaps too many in this
case,

for Philip certainly will not postpone the festival.
Even if the fatigue of his life is great, all

quality has not gone—his memory has not broken.
He recalls how greatly they mourned in Syria, when

Macedonia their motherland was devastated, what sorrow
was theirs.
Forward with the banquet. Servants, the pipes, the
chandeliers!

[68]

The second of the three poems and one of the best that Cavafis wrote is " Of Demetrius Soter [162-150 B.C.]." Demetrius Soter was one of the descendants of that Antiochus the Great who had lost his kingdom, Syria, at the Battle of Magnesia. He had been sent to Rome as a hostage while young, but after the death of Antiochus the Great, his grandfather, he demanded from the Senate that he be set at liberty. The Senate refused his demand, and so he escaped secretly, with the help of the historian Polybius. He returned to Syria, where the people declared in his favour, and in the end he succeeded in obtaining from the Romans recognition as king. He expelled the satrap Heracleides from Babylon, thus earning the title Soter. But through the disorder of his life he lost the support of his people and was overthrown by an impostor, Balas, and killed by him in battle. Cavafis pictures him as it were in soliloquy, after his overthrow and before his death, recalling all his youthful shame and resolution, his struggle, his downfall, and his stoic endurance in failure:

His every expectation has turned out wrong!

He had imagined performing famous deeds,
to end the humiliation that from the time of the Battle
of Magnesia oppresses his fatherland.
That Syria become again a powerful state,
with her armies, with her fleets,
with her big fortresses, with her wealth.

104

He suffered, he became bitter at Rome
when he felt in the conversations of his friends,
the youth of the great families,
with all the delicacy and the politeness
that they showed to him, to the son
of King Seleukos Philopater—
when he felt that none the less there was always a secret
contempt for the hellenising dynasties :
that they are fallen, that they are not fit for anything
  serious,
quite unsuited for the leadership of the people.
He withdrew alone, and he became indignant, and he swore
that it would not be at all as they imagined ;
why, he himself has will-power ;
he will struggle, he will achieve, he will exalt.

Enough to find a way of getting to the East,
to succeed in escaping from Italy—
and all this strength that he has
within his soul, all this
energy he will communicate to the people.

Ah, only to find himself in Syria !
So young he left his country
that scarcely he remembers her appearance.
But in his thoughts he has always visualised her
as something holy which with reverence you approach,
as the sight of a lovely place, as the vision
of Greek cities and of Greek ports.—

And now ?
  Now desolation and sorrow.

They were right, the young men at Rome.
It is not possible for them to endure, the dynasties
that resulted from the Occupation of the Macedonians.

It does not matter : he has striven himself,
he has struggled as much as he could.
And in his black disappointment,
one thing alone he takes account of still
with pride : that, even in his failure,
he presents to the world the same indomitable courage.

H

For the rest—they were dreams and vanities.
This Syria—almost it does not seem to be his fatherland,
this Syria is the country of Heracleides and of Balas.

[106]

The third poem I wish to quote in this group is "To Antiochus Epiphanes." One of the favourites of Antiochus Epiphanes, King of Syria, speaks to his protector on the same theme of the resurgence of the Macedonians. At the Battle of Pydna, Perseus, the last Macedonian king, was defeated by the Romans:

The young Antiochian said to the king:
"Within my heart vibrates a cherished hope.
The Macedonians once more, Antiochus Epiphanes,
the Macedonians are in the enormous struggle.
Should it be that they win—and to whoever wants I give
the lion and the horses, the Pan of coral,
and the elegant palace, and the gardens of Tyre,
and whatever else you have given me, Antiochus
Epiphanes."

Perhaps the king was moved a little.
But at once he remembered father and brother,
and he did not answer. An eavesdropper might be able
to repeat something.—Otherwise, of course,
the terrible end came, rapidly, at Pydna.

[128]

The point I wish to bring out in these three poems is that the overshadowing might of the Romans throws into relief the vanity, irresponsibility, and inner decay of the æsthetic state. They imply as much as anything else that the corruption and decadence of this state invites its own overthrow, that the Romans are simply the unconscious instruments in the execution of a sentence which those who live the superficial, self-indulgent life of the senses call down on themselves. The portrait of Philip V of Macedonia is at once that of a defeated impotent old man who has resigned everything except his fleshly pleasures and who is moved only with a vague sadness at the memory of his own failure, and a comment on the defencelessness and indifference of the æsthetic state in its last phases, a state undermined by its own artificiality and effete to the point of self-embalming among the scents and faded tapestries of its affectation. If sometimes Cavafis' poems seem to extol the life of æsthetic humanism, they more often reveal with astonishing and dreadful clarity the hollowness and inner rot of those who do in fact live it. Demetrius Soter also lost the support of his people because of his dissolute and intemperate life: the impostor Balas, who defeated and killed him in battle, is again an impersonal instrument of justice visiting someone condemned already by his own irresponsibility and selfishness, a fact which he forgets to mention when he prides himself on his " indomitable courage." And, finally, the talk of the young favourite of Antiochus Epiphanes about giving up his lion and his horses and Pan of coral and his gardens at Tyre is a bit of sentimental whimsy designed to flatter the ear of a king hedged about by plot and counterplot, suspicion and treachery, and himself fated to die in a state of raving madness, hated by Jew and Greek alike. Cavafis is perhaps at his best when he is revealing the deceit, insecurity, mistrust and frightful corruption which lie beneath the surface of the æsthetic life and which are the price it pays for those moments of pleasure and fugitive beauty which it sometimes, but rarely, achieves. Few men have charted this world of decay so vividly.

Yet from the point of view of the æsthetic humanist that temporal power which Cavafis indicates when he speaks of the Romans is not only an impersonal instrument of self-induced punishment or virile aggression. It is more than that. The Romans in Cavafis' myth are also efficient organisers, image of State interference and discipline, or jurisprudence and prudery, and as such enemies of the cultivated laxity and laissez-faire of the tolerant sentimentalist; they stand perhaps for the kind of attitude mocked in the poem "In a Large Greek Colony, 200 B.C.":

That things in the Colony do not go according to plan
there does not remain the slightest doubt,
and although in spite of everything we do go forward,
perhaps, as not a few are thinking, the time has come
to introduce a Political Reformer.

But the objection and the difficulty is
that they make an enormous fuss
about everything, these
reformers. (It would be fortunate

if they were never needed.) Into whatever it is,
into the smallest detail, they question and examine,
and at once radical reforms suggest themselves,
with the demand to be executed without delay.

Also they possess a tendency to sacrifice.
Rid yourself of that possession ;
your occupation is insecure:
precisely such possessions damage Colonies.
Rid yourself of this income,
and of the other connected with it,
·and of that third, as a natural consequence ;
they are essential, but what can one do?
They constitute an injurious responsibility.

And as they extend the range of their controls,
superfluity after superfluity they discover, and seek to get
    rid of :
things which however are difficult to abolish.

And when, with God's help, the business is completed,
and every detail is defined and circumscribed,
they retire, taking also the wages due to them,
allowing us to see whatever still remains, after
such an effective operation.

Perhaps the moment has not yet arrived.
Do not let us hurry : speed is a dangerous thing.
Untimely measures bring repentance.
Truly and unhappily the Colony has many abuses.
But what is there human without imperfection ?
And after all, yes, we do go forward.

[162]

I shall have more to say of the reformer when discussing Cavafis'
poems on Julian the Apostate.

The second power which challenges the delicate balance of
the æsthetic life is that of a dogmatic militant and moralising
Church. In Cavafis' myth of the hellenistic world this power is
of course represented by the Christian Church, which scorned
and attacked the pleasures of the flesh, the refined sensuality,

the naturalistic art with its sentimental idealisation of the human body, which burnt temples and broke idols, and which sought for justification of earthly life in a world beyond the tomb. The æsthetic humanist is of course quite incapable of any deep understanding of the religious life and in consequence the demands which that life makes on the individual appear to him to be merely so many obstacles between him and his pleasure, while those who are obedient to such demands are fit only to be mocked, as, for instance, in the following poem, " Theatre of Sidon (400 A.D.) " :

> Son of an honourable citizen, above all a good-looking
> young man of the theatre, in many ways likeable,
> I compose sometimes, in the Greek language,
> highly immodest verses, which I circulate,
> most secretly of course, verses—do not let them be seen,
>   O Gods,
> by the grey-clothed, by the moralising Christians—
> about the especial voluptuousness that leads
> to the barren, to the disapproved of love.
>
> [133]

Having, as I said, no religious capacity of his own, the æsthete substitutes a vacuous and sentimental worship of " gods " who correspond to no reality but allow him to indulge in a certain wistfulness and romantic fancy:

> Because we have broken their statues,
> because we have driven them from their temples,
> not for this at all have died the gods.
> O land of Ionia, even still they love you,
> you their soul remembers even still.
> When upon you dawns an August morning,
> your atmosphere takes vigour from their life ;
> and sometimes youthful heavenly beauty,
> shadowy, with swiftness gliding,
> over across your hill-tops passes.
>
> [37]

Or in another poem, " If Indeed He Had Died," Cavafis gives the picture of " one of the few pagans " musing on the where- abouts of the hellenistic sage Apollonius of Tyana and wondering

109

if he will ever come back to restore the graceful decorative
festivals that beautify his life:

> *"Where has he withdrawn, where has the Master lost*
> *himself?*
> *After his many miracles,*
> *after the fame of his teaching*
> *that has spread to so many races,*
> *he has suddenly hidden himself, and no one has learnt*
> *with certainty what has happened*
> *(neither has anyone seen his tomb).*
> *Some have rumoured that he has died at Ephesus.*
> *But Darius has not written; nothing*
> *has Darius written about the death of Apollonius.*
> *Others have said that he vanished at Lindos.*
> *Or perhaps that is the truth, the story*
> *that his resumption took place in Crete,*
> *at the ancient sanctuary of Diktynna.*
> *But, however, we have his wonderful,*
> *his supernatural appearance*
> *to a young student at Tyana.*
> *The time perhaps has not arrived for his return,*
> *for him to reveal himself to the world again;*
> *or, transformed, perhaps he is back*
> *unrecognised among us. But he will reappear*
> *as he was, teaching the virtuous ways; and then certainly*
> *he will restore the worship of our gods,*
> *and our graceful hellenic festivals."*

> *Thus mused in his meagre apartment—*
> *after a reading of the work of Philostratus:*
> *"The Life of Apollonius of Tyana"—*
> *one of the few pagans,*
> *one of the very few that were left. Moreover—insignificant*
> *man and a coward—he pretended to the world*
> *that he too was a Christian, and he went to church.*
> *It was the time when there reigned,*
> *with the utmost piety, the old Justin,*
> *and Alexandria, a God-fearing city,*
> *abominated miserable idolators.*

[110]

But Cavafis' æsthete, himself without any faith but living in a world where such a faith exists, even, through fear, pretending indeed that "he too was a Christian," cannot but be aware of the consolation and reward such a faith can give. Cavafis, this time through the figure of someone outside the hellenistic world, expresses this awareness in a short poem, "Manuel Comnenos":

> The Emperor Manuel Comnenos
> one melancholy day of September
> felt himself close to death. The astrologers
> (salaried) of the court were voluble
> that many other years he had yet to live.
> While however they were talking, he
> remembers ancient customary devotions,
> and from the cells of the friars he orders
> ecclesiastical vestments to be brought,
> and he wears them, and he rejoices to show
> the modest aspect of a priest or of a monk.
>
> Fortunate all those who believe,
> and like the Emperor Manuel finish their lives
> clothed according to their faith most modestly.
> [69]

And in another poem, "The Tomb of Ignatius," although the tone is more playful and perhaps even ironic, Cavafis gives the epitaph of one who was converted from his ways of luxury and indulgence:

> Here I am not the Kleon who was talked about
> in Alexandria (where it is difficult to astonish)
> for my magnificent houses, for the gardens,
> for the horses and for my carriages,
> for the jewelry and for the silks I wore.
> God forbid it; here I am not that Kleon:
> his twenty-eight years are deleted.
> I am Ignatius, the novice, who very late
> came to myself; but who even so for ten months lived
>   happily
> in the peace and in the security of Jesus.
> [83]

111

Sometimes the æsthete may dream of having the best of both worlds:

> *Said Myrtias (a Syrian student*
> *at Alexandria, in the reign*
> *of the Emperor Constans and the Emperor Constantius;*
> *in part a heathen, in part Christianised):*
> *" Fortified with theory and with study,*
> *I shall not like a coward fear my passions;*
> *I shall give my body to voluptuousness,*
> *to the dreamt-of pleasures,*
> *to the most audacious erotic desires,*
> *to the violent lasciviousness of the blood, without*
> *the slightest fear, because when I wish —*
> *and I shall have the will-power, fortified*
> *as I shall be with theory and with study —*
> *I shall at critical moments find again*
> *my spirit, as before, ascetic."*
>
> [40]

Finally in this group, Cavafis gives the portrait of a lover distraught at the death of his friend and suddenly appalled lest, in spite of the fact that although a Christian the friend lived exactly like the rest of his pagan company, he may after all never really have been one with it. Apart from anything else, this poem, " Myris: Alexandria 340 A.D.," is a remarkable re-creation of an historical scene:

> *When I learnt of the tragedy, that Myris was dead,*
> *I went to his house, for all that I avoid*
> *going into the houses of Christians,*
> *especially when they have sorrows or festivals.*
>
> *I stood in the corridor. I did not wish*
> *to enter further within, because I perceived*
> *that the relatives of the dead regarded me*
> *with evident surprise and with displeasure.*
>
> *They had him in a large room*
> *which from the corner where I stood*
> *I saw a little: all precious carpets,*
> *and objects of silver and of gold.*

I stood and I wept in a corner of the corridor.
And I thought how our gatherings and the excursions
without Myris would not be worth while any longer;
and I thought how not any longer should I see him
at our beautiful and indecent all-night sessions
to rejoice, and to laugh, and to recite verses
with his perfect feeling for the Greek rhythm;
and I thought how I had lost for ever
his beauty, how I had lost for ever
the young man that with madness I had worshipped.

Some old women, close to me, in undertones were speaking
of the last day that he lived—
on his lips continually the name of Christ,
in his hands he held a cross.
There entered afterwards into the room
four Christian priests, and they said prayers
fervently, and orisons to Jesus,
or to Mary (I do not know their religion well).

We had known, certainly, that Myris was a Christian.
From the first moment we had known it, when
the year before last he had joined our company.
But he lived exactly like us.
Of all of us most given to pleasure;
scattering lavishly his money on amusements.
Indifferent to the world's esteem,
he threw himself eagerly into the nocturnal fights of the
*   streets*
when our band happened to meet
with a rival band.
Never did he speak of his religion.
And once even we told him
that we would take him with us to the Serapion.
But it was as if it displeased him,
this joke of ours: I remember now.
Ah, and two other times come now into my mind.
When to Poseidon we made libations,
he drew himself back from our circle, and looked
*   elsewhere.*

When enthusiastically one of us
said : " Let our company be under
the favour and the protection of the great,
of the most beautiful Apollo "—Myris whispered
(the others did not hear) " with the exception of myself."

The Christian priests with loud voices
were praying for the soul of the young man.
I noticed with how much diligence,
and with what intensive observance
to the forms of their religion, they had prepared
everything for the Christian funeral.
And all at once an odd sensation
came upon me. Obscurely I felt
as if Myris had fled from close to me :
I felt that he, a Christian, was united
with his own people, and that I had become
distant, very distant ; I felt indeed
a doubt approaching me : lest I had been deceived
by my passion, and always I had been distant to him.
I threw myself out from the frightful house,
I fled quickly before it was taken away, before it was
    altered
by their Christianity, the memory of Myris.

                                                        [174]

But if a dogmatic militant church with whose creeds the
æsthete has little sympathy is bad enough, far worse is the
reformer and proselytiser who seeks to make an official State
religion out of what in fact amounts to a parody of a way of
life whose great attraction is a freedom from compulsion and
a tolerance bred in an atmosphere of enlightened *laisser-faire*
and sophisticated indifference. Any State-sponsored religion
amounts of course to a negation of that cultivated delicate artificiality which is the æsthete's substitute for religion, but to
institutionalise this artificiality so that what is a purely private
allegiance becomes a public duty ; to solidify the frail creation
of the æsthete's distilled sensibility into a world of prescribed
rite and blue-print morality : this is the final insult. There is little
so irritating and offensive as the spectacle of someone of whom
one does not approve making a public parade of, and advocating

for general practical consumption, a vulgarised version of one's own particular sympathies, especially if part of the charm of these sympathies depends upon them being the possession of but a few of the more exclusive and select members of society. Yet this, in Cavafis' myth of the hellenistic world, is precisely what Julian the Apostate does. He is one of these reformers and proselytisers, and as such is the continual butt of scorn and mockery for both heathen and Christian alike. In the eyes of the æsthetic pagans he is a ridiculous interfering and pedantic prig, and in the eyes of the Christians an uncouth and bombastic sinner. Cavafis wrote five poems of which Julian is the direct subject, and in only one, " Julian at Nicodemia," does he receive even slight sympathy. Far more typical is the poem entitled " Julian and the Antiochians." Julian had wintered one year at Antioch before setting out in the spring for war with the Persians. He was ridiculed by the Antiochians on account of his austerity and virtue, and they had laughed at the way he grew his beard in the old fashion. In return, Julian wrote a stringent satire, " The Enemy of the Beard," on the effeminacy and licentiousness of the people of Antioch. The poem expresses the response of the Antiochians to Julian's call to reform and moderation. The letters Chi and Kappa in the last lines stand, the first for Christ, the second for Constantius, Julian's cousin and predecessor on the Imperial throne, and indicate here that the Antiochians would rather have Christianity than Julian's austere paganism:

> *How was it possible ever for them to renounce*
> *their beautiful way of life ; the variety*
> *of their habitual amusements ; the brilliance*
> *of their theatre where was consummated a union between*
>   *Art*
> *and the erotic inclinations of the flesh !*
>
> *Immoral until now—and probably for a great while*
>   *longer—*
> *they were. But they had the satisfaction that their life*
> *was the much talked of life of Antioch,*
> *the pleasure-loving, the absolutely æsthetic.*
>
> *To give up all this, in order to devote themselves, indeed,*
>   *to what ?*

His vapourings about the false gods,
his tedious self-advertisement;
his childish fear of the theatre;
his graceless prudery; his ridiculous beard.

O certainly they preferred the Chi,
O certainly they preferred the Kappa : a hundred times.

[151]

And in another poem, "A Great Procession of Priests and of Laymen," Cavafis describes the relief of the Christians of Antioch after the death of Julian and the election of the Christian Jovian as Emperor:

A procession of priests and of laymen,
each walk of life represented,
passes through streets, through squares, and through gates
of the famous city of Antioch.
At the head of the impressive, enormous procession
a beautiful white-clad youth is holding
with up-raised hands the Cross,
our strength and our hope, the holy Cross.
The pagans, before so greatly arrogant,
submissive now, and cowards, with haste
remove themselves from the procession.
Distant from us, distant from us let them remain for ever
(so long as they do not renounce their errors). The holy
  Cross
goes forward. Into every quarter
where in the fear of God the Christians are living
consolation it brings and happiness :
they come out, the faithful, to the doors of their houses
and full of delight they salute it—
the strength, the salvation of the universe, the Cross.

This is an annual Christian festival.
But today it is held, behold, more splendidly.
The empire at last is delivered.
The most depraved, the appalling
Julian reigns no longer.

For the most pious Jovian let our prayers be given.

[152]

The most absolute and irresistible enemy of the æsthetic state, the one against which it is most defenceless, and the root of its *malaise* and despair is, however, the awareness of mortality, death, and of the terrible transience of all to which its affections are attached. It is here that we reach the real pathos of the æsthetic condition and it is not hard to understand why. The religious man, who looks for fulfilment to a world beyond the senses and for whom this world is at best but an inadequate shadowing forth of a supernatural world, and this life but an incident in the great life of eternity, may reach some accord with himself in which the terrors of mortality are quietened. While still part of this world he may understand and accept that he is subject to all its shifts and chances, to pain, unhappiness, disease. He is very likely to agree that this life is nasty, brutish, and short, that its pleasures are illusions, its beauties deceit, and its death a release. But such a view of life is beyond the scope of the man for whom the only reality is that of the senses, whose only notion of enjoyment and beauty is the enjoyment and beauty of things that are transitory and perishable. The religious man can see this life as a fraction of another life. The æsthete can only see this life ; for him the fraction is the whole. What he most cherishes and values, the only reality of which he is aware, is fugitive and doomed. Powerless against time and death is his world. It may be well to acclaim the delights of the flesh and to refine one's appreciation of the æsthetic surface of things to a most delicate and fastidious point, and, for the view of life for which the sensory world is the only world, there is an irrefutable logic in one's course. But to pursue this logic to its end is to terminate in despair, for then one must recognise the fundamental futility of one's own and everyone else's existence ; one has to recognise that fate and death as part of fate have the last word in life, that by no grace can they be overcome ; one has to accept the inevitable tragedy of this world without the possibility of participation in a higher state of existence where this tragedy is overcome.

There are many poems of Cavafis which illustrate in ironic terms the vanity of the purely human state, its defencelessness before fate and death. There is the somewhat didactic " Theodotos." According to Plutarch, Theodotos persuaded the

Egyptians to kill Pompey when he landed, and Cavafis uses this alleged incident to point his moral:

> *If you are among the truly chosen,*
> *watch how you acquire your dominance.*
> *However greatly you are glorified, your accomplishments*
> *in Italy and in Thessaly*
> *however much the states proclaim them,*
> *whatever degrees of honour*
> *your admirers in Rome confer upon you,*
> *neither your joy, nor your triumph will remain,*
> *neither a superior—how superior?—person will you feel,*
> *when, in Alexandria, Theodotos brings you,*
> *upon a blood-stained platter,*
> *the head of the wretched Pompey.*
>
> *And do not be certain that in your life*
> *restricted, regulated, and prosaic,*
> *such spectacular and dreadful things do not occur.*
> *Perhaps at this moment into some neighbour's*
> *well-conducted house there goes—*
> *invisible, unsubstantial—Theodotos,*
> *bringing exactly such a frightful head.*

[58]

Or there is the picture of the hedonist Nero, self-deceived by the ambiguous reply of the Delphic Oracle into thinking that he has many years yet of indulgence left before him:

> *He was not disquietened, Nero, when he heard*
> *the pronouncement of the Delphic Oracle:*
> *"Beware the seventy-third year."*
> *Time still to rejoice.*
> *He is thirty. Ample indeed*
> *the period the god bestows*
> *to concern himself with future dangers.*
>
> *Now, tired a little, he will return to Rome,*
> *but excellently tired after that journey,*
> *which, all, was days of enjoyment—*
> *theatres, gardens, gymnasiums . . .*
> *Evenings in the cities of Achaia . . .*
> *Ah, the delight above all of naked bodies . . .*

118

So much for Nero. And in Spain Galba
secretly gathers his army and drills it—
Galba, the old man in his seventy-third year.

[93]

Or, finally, there is the young man who sought to make himself immune from the attacks and vicissitudes of life:

With words, with countenance, and with manners
I will make an excellent suit of armour ;
and thus shall I face the wicked men
without fear and without weakness.

They will want to injure me. But no one will know,
out of all those that come near to me,
where my wounds lie, my vulnerable places,
beneath the falsehoods that will cover me.

Boasting words of Aimilianos Monæ.
One wonders if ever he made that suit of armour ?
In any case, he did not wear it long.
At the age of twenty-seven, he died, in Sicily.

[101]

But the æsthetic way pursued with logic to its end contains a more bitter irony. For by a sort of infernal movement within this way itself, the greater the degree to which one refines one's sensitivity, the more aware one becomes of the terrible impermanence and fleeting nature of all that upon which one's sensitivity depends for its sustenance ; the keener grow one's love of sensuous beauty divorced from any comprehension of the roots of that beauty, the more one becomes aware of its fragility and of one's powerlessness to enjoy it except in a most partial and temporary way, in such a way, in fact, that makes one's very attachment the cause of an acute and growing distress. For this distress must become greater as with age the capacity to enjoy the world of pleasure dwindles, as the approaching shadow of death threatens to annihilate even that which one can still enjoy. Begotten thus more and more by Despair upon Impossibility, the æsthete's love can find outlet only in a sort of parody, a profane and perverted parody, of that act of recollection which for the religious life is a way to spiritual realisation.

119

According to this way, the sight of beauty in the physical world may stimulate in the beholder a desire to penetrate back to that supersensual world where he may enjoy in essence and ever-lastingly what in this world he can enjoy only in appearance and for short moments. But the æsthete has no knowledge of a supersensual world. His passive nature permits that act of recollection to take place only on the psychological level, where by a quite natural and unpremeditated process of sublimation he can enjoy in image what he can no longer enjoy in the flesh. In the psyche, all those presences, those images of the perishable or the in many cases now perished bodies which cannot be possessed any longer physically, can be reborn with a new if somewhat etiolated appearance. It may seem out of place to quote Wordsworth in connection with Cavafis. But in his " Ode to the Intimations of Immortality,"[1] Wordsworth describes a process analogous to that of which I have been speaking. In this poem, Wordsworth says that there was a time when:

> meadow, grove and stream
> The earth, and every common sight
> to me did seem
> Apparell'd in celestial light,
> The glory and the freshness of a dream.

But, he goes on to say, this visionary power has now left him:

> The things which I have seen I now can see no more.

None the less, these things which have passed away are, when called back into the natural memory, the " fountain-light " of all his days, they are able to:

> Uphold us, cherish, and have power to make
> Our noisy years seem moments in the being
> Of the eternal silence : truths that wake
> To perish never . . .

It is, as I said, by some analogous process, that the æsthete resavours those delectable moments of his past that are now out of his physical reach. His whole life becomes one long and increasingly desperate " recherche du temps perdu." He does not

[1] Wordsworth: Poetical Works, ed. Hutchinson, Oxford Edition, 1920, in particular pp. 587 and 589.

of course give to his images of the past thus brought back into the memory quite the status which Wordsworth confers on them: " truths that wake to perish never . . ." ; rather he seems to see them simply as brief consolations in a life already approaching its term. But with this qualification, many of Cavafis' poems seem to describe or to result from a process of sublimation similar to that described by Wordsworth in his Ode: memories of certain youthful experiences return to uphold and to relieve the distress of the ageing man. A great number of Cavafis' erotic poems, for instance, written after 1920 and when the poet was in his late fifties or early sixties, bear such titles as " Days of 1901," " Days of 1896," or " Days of 1908," and describe incidents long past called " back from Time " into the poet's soul. Indeed, it is in this rebirth of past experience that the meaning of the experience itself would seem to lie ; it is in the poem distilled years after the physical event that the event itself is fulfilled: " But how the life of the artist has profited," concludes one poem after a description of an erotic adventure:

> But how the life of the artist has profited.
> Tomorrow, the day after tomorrow, or years hence will
>   be written
> the powerful verses that have here their origin.
> [121]

In fact, the very purpose of the æsthete's art is not to remind us of a supersensual world, of which, as we said, he has no notion, but is rather to assist in this process by which the artist seeks to deal with the dread problem of time's and his passing:

> The ageing of my body and of my beauty
> is a wound from a terrible knife.
> I have not any resistance.
> Towards you I turn, O Art of Poetry,
> who know somehow of remedies :
> attempts to numb the pain, in Imagination and Word.
>
> It is a wound from a terrible knife.
> Bring your remedies, O Art of Poetry,
> that they make—for a little—the wound not to be felt.
> [125]

I

For the æsthete, tortured by the endless dance of time and death that sweeps all that he values into oblivion, art seems the only way by which he can relieve his suffering. In his poetry, this idiotic chasing of moment after moment, this time, is frozen into a spatial form from whose contemplation is generated a sort of timeless untroubled mirth. For that is the only solution left to this tired, rapacious, over-refined man who is the generic hero of Cavafis' myth, homo Europæus, as we might call him, of our late æsthetic humanist period. From the deadly boredom and intolerable pain of his wretched existence, he suddenly raises himself and looks at himself from the outside ; and seeing a ridiculous hypochondriac, full of selfish fears and absurd vanities, ageing into impotence and ugliness, purified by every longing, sick with every vice, all sentiment and all fatigue, devoted to fate and pain as the morphinist is to his drug, lonely, hollowed out, old as the ages, animal and sage, all bare, with no ambitions, all stripped, full of a child's fear of death and full of a weary readiness to die his own death—seeing himself there in the mirror of his art, he breaks into a laughter which suddenly releases him from his self-tormenting and self-destructive nightmare, and which makes life—" for a little "—once again bearable. It is a recovery through irony. By living in such irony, by living as if he were playing a rôle which he can watch and analyse as an outsider, the sick guest of the æsthetic City can cure himself, not indeed of the disease of being alive at all, but of the more deep disease which made it impossible for him to bear living. Established at that point of contradiction, at that point of ambiguity, where he is at the same time himself and not himself, he can watch with something approaching a detached, timeless serenity the temporal humiliations of his earthly life.

This ironic solution is of course an " æsthetic " solution. It is not a religious solution. From the religious point of view, it is not a solution at all, because the kind of eternity which it achieves represents no real conquest of time and death, but is only a device within time by which time's offence is made less gross. A real conquest of time and death requires an inner sacrifice, a superhuman effort to recover an obscured spiritual state. The æsthetic solution seeks to escape this sacrifice, to avoid this effort. Instead of communing in a holy sacrament, the æsthete tastes as it were with refined awe the wine of the chalice and drowses the sense with beatific images of the sacrificial mystery. He achieves his solution, that is, by substituting himself for the high priest ; and what he officiates over is no longer a solemn symbolic drama by participation in which he may attain to union with a real living God, but the spectacle of an all too human life of pleasure, folly, misfortune, vice, and sybaritic elegance which, called back to the memory, allows him to suspend for a moment the vast tedium and pointlessness of his existence, but which is, alas, no more than a spectacle. And if in the end he leaves us with the sense of irresolvable frustration, that is because, while on the one hand his love for this life is so deep that he often lets it oppress him with craving and regret for the images he has formed of it, it is on the other hand a love which, all hope plucked up by the roots, lives on with the pure despair that comes from the knowledge that its object has long since and for ever perished.

IV. Anghelos Sikelianos

(1884-1951)

THERE are two aspects to the poetry of Anghelos Sikelianos. On the one hand, there is the lyric assertion of the natural world, and of the human body as the perfection of this world. On the other hand, there is the austere vision of the seer who knows that the natural world is full of tragedy and suffering and that the true centre of man's life lies elsewhere. There is the refusal to shut the door on the senses, and the disavowal of all renunciation and asceticism ; and there is the lifting up, as it were, into an intensity of contemplation in which all earth-life is forgotten. There is the celebration of, and the insistence on, the holiness of all life's spontaneous manifestations and anarchic energies ; and there is the formal and hieratic sense that is aware of a divine order and that mankind's failure to realise this leads to calamity and downfall. Both aspects are integral to the total experience of the poetry, and any attempt to understand this experience must take account of how this comes about.

Sikelianos' first important poem, "The Visionary," is an autobiographical poem, which describes, in lyrical terms, the poet's youth and early manhood on his native island, Leucada. It is simple, direct, unaffected. Things are seen with a clear eye, with clear senses, with feelings undulled by custom and fixed routine. There is an immediate and reciprocal relationship between the poet and the world he describes. Nature and natural events are felt as part of the poet's own subjective experience. The poet's life and the life of nature mingle:

> *The lightning I encountered*
> *before it left the cloud. At the sound*
> *of the thunder-bolt echoed*
> *first the heart-beat of my joy ;*
> *at light awakenings,*

at the sudden rustle of leaves,
at the full peal of bells,
at the night quietness of crickets,
at the first talk in the road
at morning, at the first windows
of the fishermen opening, at the rising
deep from the trees of many birds,
at dawn scents,
and at the sudden
ring of the breeze which sounds
in space, at the spring's gush
which fills
the golden pitcher of my love!

[1, 32][1]

"The Visionary" represents a phase in the poet's growth to maturity. This growth is not that of the mind alone. It is much more organic than that. It is the growth of the whole person, body and soul together, instinct and mind together, an awakening and overflowing of an organic sense of life. The stream of life that runs through the poet's veins is one with that which runs through all nature. It is the same stream that shoots through stones and grass, through leaves and flowers. Man's body and blood are part of this same dance and rhythm of life. From direct, living, sensual contact with every living thing, man draws in the vital nourishment for his own life. This is the sap that feeds his growth, that stimulates new organs of perception. Intense physical delight turns to an illumination of the mind. The deeper the roots are sunk in the earth, the richer the springs that feed them, the stronger will be the powers of vision:

> *Tighten well*
> *the girdle, that you grow*
> *light-footed, and all nature round you,*
> *luminous to your desire,*
> *will come with youthful vigour*
> *to attire your flesh;*

[1] All such references give the volume and page number of: "Lyrical Life," 3 vols., Athens, 1946-1947, where the original Greek text will be found.

126

and the body will grow strong
in thought, to live as it would throw
itself into the fight,
into the manly fight with death,
testing with light heart
all indurate opinion.
And when your grasp is firm
upon the sacred earth,
in triumph and in deliverance
will I forge wings for you
which the sun cannot destroy,
that you ascend and before it
raise up my indomitable
heart among the stars.

[1, 95]

There is, implicit even in this early poetry, a mythological attitude to life. All in the beginning was part of one whole, of a primordial unity. The coming into being of time and place, of the natural world of multiplicity, is at once the spontaneous expression of this original oneness, an overflowing of its own nature into transient and perishable forms, and its division, its dismemberment. There is a double aspect of things. On the one hand, all natural forms are the manifestation of an original divine life, and are therefore holy. On the other hand, these same forms witness to the dismemberment of this original life. Earth and sky were once one. They can be one again. Earth can mix with the stars. The sky can harvest the wheat of earth. In these symbolical terms Sikelianos represents later the falling into disunity of things, the division of time from eternity, flesh from spirit, and the possibility of and need for their reconciliation if life is to be fulfilled. Man's task is to bring this reconciliation about. Through the attainment of spiritual vision, which is the realisation of his own nature, he also brings together the worlds which have fallen apart, he restores their original unity. But the impulsion for this act of creative understanding comes from participation in the life of the senses, in the life of the physical world. We are far from the cell and the scourge. Instead of imprisoning the forces of life in well-ordered channels, man lets them act through him, so that they reveal in his mind their true original nature. This does not mean that the source of intellectual wisdom is in the senses and in sensual experience. The source of intellectual wisdom is Eternal Wisdom. There is a descending and an ascending process. The process through which Eternal Wisdom enters into manifestation is one of descent. The process through which the individual so perfects his vision that it becomes one with Eternal Wisdom, and thus restores the original unity, is one of ascent. What provides the impulse for this ascent, Sikelianos would seem to imply, is the vitality of man's earthly life.

From where did Sikelianos derive this mythological attitude to life that is implicit even in such an early poem as " The Visionary " ? The answer would seem to be that he derived it from the people of Greece and from their tradition. The lives of the Greek people during the long years of Turkish occupation may have been poor, squalid, constricted, harsh, and cruel, but they possessed a poetry, a vitality, a feeling of reverence and wonder before creation which elsewhere were rapidly being lost. For these people, the natural world was not an object suitable for experiment, analysis, and exploitation. It was not an object at all. It was alive with mysterious and powerful forces, and man's life still possessed a richness and a dignity which came from his sense of participation in the movement of these forces. Above all, the people of Greece had preserved through the centuries a wealth of song, legend, and dance in which were enshrined the perceptions and understandings, the qualities of thought and feeling, of a way of life whose roots went far back into the past. It is easy for those who do not possess a living tradition even of this nature—and most of us today do not— to romanticise it, to see it, uprooted from actuality, as something decorative and aesthetically pleasing, and to forget that, while it endures, it is the yeast which raises the individual and group life of a whole people from their earth towards the realm of imaginative freedom. What, indeed, is often preserved in such a tradition is far from merely decorative and charming, but is a genuine human and even superhuman wisdom, however unconscious, and however imperfect and fragmentary the form in which it is expressed. That the peasant himself may be unaware of the true nature of the doctrines and the symbols of which his lore is the repository, does not in the least effect their genuineness. When symbolic and doctrinal teaching has been broken

128

at the higher levels—and this is what has happened or is still happening in most parts of the world—then it is precisely in the beliefs, art, and customs of the illiterate peasantry that may be found, in however adulterate a form, the material through which the wisdom of a former age can be recovered.

Participation in such a tradition is of the utmost value for the poet. Even if he is unaware of the true nature of the wisdom it preserves, his attitude to, and sense of, life will nevertheless be permeated by the qualities of this wisdom ; his poetry, although unconsciously, will reflect it. This would seem to be what happened in Sikelianos' case. Sikelianos had the good fortune to be born into a Greece where the traditional memory was still alive, where the traditional pattern of life still flourished, and where he found an ancient soul and an ancient aura. Instinctively he turned towards it. He mixed his life with its life, his roots with the roots which nourished the lives of the people :

> *And to the people I descended ;*
> *and the doors of the houses*
> *opened so quietly*
> *as if the doors of a tomb.*
> *And it was as if they embraced me*
> *returning from the grave—*
> *thus*
> *the fates the thread had woven—*
> *or as if for me the dead*
> *had come alive again :*
> *so deep in the ground did our roots mingle,*
> *so were our branches raised*
> *into the heavens.*
>
> [1, 28]

But it is one thing to write poetry which expresses subconsciously a mythological attitude to life. It is another to have full and conscious understanding of the principles upon which such an attitude depends. In " The Visionary " such an attitude is implicit. It had been given to the poet, one might almost say, by the gods themselves, as his birthright. It was the natural and unpremeditated outcome of the life which he had lived and of the influences which during childhood and adolescence he had received. This life and these influences had at a certain moment crystallised into a coherent whole. " The Visionary" marks the first stirring of the poet's energies, his first communion with life. But these energies and this communion would require for their full development the poet's creative co-operation on a deeper, more positive, and conscious level than had so far been the case. They would require an understanding of the true nature of the doctrines and the symbols which had been preserved, even though in a confused fashion, in the memory of the people. It would require the knowledge of the principles which were reflected, however inadequately, in the people's tradition. For these people are, as I said, often the direct heirs of the most ancient spiritual wisdom of mankind, the oral libraries, as it has been put,[1] of the world's ancient cultures. Their collective memory is often the repository of images and symbols of a most profound metaphysical tradition. Their beliefs are a relic of former knowledge.[2]

Sikelianos had found such a people's tradition and such a memory of images and symbols in the Greece into which he was born. He had been nurtured and nourished by this tradition and by this memory. They had become part of him to such an extent that simply by opening, as it were, the flood-gates of his sub-conscious being, he had, in " The Visionary," given expression to the vision of life which they had generated in him. He had become their child and his responses and attitudes had to a large extent been determined by them. His task was now, working from these primary intimations which they had stimulated in him, to recover full conscious possession of that lost spiritual tradition from which they themselves were derived. " The problem was then for me," he writes of this stage of his development, " By what way and with what means could I achieve essential contact with and understanding of this tradition ? "[3] For it meant much more than being merely a student of " primitive " beliefs and " folk-lore " in the normal sense. If the fundamental sources of custom and belief, of the way of life of a people's tradition are the principles of a metaphysical tradition,

[1] Chadwick, N. Kershaw, Poetry and Prophesy, C.U.P., 1942, p. xv.
[2] Aristotle, Metaphysics, XII: 8: 10.
[3] Prologue to " Lyrical Life," Nea Estia, No. 366, 1st Sept., 1942, p. 840.

it is presumption if whoever wishes to understand these sources is not himself at least something of a metaphysician.

Such metaphysical understanding does not involve anything abstract. It requires a direct experience of the spiritual realities, an actual participation in them. Just as Sikelianos had come to know the physical life of Greece by allowing each element of his own being to mingle and cohabit with its corresponding natural element, earth with earth, air with air, water with water, fire with fire, so now, to know the spiritual sources of his country's life, he had to allow his own spirit to penetrate into her spirit, had to allow his soul, freed as far as possible from all vain theory and supposition, to enter into the rich depths of the Greek soul, " to dig up again, from out of the earth of time, her most ancient universal historical foundations."[1] In other words, there is again a double process. To understand the true nature of the doctrines and symbols of which the people's tradition was the residue, it was necessary to achieve a knowledge of the principles of the ancient spiritual tradition of which they were a part. This is an historical quest. But if knowledge of that ancient spiritual tradition was to be anything but exterior, the principles of that tradition had themselves to be experienced directly, subjectively. They had to be vital and dynamic in the poet's own inner world. This is a question of personal spiritual development. The historical quest is the external counterpart of this internal development. The recognition of such a counterpart Sikelianos regarded as indispensable for this development: " For as an eagle, each time it wishes to raise itself from earth, must first walk a certain specific distance, and if it does not have this requisite distance free before it, remains a prisoner of its own wings, in exactly the same way the spirit, . . . if it does not recognise a certain elevation of spiritual history to which it corresponds, is likewise in danger . . . of being trapped in precisely that world from which it continually aspires to save itself."[2]

In what, then, did Sikelianos recognise this ancient tradition of Greece of which the people's tradition was a survival and whose principles he sought to comprehend ? He recognised it

[1] Cited by Themopoulos, T., The " Dithyramb of the Rose " of Sikelianos, Athens, 1934, p. 116.
[2] Sikelianos, The Delphic Union, Athens, 1932, p. xii.

131

in the Greece of the pre-Socratics. It seemed to him that in that age, for perhaps the last time in Europe, the true nature of that mythological attitude to life implicit in " The Visionary " as in the art, beliefs, and customs of the Greek people, had been consciously understood. Orphism, the teachings of Pythagoras, the Mysteries of Eleusis, all bore witness to this. In these three, Sikelianos saw embodied what was essentially the same under- standing of life, an understanding which transcended the limits of blood-groups and clans, which affirmed the brotherhood of man, and which preserved a sense of unity that embraced not only all mankind but all living things. All life is one. There is a unity of all creation. The human individual is the microcosm. All that is found in the universe is found also, actually or potentially, in the individual. The individual mirrors the whole in miniature, from the grain of sand to the highest level of reality. All grades and states of being have their meeting-place in man. The shifting, changing scenes of the visible world are the varying expressions of a deeper, underlying reality, of a universal order. The world is not simply the plaything of a blind and indiscriminate chance. It is the expression of an understandable process, though what this is, is often obscured for man by a defect in his own inner organisation. The emphasis is thus on inner organisation, not on external conduct. It is not morality which is important, but initiation. The individual has to pass through various stages of development until in his own depths he experiences the touch of divinity and is established in the life of the spirit. The seer is no longer distinguished from what is seen. He is one with the centre of his life which is the centre of all and is all. The supreme reality dwells in everything and moves everything. It is the green in leaves, it is the lark's song, the terror of the thunder-bolt and hurricane, the sunset's splendour and the remote epistle of the stars. It is formless, impersonal, pure, and passionless, and yet at the same time the warm, full-blooded life in the heart of man.

Sikelianos did not claim that this tradition of which Orphism, the teachings of Pythagoras, and the Eleusinian Mysteries were an expression, was of native Greek origin. He looked eastwards, to Asia, as the source of the deep religious currents of life that had penetrated westward and filtered into Europe, "the venerable Asia," as he calls her, "that beneath the obscure masks of her numberless civilisations seems to have preserved not only her own secret but also the secret of a brotherly relationship between us within a more ancient civilisation which has vanished."[1] He was well aware of the Oriental background against which Greek culture arose, and he did not make that facile distinction between Hellenism and barbarism so dear even today to the classical scholar, for he understood that it was precisely from this so-called barbarian world that Greece drew the sustenance for her own creative life. In particular, Sikelianos looked to India, to the great teachings of the Vedas and the Upanishads for the source of that spiritual wisdom in which the ancient Greek tradition had participated.

It was, then, in this pre-Socratic tradition of Greece and in the principles which it embodied and to which poets like Pindar and Aeschylus had been the last to give full and conscious expression, that Sikelianos recognised the archetype of which the Greek people's tradition was the survival. It was in them that he found the historical counterpart to what had now become a personal understanding of life and its purpose. But this recognition of an historical counterpart was, it must be emphasised, but the reflection of the poet's own inner development. This development was that which took place in the years after the writing of " The Visionary," when the poet sought to penetrate to the sources of the vision of life which he expressed in his early poem—to penetrate, that is, into his own inner depths, since the vision of life which he expressed in " The Visionary " reflected his own primary intimations of the deeper sources of life within him. His search during those years was for the inner sources from which those intimations derived. But so completely were these intimations themselves the outcome of the quality of thought and feeling enshrined in the Greek people's tradition, that the search was at the same time for the principles from which this tradition derived. The two were one and the same thing. Moreover, this search was not, as I have said, merely abstract. It corresponded to the demand of the poet's awakening instincts and energies, it was a further stage of that development of which " The Visionary " had marked an earlier stage. It is from this point of view that Sikelianos may be said to have been simply obedient to the spontaneous demand of his own instinctive nature in his spiritual search. The impulsion of his own

[1] Cited by Themopoulos, *op. cit.*, p. 112.

133

instincts and energies took him beyond the limits of the physical world, towards the sources of life, towards his own inner depths:

> Let desire's girdle be loosed around me,
> the secret course of my deliverance
> finds the magic thread, that girds me
> with delight as the sea the land;
>
> Surrounding life I now no longer search,
> but altogether, as root within the source,
> refresh myself within the ocean's depth,
> full of hidden sweetness and of silence! . . .

[1, 205]

Thus Sikelianos writes in a short poem written at about this time. And another poem from the same period, "Hymn of the Great Home-Coming," in which the poet celebrates the Dionysian erotic communion of his whole being with the rhythmic force of the nocturnal universe, with "the secret Dithyramb, which time no longer touches," concludes:

> Deep orgy! To your universal beat, in the new
>   body I have found,
> at your power's source most deeply I breathe
>   with unheard of strength,
>
> And as, without my seeking it, Eros armed
>   descends the sky's
> depths before me, I leap and I dance
>   with the mind's armour!
>
> Because I know: more deep than the thick starlight,
>   like an eagle hidden,
> awaits me, there where the sacred dark begins,
>   my original self . . .

[1, 214]

For this journey towards the principles of life, this taking up by man in a responsible way of "some position before the demands of Eternity free from the spectre of time, a position unself-interested, proud, purely universal,"[1] is at once a liberation from the constricting categories of time and place, and a journey towards the depths of the human soul. It is also no more and no less than the struggle of the poet to raise his consciousness to the level at which the principles and energies reflected in the spiritual tradition of ancient Greece, become the active, liberated, and determining principles and energies of his own being. It is, in other words, to recover the " original self " that is not merely the individual self of time and place, the selfhood or ego, but is the profound supra-individual self behind all tradition, behind all doctrine and symbol, the root of individual life as of cosmic life, the ultimate subjective ground of being and the rhythmic force which moves in all things.

What does this recovery of the original self mean in terms of living experience ? It is this that Sikelianos sought to express in his long poem, " Prologue to Life," written some ten years after " The Visionary." " Prologue to Life " is divided into five parts, five " consciousnesses " as the poet calls them, each made up of a number of rhapsodic hymns. The images and symbols of these hymns are for the most part those of the iconography of the Orphic and Pythagorean tradition. Divine powers and principles are given the name and form of the gods of this tradition. This is both an advantage and a disadvantage. On the one hand, it provides us with an historical counterpart which may act as a support for our understanding of the poetry. On the other hand, the iconography and the gods of this ancient tradition have, since Hellenistic and Roman times, and particularly in the Renaissance and post-Renaissance world, been regarded æsthetically, or at best allegorically, and the sense that they correspond to anything real, to an intelligible reality, and that they are dynamic potencies active in life itself, has been lost. Yet if we are to understand what Sikelianos' poetry is about, it is with this latter sense that we must approach them.

The first part of the poem is " The Consciousness of My Earth." After a brief invocation it opens with the hymn, " Journey with Dionysus." The hymn recounts the poet's first contact with, and experience of, that stream and dance of life that goes

---

[1] Sikelianos, Prologue to " Lyrical Life," *op. cit.*, p. 843.

through all things ; when, surrendering himself, he lets the forces
and rhythm of life, "the mature orgies," bear him onward :

> *From the pitch-blind night,*
> *held lightly beneath the arm-pits,*
> *leaving my weight in I knew not what hands,*
> *placing the foot dancingly forward,*
> *I first entered, my earth, into your mature orgies.*
>
> [2, 12]

He gives himself into the hands of some higher power ; he, quite
literally, lets himself go. His attitude is one of relaxation, almost
that of the puppet suspended from a thread held by some inner,
invisible controller. It is the attitude of the sacred dancer and
the inspired seer. Plato wrote that as regards the best in human
beings they are God's toys, and they ought to act in accordance
with this insight, obedient only to the control of the one cord
by which the puppet is suspended from above[1] ; and one of the
Upanishads supplies a commentary : " Verily, he who knows that
thread, and the Inner Controller who from within controls this
and the other world and all beings, he knows Brahma, he knows
the Gods, the Vedas, Being, Self and everything."[2] This " inner
controller," the principle of the stream of life of which all is the
manifestation, is Sikelianos' Dionysus.

Before this kindling and upward flight, this Eros-love of
man's inner being towards the divine, and the God's possession
of his creature, the " thiasos of little gods "—the five senses and
the uncoordinated and irregular desires that go with them—also
surrender their wills and become obedient to the central and
directing purpose which governs the whole being. These " ruling
passions," as they are rightly called when the inner controller is
absent and they determine conduct, pulling and driving wherever
their blindness leads them, are not suppressed or denied.
Sikelianos, as we have already seen, is no moral ascetic, denying
the passions and the instincts. He does not, as he embarks on
the " divine journey," extinguish " the flame of the limbs "
[2, 14]. His surrender to a higher power does not involve a rejection of humanity. It is, rather, that, as he goes forward, his

[1] Theatetus, 155 D. Laws 644 and 803-844.
[2] Brhadaranyaka Upanishad iii, 7, 1.

humanity is reborn, no longer subject to the deformations of
the passions acting blindly in isolation:

> *O little gods,*
> *who, thus drunk in the dark,*
> *terrified of your own shadow, or vainly spurred,*
> *pull uncheckably forward . . .*

> [2, 13]

—but entirely co-ordinated in relation to that higher will, of
which, indeed, they are themselves the attributes.

The poet now takes his place, humble and untried oarsman,
among the other companions of the "divine journey," the
journey over the seas of inwardness towards the original self,
the cosmic Dionysus. Dionysus is the inner principle of everything, of rock, of flower, of human beings. Our normal consciousness can only respond to the outward appearances of these
things. But if we integrate our consciousness with our own
inner principle, we shall then understand the inward nature of
all that is, for that principle is the inward nature of all that is.
Thus, penetration into the true nature of things requires first
of all a penetration into our own depths. The initial stages of
the journey towards self-realisation involve a withdrawal from
creation, an opening of a gulf between us and the immediate
sensible world:

> *As the wind kissed the source of our breath,*
> *the sky emptied of thin and always moving cloud,*
> *and the dull glow of the mountains that we left far behind*
> *opened in our breast the unsmelt flower of the abyss . . .*

> [2, 15]

As they go, the companions—and they are both the crew of the
legendary Argo, and all men and women afloat on the seas of
life—pray to the gods:

> *Your wind draws us, O gods,*
> *and our whole body from head to toe awake,*
> *free from deceitful dream and the nightmare's weight,*
> *feels, in every joint,*
> *all round your passion winging . . .*

> [2, 17]

Only the poet's voice is not heard among them. For the

137

K

companions, in spite of their boast, are still in the sway of ordinary human weaknesses ; they submit to the narcotic dazzle of the midsummer sun, symbolic perhaps of the blinding splendour of the physical world at the height of its beauty, or perhaps indicative of the dazzling but deceptive light of human reason :

> But when midsea the summer came
> and the waters quietened,
> and the heat spread dead calm
> and gathered the sun's sparkle
> which before had danced numberless on the sea,
> and from their temples sweat poured
> like the drops of water from the oars . . .
> and the light seethed speechless,
> their eyes half closed and they dreamt,
> their oars fell suddenly from their hands,
> and at once all like lead slept
> the noonday sleep . . .
>   [2, 18]

It is at this moment that the god, the " secretly controlled life," appears :

> For,
> without the stern foaming,
> without the prow leaving a track,
> without wind,
> the ship went forward !
>   [2, 18]

This meeting with the God corresponds to the recognition of that living unity, that essential identity of things which underlies the appearance of multiplicity and contradiction and confusion in the world. Dionysus is the principle of unity in manifestation, the One in its becoming as the many. It is this unity which the companions, still caught in the world of opposites—self and not-self, subject and object, spirit and flesh—cannot accept. They cling to the world of logic and reason. And the image above of them sweating away in endless labour until they drop exhausted and spell-bound is a fitting description of those who with interminable persistence seek to grasp truth with the natural light of their own individual minds, gathering into one general law the results of the observation and analysis of scattered "facts" (gathering into one the sun's scattered sparkles), until they fall hypnotised in the glare and stupor of their own vain theories and opinions. They are unable to accept the revelation of the God, that creation is a living divine body, "a limitless" which we are yet able to touch with the senses,[1] for that would mean the dethroning of reason from the centre of life. Instead, they plunge back into the divided world of time and place, the world of necessity and determination. They "become dolphins," as the poet puts it. Only the poet holds fast as the storm of antinomies breaks over him, for he alone understands that the seeming oppositions and contradictions in life are a reflection of his own uninitiated state and will vanish as soon as he achieves enlightenment. Thus the poet, sitting, as he says, like a sea-gull "between two huge waves"—understanding, that is, that life can be fulfilled not through the suppression of one side of an opposition in favour of the other, but through the acceptance of both sides, however illogical such an acceptance may seem—greets Dionysus, the reconciler of opposites in a higher unity as well as the dynamic power within the tempest of opposites itself, as the deliverer:

> O deliverer! O my joy!
> while I half slept in forgetfulness of my own self,
> to find myself confronting such a tempest!
>
> [2, 20]

He affirms his acceptance of the tempest, says the Nietzschean "Yes" to life, "including even its most strange and terrible problems," to "the will to life rejoicing over its own inexhaustibleness"[2]:

> O Tempest,
> like a gull I rested on your own pulse,
> between two huge waves
> which raised me each time with their foam to the crest!
>
> [2, 20]

And the hymn ends with a recapitulation of the poet's cathartic progress and his plunge into the "Depth of Life."

[1] See Hermetica of Trismegistus, ed. and trans. by Scott, W., Oxford, 1924, Lib. V, 10.

[2] Nietzsche, Twilight of the Idols, in English trans. of Works, ed. O Levy, pp. 119-120.

The poet now turns to celebrate his native earth.

> *O soils of my earth,*
> *many and inseparable like the waters,*
> *like sleep that not only from one tree to another,*   [2, 37]
> *different, changes,*
> *but even in the olive-grove,*
> *as the shepherds know,*
> *who exchange the shade*
> *following the flock here and there,*
> *is not the same under all the olive-trees . . .*

The earth, with all her various soils, is a kind of passive power. Her beauty is in some way a reflection of the eternal feminine. By a contemplation of her beauty we may be reminded of a supernatural beauty of which she bears the faint and distant impress. It is this that Plato understood when he spoke of the contemplation of the beauty of the sensible world stimulating that process of recollection by which we can at last attain the vision of ideal beauty. It is this aspect of Plato's teaching that links it with the Orphic-Dionysian tradition, and makes Plato the " image of Dionysus on earth." For he had taught the Dionysian way of deliverance, that it is by a " recollection " of his original divine life that man achieves his realisation, a process which, from the purely individual point of view, can be likened to a death, for it involves a going beyond all those states of which individuality may be said to consist. " The only method is death "—it was this knowledge, the crown of Plato's teaching, that had become the starting point of the poet's own effort towards realisation:

> *And behold*
> *you, Plato, image of Dionysus on earth :*
> *the end of your journey*
> *has become my beginning.*
>
> *Word*
> *where Athenian thought for ages rested,*
> *to flower in my own struggle :*
> *" The only method is death ! "*   [2, 43-44]

A hymn to Hercules follows. According to Sikelianos, the significance of Hercules has been misconceived. He has been regarded as "the image of blind strength," and his true image, that of one who through severe struggle at last succeeds in delivering himself from the lower and constricting categories of life, has been lost. He is, in fact, an example of that heroic spirit of self-sacrifice which is demanded by the Orphic-Dionysian way of initiation. He is one who achieves the rebirth of his humanity, becomes that "achieved body" which represents the highest type of human development, the godlike hero entirely delivered and transformed. This is the consummation of his labours, that Sikelianos sees symbolised in his death, which is not so much a physical death as the sacrifice of individuality through which the individual realises his true nature.

Hercules not only stands as the type of the heroic destiny that Sikelianos has chosen for himself. He is also the type of the highest human destiny achieved in the Greek firmament. He is the purest and most complete embodiment of the Orphic-Dionysian teaching. It is thus that Sikelianos uses the occasion of this poem to express his own endeavour to resuscitate the lost voice of the great Greek tradition, to bring back to Greece a consciousness of her proper roots:

> O Hercules,
> the sacred Greek voice,
> which was drowned like your beloved boy
> who with the Argonauts you had taken with you—
> Hylas—
> the day he drew aside to drink
> at the foreign land's spring,
> and you everywhere sought him,
> and from the water's depths
> his small voice
> came to you like the water-turtle's
> on summer evenings,
> but you did not know from whence it came —
> until it also failed;
>
> O Hercules,
> to what depths I sunk
> to bring back
> pure as never before
> the sacred Greek voice! [2, 50]

This leads Sikelianos on to the second part of the poem, "The Consciousness of my Race," the "black unridden horse," as he calls her, that is itself a manifestation of the Dionysian life-force, unsubmitting, fierce, and proud. But life must have form if it is to be lived with dignity and purpose, and form is the outcome of a particular quality of thought and feeling enshrined in a tradition. Where such a tradition is absent, life becomes uncreative and ugly, and people, instead of being a people, become a mob, whatever their material standards or physical condition. And it was a tradition that could give such a form to the anarchic and fierce temper of his race that Sikelianos felt was lacking in Greece. The vitality of his people was without purpose. They lacked a sense of the inner meaning of life, they had forgotten the teaching and principles of their ancient tradition. It was this that they had to recover if their life was to achieve form and dignity, and if they were not to be drawn along the profane and false paths of the modern West, which had substituted ideas of material efficiency and physical well-being for spiritual knowledge. This modern mentality must be rejected and Greece must find again the profound ways of initiation by which the individual returns to a consciousness of his true nature and which had once been taught at the sacred centres of ancient Greece, at Delphi, at Olympia, at Eleusis:

> O Greek youth,
> time that we cut in two
> the risen bread of the centuries!
>
> Rivet inward the eyes,
> into the sacred precinct!
> on to the internal track . . .
>
> What are for us
> the false lights of unripe civilisations?
>
> Turn your eyes inward
> and know the eternal Longing! . . .
>
> Prepare yourself for the Return!
>
> [2, 111-115]

As we shall see, the first stages of this initiation consist of a purification that leads to a state of inner receptivity. It is the purification of the feminine and passive element in man. This passive element stands opposite to, and, at the same time, calls forth the active life and light conferring element. It is as it were a state of pure potentiality, a passive support. It is the undefined " chaos " in the Platonic sense, the shadowy pole of life in contrast to the luminous pole, whose influence illuminates the " chaos." It is the deeps over which the light moves. It follows that this condition of undefined passive receptivity is indispensable if the light, the illuminating, defining power, is to be active, if the " Let there be light " is really to happen. The image of this can be seen on the purely natural level. On this level, the passive feminine element is the vegetative element, what we call earth, which is the " mother " of the fruit that issues from her and which she nourishes. But this fruit only develops and matures under the vivifying influence of the sun, which is, so to speak, the " father." The fruit therefore may be said to be the sun's offspring, a condition of whose birth was the receptivity of the passive and feminine element. Similarly, such a state of inner receptivity is a condition of illumination by spiritual light, of spiritual engendering. It is that which the seer and the inspired prophet must have attained before he can become possessed by the God, can become " entheos "—that state of relaxation described above, and which Sikelianos writes of again in the third part of the poem, " The Consciousness of Woman," where he speaks of his own inner depths as the shadowy " blue abyss " over which the breath of the God moves, stirring, illuminating, bringing forth:

> Blue abyss,
> full-shadowy, from the spray of waves,
> to my suddenly raised look
> like the quick red-purple
> belly of a sea-gull! . . .

> O unexpected sea-wind!

> The one wave breaks upon the other
> and the foam's border
> like the spider-spun veil
> glistens on the crest! . . .

143

But O descender into my heart's depths,
tremor without beginning, violent,
rocking ceaselessly the life within me,
throwing forward whatever is heavy,
scattering behind me whatever there is to scatter,
and holding,
like continual gold rain,
in the centre
the fruit!   [2, 119-122]

The whole process of this supernatural "marriage" of the active spirit, of the "golden-lyred invisible Rhythm," with the passive substance, the "mind of innocent purity" [2, 132], of Cupid with Psyche, was mirrored on the natural level also in the beautiful rite of a traditional Greek wedding. It is here that can be seen clearly what is meant by saying that the customs and beliefs of a people's tradition have a metaphysical origin, the understanding of which is indispensable for the proper study of that tradition. A rite is that which mirrors faithfully the events of a supernatural order, and that is why, where there is a conscious tradition, every act has a ritual character. But often the rite endures even when the tradition has become largely subconscious, when, that is, its metaphysical content has ceased to be consciously understood. But this is not at all the same thing as saying that it ceases to have, or that it can be understood apart from, its metaphysical content. It is thus that the rite of a traditional Greek village marriage can only be understood in the light of the relationship, of which I have just spoken, between the active element and the passive element in the process of creation ; its development mirrors the stages of that relationship, from the preparation of the bride:

The bride sits
on a low polished throne,
neither to the right does she gaze nor to the left,

while the adorners,
standing behind her shoulders,
on the top of her head
part the hair in the middle,
and when they have combed it through,
and have shaken it out into the air this way and that,

144

powerfully,
in their three fingers separating
the soft treasure,

with gentle hands they begin
to braid the plaits
like slings
the one on top of the other ! . . .

(But from the bride, unmoving, all round,
covered now with the delicate head-dress,
let the crystal silence pour.

And virginal let the thought flow
as on deep-grassy slopes
in the windless sun
the flowering of the wild pear-tree.)

[2, 134-135]

—and from the coming of the bridegroom:

But riding on horse-back, leading the way, the bridegroom
greets all creation as his dowry !

His body drinks the sun,
drinks as a hot beach of fine sand
the ever-renewing foam ! . . .

His strength is tilled and closes
as the soil after the corn !

And at last now :
as he alights on the threshold of the house,
facing the bride,
his heart suddenly stills !

[2, 136-137]

—to the union of bride and bridegroom:

Let the bed seem as of marble
before the souls of the newly-married !

145

O cool woven sheets
like the snows of March!

O mind dazed before the open altar!

Flesh chilled at first to the finger-tips!

Breath
like a lily that the north wind has frozen!

Orange-blossom
hung in the white light of the virginal death!

As snakes from winter
from your sweet drowsiness you wake
O Virginity!

And suddenly,
in the depths of expectation,
O scent of the hive!

Sudden breath of honey
deposited on the palate! . . .

Creation of man from the beginning
in the divine Image!

From his side secretly nourished
full-bodied joy!

Now the hands, sunk in the loosened hair,
let him plunge wholly
as into a heap of corn!

Now let him reap the richest field
of creative fragrance! . . .

[2, 140-141]

—to, finally, the bride as mother of the father's child, just as the poet is " mother " of the poem he bears through divine inspiration. And in the final section of this part, the woman, as both natural creature and the eternal feminine, addresses the active and " masculine " spirit, fully conscious of her rôle as root and support; as the primordial passive ground through which that spirit generates the forms of creation:

Go forward alone
to the heart of your silent longing.

As the wing
found its root on the shoulder of the Victories,
let me root the fire
here in the house with my breath!

The wind of the stern
let it not loosen the hair
that I raised and bound
to support the weight of your word silently!

Remin directed into your own depths,
towards the Sun of eternal happiness!

While I bear your pure command
exalted
into the cave of men!
[2, 161]

The fourth part of the poem, "The Consciousness of Faith," is at once a recapitulation and summing up of some of the themes already explored in the first three parts, and a more direct identification of the poet's vision with places, rites and symbols with which the ancient tradition of Greece was connected. Thus, the first hymn of this part has the title "Partaking of the Eleusinian Kykeon," the drink of the initiated:

Ancient consecrated drink,
Kykeon,
as with soul bathed in the ocean,
hallowed, perceptive,
with clear breath,
with limbs clean in the wind's touch,
clothed in the linen of my silence,

I feel you respire before my lips,
O smell of all fruits in one,
juice of every seed . . .
[2, 165]

It is the drink of the mystic communion which signifies man's participation in life's whole, in the governing rhythm of the universe:

> Sacred Eleusis,
> I drank last your strong drink,
> and life overflowed within me
> to the limit of expectation . . .
>
> O how as I knew you
> the Rhythm came
> from the abyss
> into my vision!
>
> [2, 185]

It is this participation which is a condition of the poet's full creativeness. From the source of life with which he is now at one he can draw forth those myths, images, and symbols, those gods, through which the mysterious inner rhythm of life reveals itself. He draws forth the "holy children" from his own depths, that are now at one with the original generative power:

> Like the peasant
> who assists the birth of his cow—
> and she from the pain groans like a wild beast—
> plunging the hand into her bowels
> until the calf slips
> in one movement
> to the floor of the shed . . .
> thus was I covered with blood
> assisting with all my soul the birth of the gods,
> mysteriously!
>
> Red still,
> like the moon in its rising,
> I held in my embrace
> the holy children
> from the womb of the goddesses!
>
> [2, 171]

The human soul that thus conceives these divine ideas and forms corresponds in the individual to the feminine productive

148

element whose receptivity is a condition of spiritual engendering, of illumination by spiritual light. It follows that the first stages of individual initiation, the preliminary purification, will consist in disembarrassing the passive receptive element which lies within, from all the entanglements and profanities in which it has been caught in its mortal life. It is then, when man's inner being has been brought back to its state of original purity, and is, using Christian terms, a Virgin, that the Annunciation can take place, the planting of the divine Word in its depths. Similarly, the purified soul that gives birth to the divine Word in man may be called, again using Christian terms, Mother of the Son of Man (God created man in his own image. If the image of God is man, God is the archetypal Man, and Christ, the divine Word, is thus the Son of Man). It is with these connotations that the poet now addresses the Mother of the Son of Man:

> *O Mother*
> *You did not, as Daphne, flee*
> *the love of God,*
> *to save Your virginity on a mountain,*
> *but when, thrusting forward with the knee,*
> *the Archangel,*
> *like the north wind,*
> *opened the door of Your house,*
> *and the lily's scent*
> *at once filled the air,*
>
> *You did not move Your large eyes,*
> *nor the bow of the eye-brow,*
> *but,*
> *as a cloud-covered May-day,*
> *trembling*
> *You said:*
>
> *" Behold the Lord's servant:*
> *Let it be with me according to your word!"*
>
> [2, 197]

It is worth while pausing at this first important use by Sikelianos of Christian iconography. Sikelianos did not rank himself against Christianity. Far from it. He recognised that a great deal of the ancient tradition was enshrined in Christian myth, especially in the Orthodox East, but that this myth itself had suffered deterioration and its meaning had been almost totally lost after centuries of abuse at the hands of Church officials, who had often confused it with morality or even worse with a struggle for power and authority. He would have agreed with Blake's words: "There is no Natural Religion . . . As all men are alike (tho' infinitely various) so all Religions and, as all similars, have one source"[1]—that source being of course the life of the spirit in the human soul. Once regarded from this point of view, many of those comparisons which Christians in particular, preoccupied with the uniqueness of their own creed, like to make between Christianity and non-Christian religions, are seen to be without sense ; and it is from this point of view also that can be understood what Sikelianos meant when he spoke of "this great truth that behind all the gods and all the myths is hidden the inexhaustible generative source of myths and gods, our own soul"[2] and talked of uniting "all myths into one Myth."[3] His own soul identified with that "generative source of myths and gods," there is thus no inconsistency in the fact that Sikelianos can make use, in its original but now often forgotten metaphysical sense, of Christian iconography in the same breath as he makes use of pre-Christian images and symbols.

But to return: the purified soul conceives at the inspiration of the Word, and gives birth to the Son of Man, who, being of one nature with Man, is also Man. It is thus that Sikelianos writes that it was through the eternal feminine within him, his own soul, that he knew the divine Child, Man:

Mother, with you
I knew Man,
the Child
who leans the cheek against Your cheek,
and watches fixedly the abyss in Your eyes . . .

[2, 198]

[1] Blake, Nonesuch Edition, ed. Keynes, London, 1941, pp. 148-149.
[2] Life and work of Pindar, Anglo-Greek Review, Vol. 3, No. 7, Nov.-Dec., 1947, p. 194.
[3] The Eleusinian Testament, I, To Nea Grammata, Jan., 1936, p. 51.

—and can go on to speak of the growth of this divine life within:

Until,
a separate sun,
it spilled over Grace
and gave to Creation, which had been dead,
new rhythm,
radiant,
raised in the sacred dance of its Word!

[2, 199]

In the last part of "Prologue to Life," "The Consciousness of Personal Creativeness," Sikelianos speaks of the rôle of man in the work of creation, both in an individual and in a universal sense. The first hymn of "The Consciousness of Personal Creativeness" picks up the theme of man's task in relationship to his own personal destiny, his integration with his deep original self. This integration is something that must be accomplished before man can be said to act at all in any significant sense. The original self, while it dwells within each individual, yet in relation to individuality, may be said to be closed in the depths of nothingness and silence, for its realisation involves a going beyond all the limited states which make up one's individuality. The human individual must thus divest himself of all these limited states; must, as far as individuality is concerned, penetrate into those depths of nothingness and silence before he can realise his true nature. Sikelianos takes the human skull as the symbol of this nothingness and this silence in which man, stripped bare of all that belongs to the limited individual world of time and place, confronts his original self. The skull, symbol of nothingness and silence, is the home of divine life:

Silent light-producer of my most hidden wish,
ivory tower
from which leaps as a flag
the soul's flame!

O human skull!
O skeleton!

151

I place you before me today
as my fathers placed you
in the shrine of the Delphic Sanctuary,
measure and plumb-line,
weighing of the same huge force
which you close deeply within you as marrow
—marrow of immortality! . . .

O white image of my deepest,
of my most holy self! . . .

O skull! O chalice of all-knowing Intoxication!
Upright backbone!
Reed where Prometheus first closed,
to give it to all his brother men,
the sacred seed of immortal fire!

[2, 227-228]

Here, then, in this putting off of the individual self, in this self-annihilation, man meets and unites with his Self, with the "burning fire of life" [2, 229], the "sleepless beat of creation in my breast" [2, 230], the root of individual as well as of cosmic life, the Word which is ἐν ἀρχῇ [2, 230]. And the *is* is emphasised, for ἐν ἀρχῇ does not mean only a beginning in an historical sense, with respect to a definite and past period of time; it means also "in principle," in the ultimate source which is actually rather than temporally prior to all things, in the eternal now from which past, present, and future derive, but which is itself free from all duration. This must be grasped before it can be understood how a purely individual realisation is at the same time a realisation of the essential nature of all things. In realising himself, the human individual becomes one with the Word ἐν ἀρχή, with the Self that is in the source of all things, in the everlasting beginning; that energy from which all manifested life, all tradition, all historical and physical becoming derive, is now the active, liberated, and determining energy at the centre of the realised person. It is thus that through his own realisation Sikelianos becomes one with the source of which the tradition was the expression. This tradition, as we have seen, he recognised, as far as Greece is concerned, as most fully realised, in an historical sense, prior to the fifth century B.C. ; it was in this period that life had reflected most completely those universal principles embodied in the tradition, it was then that life was most closely integrated with that metaphysical source, that Word ἐν ἀρχῇ that now governed the poet's life. Subsequent centuries had fallen away, had lost contact with the Word, and had reflected less and less distinctly the principles of the tradition. Now the poet, through his own creative effort, had brought the Word to life within him, so that it shone with full radiance ; he had, seen in an historical perspective, recovered contact with those principles which for the centuries since the " fall " of ancient " pre-Socratic " Greece had been obscured. All these centuries had been as it were " unsatisfied," unrealised, and only now were able to achieve their realisation in this new birth of the Word:

> *Here now altogether descend,*
> *descend like burning lions,*
> *to drink and to quench their thirst*
> *from the steep slopes of Time,*
> *the one following behind the other,*
> *twenty-five centuries!*
> *To drink and to quench their thirst*
> *at Your fresh source, O Word,*
> *Word of Greece!*
> [2, 231]

This was the Word which had revealed itself to the poet when, established in his own nothingness, he prayed before the anvil of Silence:

> *Thus I prayed, thus*
> *before the steel anvil of Silence,*
> *and behold, suddenly,*
> *the gigantic hammer-stroke,*
> *manful, peaceful, rhythmic, deep,*
> *began ceaselessly to sound!*
>
> *The most ancient silenced heart-beat*
> *began once more to sound!*
> [2, 231]

L

Yet at the same time this " heart-beat," while it is the original
self of the individual, of the poet as an individual, is so much
more than merely individual, that the poet denies that it is in
any sense his own. He sees it rather as the " heart-beat " of his
earth, as the stifled heart-beat of the Greek people—as, that is,
the source both of his physical world and of that people's life
in which was still reflected some of its qualities [2, 232]. It is in
fact the " Word of Greece " [2, 235] of which the centuries of
Greek history were the scattered limbs, the scattered drums of
that original column :

> *Scattered drums of a Doric column*
> *razed by unexpected earthquakes*
> *to the ground !*
> [2, 237]

For all history is simply a part, a limited expression of universal
life, a passage of its great melody :

> *Part only of the great melody*
> *which sounds in the depths of my veins,*
> *unconquerable rhythm and ocean !*
> [2, 238]

It is the realisation of this melody, of the Universal Spirit, that
the initiate after long discipline and purification finally attains ;
he knows and merges with a higher power, his own consciousness
becomes one with the inner consciousness of the universe. In
ancient Greece, at Eleusis, this divine power was symbolised by
the corn-ear, the " corn-ear reaped in silence," and at
the most solemn moment of the initiation, this ear of corn, which
" the Athenians hold to be a great and perfect light, from that
which has no form,"[1] was shown forth as a sign that the initiate
had now achieved enlightenment, had merged his consciousness
with that of the God. So it is that Sikelianos asks that he too
may achieve this full all-seeing consciousness, reap the
Eleusinian Corn-Ear, and then, as Hierophant, hold it up before
the Greek people, that their life, and through them, the life of
mankind, be once more integrated with the universal principles

---

[1] Cruice: Philosophoumena, Paris, 1860.

of life and once more possess the dignity and grace it had in the great traditional communities of the ancient world:

> *May I behold once again,*
> *not now vision, but life, fruit and truth*
> *before my eyes*
> *the mystic Eleusinian Corn-Ear,*
> *greater, more full than the corn-ear of Apellis,*
> *upon which perched heavily a pigeon,*
> *and which yet supported it*
> *unbending and firm !*
>
> *And may I, finally, stoop,*
> *a Hierophant,*
> *to reap it in silence,*
> *and to hold it up among all the people,*
> *among Humankind,*
> *pledge of the new*
> *victory of Apollo*
> *over the Snake, Time,*
> *of your own unreigned age,*
> *of your new engagement,*
> *O Greece, with life !*
>   [2, 239]

We are now in a position to see more clearly the understanding Sikelianos seems to have had of the rôle of man in the work of creation, and in particular his understanding of the relationship between the human individual and the divine on which this rôle depends. For Sikelianos, this relationship is a reciprocal one. For if on the one hand the human individual only has a full existence when he has united himself with the divine principle, yet this principle itself can only become fully active in man's own creativenes. One reaches the paradox that while the divine principle is given life in man's creativeness, yet, divorced from this principle, man is incapable of creation. This principle, the original self, is the principle of creation in man, as in the whole universe, but it remains unrealised in man unless he develops his creative powers. The preservation of this paradox is essential if one is to escape on the one hand an impersonality and a sense of human paltriness in the great processes and purposes of the cosmos, and on the other hand that assertion of the mere individual *qua* individual which is a feature of the "humanism" of Renaissance and post-Renaissance Europe. The individual, like everything else in the divided world of place and time, is a fraction of the whole, a single scattered limb of man's immortal body, of the great Dionysus:

> *And yet I know*
> *how in this deep silence,*
> *over the surface of the world,*
> *are still after centuries scattered*
> *the peaceful limbs of my God,*
> *the peaceful limbs of the great Dionysus,*
> *the peaceful limbs of the great Poetry,*
> *the peaceful limbs of the world's deepest Unity!*
>
> [2, 242]

In the divided world of time and place both the Self and man, the human individual, are incomplete, imperfect, lacking fulfilment; the Self is "dismembered" in the individual's separate, self-centred existence, and in the absence of the Self the individual is a mere fragment, almost a fiction. In fact, the fulfilment of either is something incompatible with the world of time and place. In that world, the Self, the unity, is scattered into a thousand pieces, while the individual is divided from the inner principle, that same unity, which gives his life form and purpose. It is man's realisation of this that marks the beginning of his creative life. He begins to try to realise the Self, the unity, which in a potential state dwells within him and whose realisation is at the same time the realisation of his own life. But as the Self *is* the creative principle in man, the development by man of his creative powers in an effort towards realisation is at the same time the development of, the giving of life to, the Self. This is what is meant by saying that the Self can only become fully active in man's own creativeness, while at the same time man is incapable of creating without the co-operation of the Self. The more fully creative man becomes, the more completely he realises the divine principle in him and the unity which goes with it. At the same time, as the Self becomes "actualised" within the individual, so is the Self beginning to heal that breach in its own nature which the individual's separation implied. This is

156

the reciprocal relationship between the human individual and the divine as Sikelianos seems to understand it; the one needs the other. Yet the first movement towards mutual realisation comes from man; it is he who makes the journey whose fulfilment is the vision of life's wholeness:

> And again I know
> that in this Silence
> I must go forward,
> forgetting the Word's ferment within me,
> silent, as if I feared to wake someone,
> to see the world's face,
> the whole world's
> from the beginning.
> The face of all creatures,
> of all peoples, of all ages, from the beginning!
>
> [2, 243]

Nor is this journey, which is the justification as well as the realisation of man's life, one which has an end within the limits of the single person. The work of creation is without end. " All creation groans as a woman who gives birth . . ." [2, 247], waiting for deliverance. Purely individual realisation is only a prelude to the greater effort man is called upon to make for the realisation of all. In fact, man's full creative rôle in the world can only begin after he has achieved his own realisation. Only when saints are saints do they begin to undertake the larger task of helping others, the rest of creation, towards the fulfilment they know is possible. " Prologue to Life " closes with the poet's celebration of his own " secretly achieved body." Now could begin the struggle that was to fill the greater part of Sikelianos' remaining creative life, a struggle not only to revive in his people and, beyond them, in mankind, a consciousness of the true sources of life, of the principles of the great tradition, but also " with dominion, with authority, with the blind world-rulers of this life, with the spirit of evil in things heavenly."[1] In other words, it was now that Sikelianos himself could attempt to fill the rôle of the poet as he had seen it fulfilled by certain of the poets of ancient Greece and which was once the understood rôle of the poet in society.

1 Ephes., 6, 12.

Before going on, however, to speak of Sikelianos' effort through his poetry to make the principles of the great tradition the living and conscious principles not only of his own life but of the lives of others as well, something must be said of a movement of which Sikelianos was the centre and which formed an intimate part of his purpose. Sikelianos regarded Delphi as one of the spiritual founts of ancient Greece, a centre of wisdom and inspiration derived from the Orphic tradition. The function of Delphi in its creative period had been the sowing of this wisdom and inspiration among the peoples and cities of Greece and through them among the rest of mankind. Sikelianos felt that the time had come for the restitution of Delphi. In the face of the debased values which govern the profane education of today in school or in university, where students are prepared for " life " without the slightest reference to the principles on which life in fact depends, he felt that the time was ripe for the foundation again of a centre of education based on these principles, of a living and sacred kernel which would focus the efforts of the few enlightened but isolated spirits of today towards the regeneration of man. He did not mean by this that he wanted to " vulgarise " or " popularise " ideas which in their nature cannot be understood except by a few. He wanted on the contrary to embody the esoteric teaching of the tradition in exterior forms through which each individual, according to the measure of his or her capacity, might comprehend what he or she could, and would at least re-experience the atmosphere of creative purpose. In this way, there would be something which corresponded to the level of the possibilities of each individual, however high this might be, and would thus provide the appropriate " support " necessary to his or her development. Thus, for instance, at the centre of this hieratic order would be the direct teaching of the esoteric doctrine itself, with its corresponding " artistic " form, the theatre and its sacred drama. Round this would be gathered what elements still remained living of the Greek people's tradition, both of its crafts and of its festivity, its music, its song, and its dance. These elements of the people's tradition, being the surviving relics, as has been already remarked, of the world's ancient and sophisticated cultures, would form as it were the base from which the feeling and rhythm of those cultures could begin to penetrate into the hearts and minds of modern men and women. They would thus form the starting point of the initiatory process. From their contemplation would slowly develop the desire, which we have seen paralleled in Sikelianos' own life, to penetrate back to the roots of the people's life, back, that is, to the principles which gave the quality and distinction to those ancient cultures themselves. Forming the graduated connecting link between the centre and the base would be the Delphic University, where, in the light of the tradition, would be taught the sacred Science itself, Art, Communal Life, History (again in the sacred, not in the profane sense), Agriculture and Handicrafts. In this way, Greece, and, beyond Greece, other peoples of the world, would have before them a living image of the ancient and sacred order of life which would at once make it possible for them to judge the debasement and profanity of modern civilisation and at the same time provide a pattern on which to model their own particular efforts towards regeneration.

This movement took shape in what was called " The Delphic Idea," and had as its immediate consequence the two Delphic Festivals, one of 1927 and the other of 1930. These two Festivals, for which Sikelianos and his first wife were largely responsible, were intended as a preliminary to the real purpose of the movement, the founding of the University at Delphi as a centre of spiritual and communal teaching. They were received with considerable enthusiasm. But the government, while it was willing to lend its support to the artistic side of the programme, and to recognise the actual site of Delphi as international territory, did not support the idea of Delphi as an educational centre. Thus the movement found itself in a difficult position: either it was to continue as an artistic " spectacle " for tourists, or it had to come to an end. It was decided, at least for the time being, to bring it to an end. But it was in the spirit of " The Delphic Idea " that Sikelianos wrote the great part of his later work—" The Dithyramb of the Rose," his tragedies " The Sibyl," " Dædalus in Crete," " Christ at Rome," " The Death of Thigenis," and his still unpublished " Asclepius," and the rest of his lyric poetry. It was in this work that he sought to embody the esoteric teaching of the tradition and its consequences for the life of the individual and of society. It is to this teaching that we must now turn.

In the discussion of Sikelianos' earlier work, the method by which I have progressed has largely been analytic; in the consideration of his later work, the method will not be analytic so much as synthetic. I will not, that is, speak of these works in the order in which they were written, as was suitable when it was a question of tracing the poet's development. I will, on the contrary, take them as a whole, and, with the help of what has already been said in connection with the earlier poems, will try to distinguish the essential lineaments of the full understanding of life which lies behind them all. For we must remember that now it is not so much a question for Sikelianos of attaining for himself realisation, as of communicating to others the need and possibility of such realisation, as well as an awareness of the true human condition, of the dangers and obstructions which prevent its fulfilment, and the splendour of the fulfilment itself.

First, then, this teaching from the universal point of view. Sikelianos seems to have recognised at the centre of all life a single divine principle, what he calls, in the early poem cited, the "original self," and what we may call, for the sake of brevity, simply the Self. This Self is something different from the individual ego or selfhood. It might even be said to be opposed to the ego, though the relationship between the one and the other is perhaps not so easily reducible. It would be better to say that while the Self determines the centre of individuality—not only of man, but of all states of being—the individual, if isolated from its principle, has only a very partial, almost a fictional, existence. The individual derives its reality from the principle and therefore effectively possesses this reality only by participation in the principle. The Self is thus the permanent principle of which all individual states of being, each in its own domain, are modifications, transient, and contingent. It is the Universal Spirit, with the proviso that one must guard against falling into the dualist error which regards the spirit as something opposed to matter (matter, indeed, in the conventional dualist sense of the word, which is generally nowadays the only one understood, does not exist for Sikelianos). It permeates all things, all things are as it were its body, and yet it remains at the same time beyond all things. The individual and all manifested states exist only through the Self, and yet the Self transcends all manifestation. It is important to stress this point, for otherwise one is in danger of supposing that Sikelianos, in avoiding an erroneous dualism, has fallen into an equally erroneous pantheism. All manifestations are modalities of the Self. Everything exists in the Self, but the Self is not limited by things, which themselves, separated from their original source, have no real existence. The Self is a unity which includes multiplicity, standing in relation to multiplicity much as the sea stands in relation to the waves, the foam, the water-spouts, whirlpools, ripples, and so on, which are its various modifications but which do not affect its essential nature.

This Self Sikelianos also designates as Dionysus. Dionysus is the Lord of created beings, the great cosmic power, the great stream of life flowing through all, life itself in its dance and dizzying change from state to state, the heart-beat, the sap, the great tidal currents, winds of earth and the stars' measure. He is life in its flow and succession and ceaseless outpouring, in all its forms, with all its contradictions, in its joy and its suffering, its cataclysms and its splendours. But if Dionysus is the life of all created forms, he is not dependent on them. If he is the all in multiplicity, he is also the unity behind multiplicity. If he is the changing, destructible power divided out among beings, he is also the indestructible, immutable power, perfect and undivided consciousness. He is the inner harmony of life, that remains unchanged through all change. From this point of view, he appears as Apollo, the eye with which the universe beholds itself and knows itself divine, and the supreme organising power behind as well as within creation. Thirdly, Dionysus, or the Self, appears as Christ, as the supreme subjective source of individual life. Dionysus-Christ is the Word " in the beginning " of the individual, revealed in the depths of the human soul. Then again, as another of the " personalities " which, depending on the aspect under which it is viewed, it has, the Self is Eros. Dionysus-Eros is the communicating energy between higher and lower states, between the divine and the natural world. It is the energy that descends from above into each individuality and is that which in each individuality aspires and inspires to union with the Self. Eros is of course intimately linked with sexual love, for the real object of sexual love, Sikelianos would seem to imply, and therefore of Eros in relationship to the individual, is to stimulate that desire for procreation which can only really be fulfilled with the individual's realisation of his total androgynous nature. Eros, then, in the individual, is the desire for that union with the Self in which the individual realises his complete and original nature.

Man's complete and original nature is, Sikelianos recognises, androgynous. The Self is androgynous. This brings us to a consideration of the feminine element or principle in Sikelianos' poetry. From one point of view, the Self would seem to be beyond any such division into masculine and feminine. It is only when it enters into creation that it polarises itself into a masculine spirit, Dionysus, and a feminine element or substance, for creation is the outcome of the " marriage " of these two. The feminine substance actualises itself under the inspiration of the active spirit. This substance is thus the " mother " of all that is created, the passive and infinitely caring support of nature, of everything that lives. She is the " natura naturans perpetuam divinitatem " who is the subject of Sikelianos' long poem, " The Mother of God ":

> *Ah, this warmth is deep; it is unlike, you feel, that*
> *where in the sun's spring-head like swans the lilies sail!*
>
> *This is the rose begun and which ever spreads*
> *on a silk embroidery needle-worked for years . . .*
>
> *And if I close my eyelids, then I see her : O how many*
> *around her sacred lamp are the tassels of the dark . . .*
>
> *As an eagle is she in the eagle's nest ;*
> *from birth she rises up, and virginal is her womb.*
>
> *Motionless in her patience is she in her child-bed,*
> *clasping, as a lion-cub, her only-begotten child!*
>
> [3, 11 & 13]

She is not herself nature, still less matter, in that profane sense in which these words are generally understood. Rather is she the passive root or ground of creation, a state of pure potentiality and receptivity, into which the spirit pours its fertilising seed. She is the human soul in its state of original purity, through which the forms and ideas of eternal Wisdom are born in man's mind. She is this eternal Wisdom itself, the divine Mother, or Mother Earth, from whose ever-virginal womb issues, after the penetration of the spirit, earth and everything that lives. It is this supernatural marriage of the spirit and the eternal feminine

which was mirrored in the ritual of "The Village Wedding";
and elsewhere Sikelianos likens these two intercoursing powers
of creation to two black pigeons:

> *black like the Erebos of Orpheus, more black*
> *than the Night, one with the Holy of Holies*
> *of the uncreated dark—*

locked in eternal embrace in the depths of the androgynous Self:

> *there where, in eternal copulation,*
> *immortal pair of pigeons,*
> *the Divinity itself, sleepless, multiplies,*
> *in its most rich darkness, the Marriage!*
>
> [3, 257-258]

And these lines, which speak of an "uncreated dark," give an
indication of another aspect of the eternal feminine in Sikelianos'
poetry, where it is not something contained within the Self and
into which the Self divides on entering into creation, but where
it is something beyond the Self altogether, a limitless world of
unfathomed possibilities, of unfathomableness. It is something
beyond all ideas of God or Being, a Divine Darkness that is
absolutely infinite, the Nothing, Boehme's Ungrund or the Greek
apeiron, an unformed Ocean or Inconscient Chaos in which
Being itself lies hidden and unknown. It is important to remember
this aspect if we are to understand the fulness of Sikelianos'
vision.

Such then, briefly, are, from the universal point of view, the
main principles of life as Sikelianos sees them. If we regard this
universal order as the macrocosm, then the human individual is
the microcosm; he contains, that is, these principles within him,
either in a potential state or realised to the degree of his own
realisation. The human individual is therefore both much more
and much less than he is normally considered to be. He is much
more, because he is not simply his corporeal self, but contains
within himself the possibility of enormous development. He is
much less, on the other hand, because he is only real in a relative
way, in so far, that is, as he participates in or reflects something
of the universal. He is as it were the image in the mirror, that
only derives its reality from the object of which it is the reflection
and that without the object does not have any existence—

although it must be remembered that, according to the all-important paradox which lies at the heart of Sikelianos' teaching, this is a false analogy, and can only become more exact if we add its correlative, that, as the divine principle in man, the Self is "dismembered" until it is realised in the lives of individual men and women. The crucial reciprocity of this relationship is implicit throughout Sikelianos' work, and gives it, especially where the later poetry is concerned, its tragic tension.

The Self, then, dwells at the vital centre of every human being. It dwells there at first in a potential state, awaiting its deliverance:

> *From the beginning until the end who guesses*
> *that the worm suddenly will put on wings?*
> *Thus the soul of every man conceals complete*
> *within it God, who should be delivered wholly . . .*
> *And if man puts on wings, how will he not*
> *even from the Sun's[1] hands themselves take up the reins?*
> [D. in C., 143][2]

Thus imprisoned within the individual, captive in the largely false and wholly partial world of time and place to whose categories the individual is subject, the Self is as it were "crucified": it is nailed on the cross of the individual's egocentric ignorance and uncreativeness. Its deliverance, which is at the same time the deliverance of the individual from the same categories of the lower world, depends now on the individual's own creative effort and affirmation. It is here that can be seen how Sikelianos' attitude to Christ differs from that of much "official" Christianity. Christ, as the Self, is "crucified" within the ignorance and uncreativeness of the individual, within the ignorance and uncreativeness of the world as a whole:

> *South, North, East and West—*
> *a great cross and upon it Man's*
> *Spirit I see now nailed.*
> [S., 108][3]

[1] In all cases in which "Sun" is capitalised, the reference is, of course, to the inward sun of which the outward sun is the visible image, Apollo as distinguished from Helios—Plato: Laws, 898 D.

[2] "Dædalus in Crete" in Vol. 1 of: "Thymele," The Theatrical Works of Anghelos Sikelianos, Collection de L'Institut Français d'Athènes, 1950.

[3] "The Sibyl" in Vol. 1 of: Thymele, *op. cit.*

And again:

> *Desolate splinter of Divinity, the Word*
> *hangs, alas, with hands punctured,*
> *with his head lowered upon the breast,*
> *like an eagle which as it flew an arrow*
> *suddenly brought from the skies to the ground,*
> *and the whiteness of his visage is before us*
> *to light for us the whole abyss of suffering.*
>
> [C. at R., 12][1]

This crucified state of the Self is the responsibility of individual men and women, a consequence of their selfishness, narcosis, and uncreativeness. Sikelianos paraphrases the words of Isaiah:

> *I see him*
> *suffer for us, groan for our error.*
> *I see him, bitter, wounded, in despair,*
> *because of our own sins drop blood,*
> *lose his strength because of our own crime . . .*
>
> [C. at R., 16]

But the human individual, since he only achieves any very real existence through participation in the Self, condemns himself to virtual unreality and non-existence if he keeps the Self captive, crucified, within him, and refuses to make that creative effort on which the deliverance of the Self and, correspondingly, his own deliverance depends. Christ's crucifixion is the individual's lack of any real life. But Christ is, potentially, even when thus crucified, far more than the crucified one. He is the individual's possibility of full realisation of, and participation in, a higher order of life. He is, in his delivered state, this order itself:

> *For I am above my cross and above my nails,*
> *like a great vine whose grape-clusters hang heavily*
> *and wine of the most strong Intoxication will it give you.*
> *With me if you are united, do you with all the world*
> *unite . . .*
>
> [C. at R., 46]

It follows that for the human individual to worship the Christ

---

1 " Christ at Rome," Athens, (Skaziki), 1946.

crucified is to condemn himself to that virtual unreality and non-existence which Christ's crucifixion within him signifies. It is to confuse the moon with the finger which points at the moon. For it is only through delivering the Self, through taking Christ off the cross of individual selfishness and ignorance and uncreativeness, and through the development of the sacred seed within from its potential to its fully realised state—it is only thus that the individual himself can partake of existence in a more than relative sense, and can free himself from the constricting categories of time and place and all the illusions and fevers that belong to them. And this deliverance requires not the individual's passive acquiescence in his own paltriness and ignorance ; not, that is, the worship of the Christ crucified, but his creative co-operation in a process whereby, through a development of his own inner powers, he is able to confer on his life a fulness and splendour which he might well have imagined beyond his reach ; a process which corresponds not only to the deliverance of Christ, the Self, from the cross, but also to the individual's becoming himself Christ, the realised and liberated Self.

Sikelianos points the distinction between the worship of the Christ crucified and the attitude of those who seek, through personal creative effort, to deliver Him from that crucifixion in a conversation between the hero of his play, " The Death of Thigenis," and a priest of the Church. In this play, the Church is presented as one of those tyrannies which, from motives of self-aggrandisement and love of power, seek to persuade the individual to worship the finger and not the moon. Instead of encouraging the development of the individual according to the laws of his own inner being until he had attained full realisation, it sought to make him submit to a discipline that crippled his creative powers and prevented the plenitude of his life. It sought to implant in the individual the idea that realisation could be achieved not so much through a personal creative effort in which the individual was his own priest and was not dependent on any Church, as through the practice of observances enjoined by a priest for whom an acceptance of the other point of view would be tantamount to admitting that both his own position and the Church he represented were superfluous. The hero addresses the priest:

166

> *The very*
> *instrument of martyrdom you worship, priest,*
> *you kiss the hand that struck the Christ, the foot*
> *that kicked Him, the great yoke they laid*
> *across His neck as though He were an ox . . .*
> *And slowly for the cross do you forget*
> *the Crucified, yourself become its servitor,*
> *worship the very martyrdom, more, even he*
> *who crucifies Him, His very tyrant . . .*
> *And for the gains in heaven or on earth*
> *do you contract with him . . .*

And he contrasts his own attitude and that of his companions:

> *But we, here, Ilarion,*
> *these and I, in the world we seek to bring*
> *the Christ again on earth, as He was*
> *when thirty-three years old the great wave*
> *swelled his heart, to overthrow the tyrant . . .*
> *Him we seek—you hear?—when thirty-three years old,*
> *before you drew an old man at His side,*
> *and over Him a bird, the Spirit, that should*
> *scatter the Word from the one end to the other*
> *of the earth and that you shut with a knot*
> *in the Four Gospels, in a case of heavy gold,*
> *that the world bend to kiss the gold and your own hand . . .*
> *We, we seek to cut the cross up by the root,*
> *strong tree of life in its place to ascend*
> *and the Paradise of Man to flourish round it . . .*
> *For every Christian can become the Christ,*
> *Ilarion, every Christian woman the Holy Mother . . .*
>
> [D. of T., 21-22][1]

The creative process by means of which the individual attains realisation, delivers the crucified Self, is one of initiation. It corresponds to that process of recollection, of anamnesis in the Platonic sense, of which I speak more fully in the next study. Thus Orpheus seeks to awake in his disciples "the perfected Memory" [D. of R., 21].[2] In this process the individual has to

---

[1] "The Death of Thigenis" in Vol. 2 of: "Thymele," *op. cit.*
"The Dithyramb of the Rose" in Vol. 1 of above.

pass through a series of stages which correspond to an ascent from the dark underworld to the pure sky above ; from, that is, a state of inner darkness, ignorance and confusion, to a state of fully enlightened consciousness, where " Freedom is Knowledge and Knowledge Love " [D. of R., 32]. The whole process of the growth of the divine seed within from potentiality to realisation, which is at the same time the growth of the individual towards fulfilment, recalls the Gospel passage : " The kingdom of heaven is like unto a grain of mustard seed, which a man took, and sowed in his fields : which indeed is less than all seeds ; but when it is grown, it is greater than the herbs, and becometh a tree, so that the birds of heaven (the higher states of being) come and lodge in the branches thereof."[1] Sikelianos, in a description of an Orphic initiation, where the Self as Dionysus is the principle of initiation and where the Muses correspond to the various faculties which, as the " living soul " passes on its upward course from stage to stage, are not rejected but reabsorbed into it, compares the process to the growth of the Dionysian Vine :

which, as it sucks the Earth's
darkness and drinks from the sky dew,
reconciles in its veins the darkness
with the light in fervid blood, destined
to give out the sacred Intoxication by the hand
of the divine Muses, who stand one
on each step, to ascend with You
to the summit, and to change her name
as Your own changes . . . And thus,
from intoxication to intoxication our thought,
our senses and our courage and our breath
from the one Dionysus to the other
suddenly ascend, to where the sacred wine
no longer reaches, for there opens in our mind
the exhalation, which now joins all in One,
soul and body, blood and spirit, enmity
with love, peoples with peoples, place
with place, with life death, centuries
with the centuries . . .

[D. of R., 24]

[1] Math. XIII, 31 and 32.

It is significant here that Sikelianos speaks of the sacred Vine as drawing its sustenance from "the Earth's darkness." Just as the Vine, so the individual, if he is to be fruitful, must not sever his contact with that higher source of wisdom and understanding which Sikelianos represents as feminine, as a Mother Earth; he must not sever the Earth-roots in him, for these supply the very sustenance which nourishes his inward growth. It is from Earth that the trunk draws the food which raises the branches up into the sky of disembodied reality where the "birds of heaven" inhabit. It was such separation from Earth and the exclusive development of the individual "masculine" reason which Sikelianos saw reflected in western civilisation, reflected—for things below are copies—in the growth of great industrial cities and the mechanisation of nearly every aspect of life and the severance of men and women from the earth. That is why the whole "scientific" civilisation of the West seemed to him an anomaly, not to say a perversion, for it was the projection of the mind severed from its Earth-roots and thus incapable of any organic and therefore significant development:

> And do not separate from Earth, thinking
> higher than this to seat yourself
> on a throne of false glory, when
> on Earth's throne you have all; but whatever
> comes from Earth, support it, whether vine
> or tree; and if it sinks, give it
> your own stick to strengthen it,
> your own lance . . .
> [D. of R., 28]

In the West, man had separated himself from Earth and had established himself on a "throne of false glory," his individual mind. But deprived of its maternal nourishment the mind is incapable of becoming spiritualised and thus loses bit by bit its contact with reality. Dissociated in this way it becomes a "false king":

> Other
> hidden power is it that supports
> the world's depths. If the mind with this
> does not unite, from its own purpose
> it declines, which is sleeplessly to knit

169

M

earth's heart-beat with the radiance
of the cloudless sky. For, alone,
often by its own light bedazzled,
the mind forget itself in whatever glitters
closer to it rather, while within
the darkness, which it cannot reach, Fate
ripens by herself, until the hour when
suddenly she feels the birth-pangs . . .

[S., 50]

This last image recalls Oedipus who, trusting in his logic and reason, lived in blind ignorance of any true reality, while in the darkness Fate was preparing the suicide of his mother, his own mutilation and all the long term of his exile.

This " other hidden power" in union with which only does the mind function in a purposeful way, is again the feminine principle, the passive ground and root of all manifestation and the container, as it were, of all the ideas and forms and energies through which the spirit creates. The mind thus in union with this " Mother " is in a position to receive and to perceive true knowledge, Gnosis ; it can, that is, become illuminated by the light of perfect consciousness, instead of being blinded by its own natural light. Apollo, the Self as perfect consciousness, has his roots " above the stars." Such consciousness cannot be ours until we have come to know the holy Night, the Mother ; until then our eyes are as mere holes, for we are blinded by the natural light of our own human reason, symbolised by the natural sun, and by the illusions of our phantasy world, symbolised by the moon :

Companions,
before the light comes and traps us in its net,
ah, let us hasten to see into the darkness,
with an eyelid's flutter . . . For, alas,
these are not yet eyes, only they are holes
within our skulls, and more high than all
the stars Apollo has sunk his roots ! . . .
But all your power pledge it to the dark,
for the sun arrives and entraps your soul
in a golden net, and the moon comes out,
and you dissipate your mind in dreams.

170

But you, your mind has roots within the Aether,
and it should break the gold net of the sun,
and grasp above the dreams its source!

[D. in C., 164]

And in another passage, Orpheus, as the fully realised person, recalls how he only received enlightenment after he had known the Mother, known, that is, the feminine principle in himself, in its original state, so that, as we saw above, she could give birth to the divine Word within him, the divine Word being thus her son:

And how can one ever know the son
if first one does not know the mother?
For I too am her son; and from childhood
orphan I seized upon the nipple
of her sympathy, beneath her black
enclosing veil; and as I held
the holy breast, goat-like I leapt
in the sacred darkness . . .

[D. of R., 21 & 22]

For the Mother, in her universal aspect, is, as it were, the receptacle in which are contained all the ideas, the logoi, through which each particular individuality is created. Thus, while in relation to individual men and women, who are all her "children," she is, in their disregard, in the suffering and distress they bring upon themselves through their separation from her, "dark, sad, dressed in black" [D. of R., 23]; is, in fact, as the divine Word itself while it remains nailed upon the cross of the world's egocentric ignorance and uncreativeness, "crucified"—

On the cross of Your sacred Femininity,
on the great cross of Your Loveliness,
more sorrowful than the Son of Man,
than "he who hung the earth in water,"
than "he who encircled in cloud
the heavens" . . .

[3, 265]

—yet in relation to the spirit she is "pale, silent, and dressed in white," because:

from the black and indissolvable richness
of the paternal depth . . .

171

she sees always (the poet is addressing her):

> *there above, dancing slowly over*
> *the dumb abyss' breadth the Armed*
> *Eros like a gull proceed, and always*
> *you await him. And his wing's passing*
> *above you is enough for fresh*
> *worlds to blossom in you, fresh*
> *flowers, a thousand new-born wonders . . .*
>
> [D. of R., 23]

And in this connection, it is worth pointing out that just as it is a mistake to take " ἐν ἀρχή " as meaning "in the beginning" with respect only to a period of time, so it is a mistake to take those events which Christian myth has mirrored in the Annunciation and the Divine Conception as significant only in terms of temporal succession. From the point of view of the universal order, and thus potentially in each human individual, these are ever-present, ever-occurring events of the eternal now.

This understanding that action, if it is to be of value, must issue from deep contemplation (an understanding almost entirely lacking in the modern world, where action has been made an end in itself, and contemplation, without which action is purposeless and wasteful, is scorned as an escape from the "real life" of action)—this understanding Sikelianos saw mirrored in the part which the Sibyl played at the great religious centres of the ancient world—

> *the sacred Sibyls,*
> *the Lybian, the Cumæan, the Erythrean,*
> *the Sicilian, the Chaldean, the Cimmerian,*
> *the Thesprotian, the Egyptian, the Hebraic . . .*
>
> [S., p. 66]

—and, of course, the Delphic Sibyl. He distinguishes two "sensibilities," two modes of understanding: "one which sees in a general reality, on an ever-increasing scale but almost on the surface, a thousand shades of life, and which differentiates its meaning to an ever greater extent into thousands of analytical values; and another, which, rooted in the most subconscious depths of Man, compels him to feel situated within a Whole which perhaps exceeds him, but which makes him absolutely aware of interdependence with it."[1] This second " sensibility," that of the Prophet, the Creator, the Poet, was embodied permanently for the ancients " by the feminine sensibility in its non-temporal and non-sexual aspect in the world, and this embodiment constituted for antiquity one of the most ·olemn and most central communal creative institutions."[2] The part this feminine "sensibility" of the individual Prophet, Creator, or Poet, played in relation to his inspiration, the Sibyl played in relation to the inspiration of such religious centres as Delphi. After a long period of seclusion and purification, corresponding in the process of the individual initiate to the disembarrassing of the passive receptive part of his nature from all the entanglements by which it has been overlaid by habit, education, and general misguidance, the Sibyl is ready to receive the revelations of the God, the divine speech:

> And at last, when
> with time, as swell a young girl's breasts—
> first pain that touches her of mortal fate—
> and overflows within her the foreboding
> of someone who will come, first touched my mind
> that secretly in its depths enclosed
> the dawning divinations, the desire
> for unripe oracles, and by themselves
> did my lips open as unexpectedly
> opens some bud, to give its scent
> all round, to speak their first
> divining love-words at the God's desire . . .
>   [S., 63-64]

In the same way must the soul of the individual Prophet, Creator or Poet be prepared before it receives the inspiration of God, before it can become " entheos." And in a passage in which the God addresses his priests at Delphi, describing the relationship of the priests to the Sibyl, Sikelianos gives an image of the relationship which the human individual must preserve with the passive and receptive, the contemplative, side of his nature, if

---

[1] Introduction to " The Sibyl," *op. cit.*, p. 40.
[2] *Ibid.*, p. 43.

his mind is to be " living," not " dead " as it is when it trusts to its own natural light:

> And as the thought
> of the simple man, which only
> considers all that the market offers,
> should have as close support the woman's
> depths, who remaining in the house
> becomes engaged to Earth, in a like way
> to you, who pledged yourselves to be
> the world's sentinels, I give, emblem
> of the same Earth, the spotless woman,
> whose virginity and unquenchable desire
> for the Sacred Hymen rouses her, of all
> mankind the daughter and the mother,
> to convulse with unsubdued concern,
> soul and body together, with the single
> pulse of God, who always closer
> to him summons man, that you sink
> your thought into her depths, your mind
> to be for ever living . . .
>   [S., 50-51]

Just as the human individual must preserve this relationship with the feminine principle of life if he is to be creative and fruitful, so must society as a whole preserve it if it also is to be creative and fruitful; if, that is, it is in any way to reflect the universal order through which alone life can become something of value and beauty. It follows that ages which are creative, just as individuals who are creative, are those in which the human mind keeps, through contemplation, its contact with the ideas, or forms, of an Intelligence which is itself beyond the mind's natural reason. To exalt the reason at the expense of this Intelligence to the extent to which the West has done, is to invite destruction, since then society is swept along paths of meaningless blind activity which issues from minds divorced from the universal order and so completely unaware of the real causes of things and of the real consequences of what they do. There is a slope of descent away from reality which can be traced with an almost monotonous exactitude. In its creative phase, a society derives its vitality from, and reflects, the truths

174

and ideas of a transcendent Intelligence, of that "Wisdom uncreate, the same now as it ever was, and the same to be for evermore,"[1] which the human mind can, through contemplation, intuit, and in the light of which it can then give form and rhythm to every aspect of life. Sikelianos sometimes compares the relationship of the mind to this transcendent Wisdom to that of a child which draws milk from the breast of its mother. When this relationship is broken and the mind proclaims its own supremacy, denying its dependence on anything higher than itself, it at once becomes impossible for it to have any contact with reality in a living sense, just as the child cannot continue to draw milk from its mother's breast when taken from it. Instead, the mind seizes upon that knowledge which during the creative phase it has gained of reality, abstracts it from its living roots, and forms it into a system of mental concepts, which it then calls absolute truths and which, if it is allied to a desire for power and authority, it seeks to make everyone else call absolute truths, proclaiming them in dogma and embodying them in authoritarian institutions for which it pronounces divine sanction and to which it demands unconditional submission and obedience. Such a process of "materialisation" of the spirit continues with ever-increasing momentum until the point of maximum solidification and inertia is reached, when new forces, mounting unperceived from within and taking the form of natural cataclysms or wars or revolutions or other violence, destroy the whole fabric and a new phase of life is inaugurated.

It was this process of "materialisation" which Sikelianos saw mirrored in, for instance, the history of Delphi. According to his myth of Delphi, it was Orpheus who had delivered full knowledge of the divine mysteries to the priests of Delphi, that Delphi might become a centre of inspiration and wisdom for the whole people, leading them from the valleys of darkness up to the peaks of enlightenment. But with time the priests fall from their high task of keeping the sources of inspiration open, of keeping, that is, their mind wedded to that feminine "sensibility" through which alone, by direct perception, living contact, it can grasp truth. Instead, their thus dissociated mind forms that knowledge of the mysteries which it possesses into a system,

---

[1] St. Augustine, Conf. IX, 10.

proclaims that system to be Truth and, exploiting the ignorance
and superstition of the people:

With word,
with deed or other means to others closes
the ways of the sacred ascent, where the pure
soul of the higher world shines limitless . . .

[D. of R., 32]

Thus it is that tyrannies come into existence. Such tyrannies of
course vary enormously. If they occur near the beginning of the
descent, near the beginning of this process of "materialisation"
of the spirit, the order which they seek to impose may embody
concepts which reflect in an abstract and theoretic way principles
of the universal order itself. This is so in the case of certain
theocracies, like, for instance, that of Delphi. If they occur near
the end of the descent, the order which they seek to impose may
simply embody ideals of physical welfare and material prosperity
and power, as is so in the case of certain modern State dictator-
ships. But in all cases a tyranny is the product of a mind which,
divorced to a greater or lesser extent from the real sources of
knowledge and wisdom, asserts its own supremacy and, allied
to a desire for power and authority, seeks to impose its own
distorted conception of truth on, and to stifle the sources of
knowledge and wisdom in, others.

A full picture of such a tyrannical state of mind and of its
development Sikelianos gives in his portrait of the Cretan law-
giver, Minos. Crete had been the seat of worship of the Great
Mother-Goddess. She, as the primordial receptive power, had
been the element through which the God, the divine Self, in this
case Zeus, had revealed himself to man. Through contact with
the Mother, man had kept in living touch with the principles
of the universal order. His life had thus that ritual character
which it has in all creative ages ; it had reflected faithfully its
highest rhythms and purposes ; its masculine and feminine, active
and passive, elements had been held in fruitful reciprocity.
Sikelianos in symbolic terms describes this state, describes the
Mother's reception of the "great inheritor," Zeus, the spirit
(without which she is unproductive), her revelation of the divine
order to the people and the people's communion in the highest
mysteries of life:

And the great inheritor came, Zeus came,
and she opens her breast that many years has been dry,
she gives to him the holy breast beneath the stars,
and the black nipple suddenly pours forth milk . . .
And the milk came and overflowed the mouth
of the young God ; but as if the snows were melting
abundant was the milk and descended down to Crete.
And all the Cretan mothers raised their children
to the divine breast, and all from that
as if they were possessed, drew in the milk
of the Mother Goddess, who seemed to weigh
before her moon with sun, the day with night,
woman and man, the little with the great,
for all set off by the same path to reach her . . .

[D. in C., 144-145]

It is this order which Minos seeks to disrupt. Asserting the supremacy of his own mind over every other aspect of life, including over that higher Intelligence which is symbolised by the Mother Goddess and in union with which alone the mind is capable of perceiving truth, he " usurps the place of the sun " [S., 67], sets his mind up on a throne of false glory, and regards the conclusions of its discursive and theoretic reasoning as the counsel of Zeus himself. Now follows the second stage in the process of the " materialisation " of the spirit. Abstracting from its living roots that knowledge of the universal order which has been gained during the creative period of Cretan life, he forms it into a system of concepts. He is now in possession of an ideal order which reflects in an abstract and theoretic way principles of the universal order. This order he now " for the common good " proceeds to embody in institutions and laws for which he pronounces divine sanction and to which he demands unconditional submission and obedience:

And he placed the peasants there
to labour hard, and here the polemarchs
he rigidly established, and the priest
took his appointed place, and the women
for the ancient Shrine alone he left them
to govern themselves, but before the door
of the women's quarter deeply he engraved the spindle . . .

[D. in C., 130-131]

177

He has now in theory an ideal system of government, which reflects perfectly the principles of the universal order. In what then, it might be asked, does the tyranny consist ? If, as was said, the human individual contains within himself potentially the whole universal order, surely a system of government which embodies and establishes that order uniformly for all will be the means whereby the individual can best realise himself ? What need is there any longer for this " Mother " worship, which since it involves a personal, subjective relationship with the divine, is likely to result in individual error and communal anarchy, and in any case throws upon the single individual a burden of responsibility which may well be too much for him ? This new order, entirely logical, entirely reasonable, not only prevents the possibility of individual error and communal anarchy. It also fixes once and for all the principles of the universal order in intelligible dogma, in moral law, and in authentic institutions which, since the universal is contained entirely within each individual, apply to all without exception. It thus provides the discipline necessary for the full development of each individual without the individual having the responsibility of imposing on himself that inward self-discipline as before he was called upon to do.

The falsity of this argument can be indicated in a few words. It is true that the individual contains within himself potentially the whole universal order, but the way in which it is contained varies from individual to individual, according to the particular qualities which belong to those individuals, and which, united in them in a specific order, constitute their unique integrity. There is, in other words, contrary to what Aristotle, Aquinas, Kant, and others seem to have thought, no such thing as uniform unvarying man. To disregard this truth is to assume that all human beings are alike and therefore that an order which applies to one person applies equally well to another. But this is not so. The laws which govern the true development of the individual are particular to that individual alone and do not in their particularity apply to any other being. It is for this reason that all systems, religious, moral, political, legal, which apply general principles to particular cases, without exception and in their very nature do more harm than good. Assuredly, the greater harm is done to those who do the applying, for each extension of their usurped and illusory authority draws them further and further into the quagmire of abstraction. It was Satan, we are told, who, seeking to occupy the throne of God, fell to the deepest pit of Hell.

This tyranny of the mind which has transgressed its measure and which with ever-increasing momentum is dragging the world further and further down the slope of "materialisation," Sikelianos saw reflected in the history of modern western civilisation. He was also increasingly aware of the Fate which "ripens by herself, until the hour when suddenly she feels the birth-pangs . . .", of, that is, the new forces which are mounting unperceived within and whose eruption marks the dissolution of the whole fabric: "And have not so many struggles brought you finally," he asks himself in a poem in 1936:

> And have not so many struggles brought you finally
> to the edge of the precipice, widening
> the pupil of your eye, that it may take in
> the vision of a thousand destructions that will come,
> the vision of your own, your own destruction,
> as the black eye of Cassandra, that beheld
> the ruin of Troy and at the same time
> the black frontiers themselves of her own life?
>
> [3, 237]

And in a later poem the Self addresses his soul:

> Behind you the world like Troy is burning,
> and its conflagration glows within the depths
> of the past as with the setting of the sun
> the windows of a city glow blazingly, and,
> suddenly, sink into the dusk. . . . And beyond,
> smoke and cloud of the same conflagration,
> slowly dissolve and disappear whatever
> by man is considered to be future . . .
>
> [3, 273]

And it was to prepare for the new flowering of life beyond the destruction that Sikelianos, like Nietzsche, counselled: "Remain true to the earth," though Sikelianos meant by this not so much true to the physical earth, as to that deeper primordial Earth, the Mother, the passive ground and root of all manifestation.

179

For only the recovery of contact with this source and support
of understanding and enlightenment would make possible man's
realisation of the Self ; only then would the mind, led by intuition,
realise the true nature of things, and would action, issuing from
profound contemplation, reflect once more the divine order and
the universal rhythm. It is thus that the Sibyl, when she gives her
last oracle before the coming destruction, gives it, not to the great
ones of the world, the rich, the mighty, the learned, but to the
simple peasant, tiller of land or shepherd, for he, the central
nerve of his being rooted in earth, still preserves contact with
that deeper ground, support of all growth, through which the
divine Word can once more be born in man:

> *Plants*
> *take root in the ground and are supported.*
> *And you, who plough all your life the earth,*
> *root in the earth have not taken ! And yet*
> *Phœbus came down to the fields of Admetus*
> *servant among the slaves, and he said :*
> *" What is passed is what is passed . . .*
> *Earth and sky are one. And one*
> *let henceforth your struggle be. Rise up,*
> *new creations, to the new Word that flashes out !*
> *For earth may be united with the stars*
> *for you, as deep field with deep field,*
> *that the sky reap also corn. . . . Yours*
> *one day will be the world, peasant ! "*

[S., 56-57]

The individual, then, in his process of realisation, must first
attain that state of inner receptivity— ἀπάθεια —in which the
truths of a universal order can again feed his life. The attaining of this state demands the realisation by man of a divine
principle which Sikelianos represents as feminine, as the "eternal
feminine." If man is to be entirely reflective of, if he is to participate entirely in, the universal ; if, that is, he is fully to realise
the Self, he must first realise this feminine aspect of the Divinity
in its original purity ; he must, that is, realise it in its universal
state, as the pure receptive power. For, as was said, only in its
universal state is this " eternal feminine " entirely receptive to the
spirit. It follows thus that only when the individual has realised

this universal femininity, that which "rises from the depths of the pre-ontological abyss as a power absolutely and substantially erotic and at the same time religious,"[1] only when he has integrated it completely with his nature, will he too receive in its entirety and become wholly conditioned by, and expressive of, the spirit, the inmost Self ; only then will he participate fully in the universal order. But, as we have also seen, this eternal feminine in its universal aspect is prior to all manifestation, free from all differentiation and individuality, pure substance and pure potentiality. It follows that what prevents the individual from the realisation of this undifferentiated state in its universal aspect is all that part of himself which is manifested ; is, in fact, his own individuality. The individual has, therefore, if he is to become one with the Self, to surpass his own individuality, and this is why it is said that the Self is in some way opposed to the individual. But here again is another difficulty. For it is only in so far as he is manifested, only in so far as he possesses individuality, that the individual, generally speaking, says that he possesses life, that he is alive. If, to realise the Self, he has to pass beyond all manifestation, all individuality, then he has to pass beyond what he calls life ; he has, that is, to pass into that state which he calls death ; he has to die. " The only method is death "! But seen in this light, death is not a limit or a cessation ; it is on the contrary " the most deep and rich mystagogic starting place for the complete understanding and also realisation of the greatest and most inward demand of Life—the demand for the most perfect and ' religious ' conscious participation of man, beyond phenomena, in the universal unfolding erotic breath and force of Creation."[2] Death is in fact simply a cloud through which the individual must pass if he is to free the eternal feminine from the " cross " of his own individuality, and thus become totally ripe for union with the Self :

> *For a cloud,*
> *a yellow cloud is death before me*
> *at this moment when, filling the sphere*
> *entirely of nostalgia for me,*
> *O great archetype of my passion,*

[1] Sikelianos: Prologue to " Lyrical Life," *op. cit.*, p. 851.
[2] *Ibid.*

You call me beyond the written circle
of History, further than the Word,
to deliver, above the mystic silence
of Your Cross, and from the darkness
of the centuries, alone, Your Loveliness! . . .

[3, 267]

The living soul must be stripped free of all manifested states, of all that belongs to time and place, must go out of its created nature. But it must also go out of its uncreated nature, "further than the Word," "forgetting the Word's ferment within me," for the divine Word is, as we have seen, the fruit, the Son, of the union of the passive substance, the Mother, with the spirit, the Father, and thus the Word is not this spirit, the Self, in its unity but still in its separation, still in some sense derivative. The divine Word is the image of the Self, what Meister Eckhart calls the soul's exemplar, going on to say that " the soul is conscious that what she seeks is neither her exemplar nor its nature, wherein this final attribute of divinity is multiplicity. And since the eternal nature (the Word) . . . is characterised by multiplicity—the Persons being in separation—therefore the soul breaks through her eternal exemplar to get to where God is a kingdom in unity."[1] In other words, " No man cometh to the Father but through me."[2] And thus it is in the last stages of initiation that the state of death, which seen from the point of view of individuality is all that lies beyond its created and uncreated nature, becomes the state where the sacred marriage of the living soul with the eternal feminine and through her with the Self in its essential unity takes place. This is the significance of the Heracleitan phrase, " Dionysus and Hades—one and the same,"[3] and why in the Eleusinian Initiation, Death and Eros " were the consubstantial power which orientate all phenomena beyond accident towards the eternal sphere of fulfilment and of creative Exaltation."[4] For it is in the attainment of a state of total undifferentiation and absolute potentiality, beyond all manifestation, visible and invisible, beyond the image of the Self in the living soul, beyond the death of the individuality, in Hades—

[1] Meister Eckhart, ed. Pfeiffer, trans. Evans, London, 1947, Vol. 1, p 275.   [2] John 14, 6.
[3] Heracleitos, Fra. 15 in: Diels, Die Frag. der Vorsokr., 1934, 1.
[4] Sikelianos: Prologue to " Lyrical Life," op. cit., p. 851.

Ah, not even the Sulamite lay thus
to give warmth to David's frozen limbs
within the bed . . . as You close to me
when my heart sunk down to Hades! . . .

[3, 270]

—it is in the realisation of this primordial femininity that the initiate can become perfectly receptive to, can unite himself with and participate in, the life of the Self, of the universal spirit:

that above the waves of time
and above the closed Rhythms of creation
flies rapidly, flies with power, like an arrow!

[3, 271]

It is in this union with the universal spirit that the individual achieves his deliverance. He becomes integrated with the Self. He reflects and radiates all which is contained in the Self. He is illuminated by the splendour of the Self, shines with the light of perfect consciousness and fulfilment:

It seems you are a life-kindling soul within
the sun's depths, it seems you are within
the sun, and the flames that light the other stars
and light the world are outside you, are outside.
You see the stars; these do not see you.
You see the world; the world does not see you.
You seem all hidden within your passion's
sun, and from thence that you shoot
there where do not yet rise
creation's stubbornnesses! Study,
study is this passion for you of death,
and meditate upon it as is owing to the divine
fire which is in you, which not as creature
but as Creator you contain within your mind.

[3, 272]

In this light the fulfilled person contemplates all things. He perceives the inner identity of all things, their participation in that life which is now his life. All has become one, the One has become all, in an all-embracing singleness; and man, in achieving his own unity, has become everything.

V. George Seferis

(b. 1900)

THERE are, it has recently been observed, two separate
and contrary directions in the mælstrom of currents which
make up the literature of our time: " There is the centri-
fugal and the centripetal movement. There is the literature of
action—' in the destructive element immerse ' ; there is the literature of recollection—' be still and know.' One current, it seems,
goes with the age ; the other opposes it. Yet both are integral
to our time, the mælstrom could not exist without them."[1]
Writers like Joyce and Lawrence represent the first and active
current ; those like Forster, Woolf, Eliot, represent the second
and more passive current.

This distinction obviously cannot be taken in too absolute
a sense, and many writers, as, for instance, Yeats or Sikelianos,
seem to reach the still centre through immersing in the destructive element. Indeed, the highest genius would seem to depend
upon a reconciliation of the two directions. But if we take the
division as a convenient way of indicating the tendency of a
certain writer, then we can at once say that George Seferis is
representative of the second group, of those who move away
from the swirl of events towards an inner world of awareness
and understanding. His poetry stands as a record of the stages
in this strange and difficult pilgrimage.

But before going on to trace this " progress of the soul " of
which the poetry is the outward and visible sign, it will help
matters if we get a clearer picture of the starting point. The
starting point is of course the contemporary world and man in it.
Every artist must start with the world before him, with a real
situation. If he does not, he merely verbalises himself away into
an ineffective void. This is a great temptation when the world
seems to present, as it does today, such " unpoetic " material.

---

[1] Blackstone, B., Virginia Woolf, London, 1952, p. 7.

N

All round man in the contemporary world is a chaos of forces and events which seem on the surface to be utterly unrelated, unregulated, impersonal, and pointless. What are they all about? Where do they lead to? It is over a hundred years ago that Shelley wrote: "The cultivation of those sciences which have enlarged the limits of the empire of man over the external world, has, for the want of the poetic faculty, proportionately circumscribed those of the internal world; and man, having enslaved the elements, remains himself a slave."[1] We may be a little less certain today about whether man has enslaved the elements, but otherwise Shelley's words would seem to be as true now as at the time he wrote them.

"For want of the poetic faculty," Shelley had written. Why for this want? Because it is this faculty which is capable of throwing some light upon the black world of phenomena about us, of giving us some sense of what we are and of where we are going in the great chaotic flux of things. It provides a scale of reference, it, again in Shelley's words, "creates for us a being within our being, it purges from our inward sight the film of familiarity which obscures from us the wonder of our being."[2] The poet is not only someone who makes a beautiful or convincing pattern of words, the possessor, that is, of a specialised technique. Certainly, he must have such a technique. But a technique is, or should be, a means of expression, not an end in itself. That is why the poet must also be something of a philosopher, a seer, one who seeks to divine some meaning in the world and in human life, and to express this in words. But to this end, he differs from the conventional philosopher in that he conducts his inquiry not so much with his reason, as with that far more perceptive faculty, his intuition. This is the poetic faculty. Nor does the poet, in his quest, aim at reducing the chaos to an ordered symmetry, at finding a scheme which is all-embracing and logically watertight. "My task," writes Seferis, "is not with abstract ideas but to hear what the things of the world say to me, to discern how they interweave themselves with my soul and with my body, and to express them."[3] But through this

[1] Shelley, A Defence of Poetry, ed. Brett-Smith, The Percy Reprints, No. 3, Blackwell, Oxford, 1921, p. 52.   [2] Ibid., p. 56.
[3] Seferis, A Letter on the "Thrush," Anglo-Greek Review, Vol. 4, No. 12. July-August, 1950, p. 504.

expression, the poet will alter in some measure our perception of the whole, he will increase our awareness of life as a whole. This is his claim to our attention: that he is making us known to ourselves, he is revealing to us something of our condition and of our potentialities. If he does not do that, we can safely take no notice of him. But if he carries out his task as he should, we ignore him at our own risk, for what he has to say concerns our very existence. In the study which follows I shall attempt to discover what is the understanding and awareness that Seferis is seeking to communicate in his poetry. "I am a monotonous and stubborn man, who for twenty years until 1946 have not ceased saying over and over again the same things," Seferis remarked a few years ago.[1] What are these same things, and why has he felt it so important to repeat them for so long? In trying in part at least to answer this, it will help us to bear in mind that Seferis is representative of those artists whose orientation is towards a still centre of contemplative understanding.

> *Here, in the earth, is a cistern rooted.*
>
> [41][2]

Thus opens one of Seferis' earlier poems. He wrote poems before this one, poems of personal love and the memory of love, and I shall say something about them later. For the moment, we will concern ourselves with "The Cistern." It is rooted in the earth. It gathers only secret water. Outside and above it, the vast tumultuous life of the world goes on. Worries and joys pass over it, at the rattle of fate faces appear, shine for a moment, and disappear; hours, suns, moons, go by. But the cistern remains untouched, a still heart in the centre of life, a source which gathers to itself the pains and struggles of the outside world:

> *O closer to the root of our life*
> *than our thought and our conception!*
> *O closer than our harsh brother*
> *who watches us with closed eyelids*
> *closer than the lance still in our side!*
>
> [43]

---

[1] *Ibid.*, p. 506.
[2] All quotations from Seferis' poetry are from: Poems, 1924-1946, Athens, 1950. The figure in brackets gives the page number of this work.

N*

This cistern, this still heart, is, then, the image of some presence which lies within us ; it is in some sense our most intimate being, an aspect of our life hidden beneath all the violent and hysterical gestures of the everyday world, and ignored and denied by that world, by some human crime:

> *O to soften suddenly at our touch*
> *the skin of silence which constricts us,*
> *to forget, gods, the crime*
> *which multiplies and overlays us,*
> *to issue out of knowledge and of hunger !*
>
> [43]

And the poet goes on :

> *Gathering the pain of our wound*
> *to issue from the pain of our wound*
> *gathering the bitterness of our body*
> *to issue from the bitterness of our body*
> *roses to flower in our wound's blood.*
>
> *All to be as in the beginning again . . .*
>
> [44]

Finally, there is another picture of the hysterical outside world of disintegration and fragments, where the great crowds of death go up and down so absorbed in their own self-interest that they do not notice the cistern rooted in their midst and seem infinitely less living than the white statues past which they hurry.

This brief prosaic outline of " The Cistern " has been made in order to show that Seferis from the start of his mature work expressed an awareness of a certain contradiction in life. On the one hand, there is the endless movement of a time-ridden world, with its vanishing forms, its hungers, thirsts, and pains ; and on the other hand, there is the sense that somewhere within all this —within it, yet outside it ; suffering through it, yet withdrawn from it—is an unmoving and timeless presence, the cistern, which, like the liberated soul, " teaches silence in the midst of the fevered city " [45]. The fact that for the purposes of the poem these two aspects of life are made to appear opposite and irre-concilable should not lead to any hasty conclusion about the poet resorting to a kind of Manichæism in an attempt to explain something which he has felt and which is really beyond explanation. In "The Cistern," the relationship between the one aspect and the other, which is, from many points of view, the theme of all Seferis' poetry, is, indeed, presented in a way that his later poetry would suggest is slightly false. It is presented as something abstract and static, and not as a living experience transmitted with a directness, movement, and intimacy that compel us to acknowledge its significance.

If we now turn to the poem "Mythistorima," written a year or two after "The Cistern" in 1933-34, we shall find that the sense of life pivoting on a contradiction has not changed, but the way in which it is expressed has so altered that it is made real and convincing as before it was not. The poem is made up of several short sections. In a note to the poem, Seferis indicates why he chose the title, "Mythistorima," and in what way the sections are connected: "Myth, because I have used in a fairly obvious way a certain mythology; History, because I have tried to express, with some connection, a situation as independent of myself as the figures of a myth-history" [235]. Once again, the starting point is the contemporary world, this drifting and bewildered world, and the human person who inhabits it. I say "human person" in case Seferis' words about expressing a situation as independent of himself as the figures of a myth-history give the impression that one is going to be presented with a sort of objective, impersonal world in which the human element is used simply as a cipher for the communication of a set of abstract ideas or the author's political or religious philosophy. This is not the case. The human person is the centre of the scene, it is he who as a concrete, living, suffering and perplexed being, speaks. He is not simply a device. He is someone both inside and outside the life he experiences ; he both suffers that contradiction which Seferis expressed in "The Cistern" as an individual, and at the same time can see himself *sub specie æternitatis*. In this way he combines the characteristics of a man of our time living in our world with those of an archetypal man living a universal human destiny.

It is thus that Seferis aviods both those pitfalls which trap so many modern writers. He neither gives the feeling that his pro-

tagonist is the product of an Olympian mind uncontaminated by
the fury and the mire of this world and of living men and women;
nor does he give the feeling that he is so overwhelmed by the
pressures and persuasions of this world that he loses sight altogether of the larger, imaginative framework within which it moves
and from which it and the lives of individual men and women in
it derive significance; his poetry, that is, neither becomes
grandiose inflationary jargon nor is mere versified reportage.
Consequently, as we read, we become aware that on the purely
individual level we share a great deal with this person who is
the subject of the poetry; he speaks in many ways with our own
voice, he is in some sense ourselves, and we identify ourselves
with him. But in identifying ourselves with him on the purely
individual and contemporary level, we suddenly find ourselves
linked with him in his other aspect, that of an archetypal man
conscious of a universal human destiny. In other words, the
poetry, by stimulating in us an imaginative sympathy which
allows us to recognise our individual and purely natural thoughts
and feelings expressed by the protagonist of the poem, initiates
us at the same time into a consciousness of that universal destiny
of which this protagonist is likewise an emblem. Seferis' poem,
like many of the old Greek dramas, has the function of a ritual
myth.

Contemporary man in a period of catastrophe: this is Seferis'
starting point. He himself grew up in an atmosphere of disaster
which finds its parallel in most lives of our era. He was born and
spent his childhood in Smyrna, that ancient Greek city on the
coast of Asia Minor, on that Ionian coast where, many years
before, those pre-Socratice soothsayers and prophets uttered their
wisdom. In 1922—Seferis is as old as the century—Smyrna and
that whole coast were lost to Greece. There, in that catastrophe,
men and women and children suffered a pattern of despair and
tragedy which some years later was to become the common
pattern of Europe: homes destroyed, files of refugees, forced
marches down endless roads to unknown and often lethal destinations, separation of families, detention camps, boats over-
weighted with desperate human cargo capsizing in open seas,
the end of a world, the end of life, destruction and wreckage.
Against this background, or, rather, within this scene, the contemporary man speaks. This man is, of course, first of all a Greek,

and his background is also Greek: behind him and about him are the broken statues and the Venetian forts, the white shores of the Aegean Isles and Alexander the Great, the bony mountains and the argonauts, Byzantine churches and plane-trees, Helen and Odysseus and the heroes of the Greek revolution, rocks and olives, Missolonghi and Salamis. It is against all this that the contemporary refugee who is also the immemorial hero, this exile both from a terrestrial homeland and from an eternal Ithaca, explores his own suffering and that of those about him and ceaselessly questions the purpose of the mortal journey:

> *But what do we seek travelling*
> *on decks of decrepit ships*
> *huddled with yellow women and screaming children*
> *not able to forget ourselves either with the flying-fish*
> *or with the stars that the masts show at the top.*
> *Grated by gramophone records*
> *bound unwillingly to non-existent shrines*
> *murmuring broken thoughts in foreign tongues.*
>
> [58]

The scene is that of any refugee ship travelling through the waters of the Eastern Mediterranean; it is also in miniature the whole raucous, undirected modern world with its inhabitants so engrossed in their own trivial interests and affairs that not for one moment can they forget themselves in the contemplation of some sudden beauty, in the perception of something outside themselves. A babel of mixed languages but no complete thought, destinations which are illusory, birth and death.

Yet the hero at the centre of the poem is, as I said, both inside and outside the life which he experiences. He is inside simply because as an individual his fate has involved him with it, has projected him into a time and a place which is this particular time and place and no other. He is outside it because he is already aware that this life is not the only life or even at all the real life; he is aware that perhaps the great truth about this life is that it is somehow an absence of life, and that real life lies elsewhere. This awareness separates him, and gives his life a pathos which those who feel no lack do not share. He knows that life was once other than it is now, was once limitless, full, and creative, and not, as it now seems, closed, empty, and sterile:

> *Our country is closed in among mountains*
> *roofed night and day by the low sky.*
> *We have not rivers, we have not wells, we have not springs,*
> *only a few cisterns, these empty, which echo, and which*
>   *we worship.*
> *Stagnant hollow echo, like our loneliness,*
> *like our love, and like our bodies.*
> *It seems strange to us that once we could build*
> *our houses, our huts and our sheepcotes.*
> *And our marriages—fresh garlands and fingers—*
> *are become inexplicable puzzles for us . . .*
>   [61]

This is the crux of the hero's situation. He feels the world around him to be closed, imprisoning, and without sense. But in the very act of feeling this, he feels also that it need not, should not be so, and that it should on the contrary be free and full of meaning. Already he aspires, however obscurely, to a liberty and realisation that the world denies him. Hence his sadness and feeling of distress, all the greater in his case because, being a Greek, not only does he possess a deep belief in freedom, but he also possesses an ancient memory which makes him more conscious than most of man's transitoriness and vulnerability and hence of his poor chances of ever attaining that freedom. Nevertheless, he does feel that some escape is possible from the forces of constraint which beset him, and that through his own efforts he is capable of realising the liberty and coherence the present world denies. His attitude changes from one which accepts as inevitable the closed world, to one of struggle. His sadness and distress, at first without direction and floating, change now to a tragic sense of life whose solution demands heroic action: he must fight against the forces that hedge him in, he must seek to reintegrate his own individual consciousness to the " other life " of freedom and coherence which he feels has once existed and can exist again, though often he will doubt this and be reduced to heart-breaking despair. We must now examine more closely what such reintegration involves.

In " The Cistern," Seferis had spoken of a dark, hidden source at the centre of life, ignored by the life which flows past it and over it, in-drawn, plunged in gloom, a void of motionless depth. But it is not lifeless ; rather is it the interior origin of the river of life which streams out of it and which, being out of it, turning away from it, loses life in the real sense of the word. This depth has in fact the nature of an obscure, unmanifested intelligence which is at the root of life. It is a kind of understanding without action, yet at the same time a nameless actuality, an indwelling presence. It preserves an unbroken silence, and yet it is the essence of speech. It is beyond time and place, and yet without it time and place would not exist. It is totally collected in itself, and yet is linked to the life of creation, although creation itself may not recognise this. It is the image of another, a mysterious and silent presence lying hid in the depths of stillness, and yet also the most primitive and simple form of man's nature.

At the same time, we are made aware that the surface life of the present has fallen out of contact with this unknown source ; it has become estranged from it, and in so doing has become fragmentary and scattered, driven round and round in meaningless circles, in a delirium, like that of the scene on the ship's deck, which amounts to death. Man is part of this process of fragmentation and dispersal, of exile from the source. He is a refugee from the land of his origin, he has lost his inner unity, and his present life is really a nightmarish absence of life in consequence. And the only way in which he can recover himself and his true nature, is by turning away from the great flux of the outside world and back towards that dark source which lies in his inmost depths. By a gathering together of himself, by a concentric application of his scattered forces, he will once again make contact with that obscure intelligence and undivided presence at the root of life. When that is done, and only when that is done, will life become once more full, expressive, new-born with light. This process of realisation is what I have called the universal destiny of man.

How is this realisation, and recovery by man of his true nature, effected ? How can life ever be anything else than confined and unsatisfying ? We may find a clue in a short phrase from Plato's first " Alcibiades " with which Seferis opens one of the sections of " Mythistorima " [52] : " The soul, if she wishes to know herself, must look at a soul." The phrase occurs in the part of the dialogue where Socrates has convinced Alcibiades that he cannot be wise or give good counsel if he is ignorant of what he is himself; until, that is, in obedience to the Delphic inscription, he has learnt to know himself. But man, to know himself, must first know what he is. Now, just as the thing using is different from the thing used, so man, who uses his body, is different from his body. What, on the other hand, itself uses the body, is the soul. Thus man, in himself, is nothing less than soul, and soul is man. This is the first step towards the knowledge of self: man, since he is in essence soul, must, to know himself, know his soul. How can this be done? If an eye were asked by the Delphic inscription to " Behold itself," it would have to look at that in which it could see itself. This it can do by looking in the eye of another person, in which, as in a mirror, it will see itself reflected; in other words, an eye, to see itself, must look at an eye. So, in the same way, the soul, if it is to know itself, must look at a soul. Above all, it must look at that part of the soul where wisdom lies, for that is the divine part of the soul, and he who has knowledge of that would know himself most. It is, then, through knowing what is divine in himself that man knows himself most perfectly.[1]

It is in connection with man's knowing himself through knowing what is divine in himself that Plato develops his theory of recollection, anamnesis. The soul is the immortal part of man. Before it entered into creation and became lodged in a human tenement, it had already contemplated all truth and beauty in the immortal world. In the company of the Twelve Gods it had passed outside the sphere of the visible heaven into the supra-celestial region of colourless, shapeless, intangible reality.[2] Dragged down and lodged in an earthly prison-house, this divine knowledge of the soul—which is also man's knowledge of himself and his true nature—is obscured. It is obscured but it is not obliterated. Man still possesses it within himself, only, distracted by the world of the senses and transient things, he forgets it. Thus man, to know himself and to recognise that divine nature which is what he really is, does not have to learn something which he has never known. He has, on the contrary, only to learn again

---

1 Plato, Alcibiades (I), 133, B.C.
2 Plato, Phædrus, 247, A.ff.

what through the accident of birth he has forgotten. Learning is nothing but recollection, the recovery of that truth once seen by every soul before it became incarnate: "For man must have understanding by way of what is called the 'form'—a unity gathered by reflection from many acts of perception; and this is recollection of the things formerly seen by our soul when it travelled in the divine company, despising the things we now call real and looking upwards to true reality. Hence it is just that only the mind of the philosopher should get wings; for he is always, as far as he can, dwelling in memory on those things, the contemplation of which makes divinity divine. So the man who makes right use of these means of recollection is always being initiated into the perfect mystery, and he alone becomes truly perfect. . . . "[1]

Plato goes on to link this recollection, this anamnesis, with the sensuous intuition of beauty. The perception of beauty which comes through the bodily eye and stirs the wings of love is also that which first awakens man's memory of his forgotten life. The sight of something beautiful in the world around us calls back into consciousness our latent memory of supersensual beauty: "For, as we said, every human soul has by nature beheld the things that are; else it could not have come into the human creature; but it is not easy for every soul to recover the memory of them from things on earth. It is hard for such as had then but a brief vision of that other world, and for those, who, after their fall hither, had the ill-fortune to be turned by evil conversation to unrighteousness and to remain in forgetfulness of the holy things which they then saw. Few indeed remain in whom the power of memory is sufficient; but these few, whenever they see some likeness of things in that other world, are struck with amazement and lose their self-possession, though they know not what this condition means, because their perception is not sufficiently clear. Now Justice and Temperance and all things else that are of value to the soul have no indwelling light in their likeness on earth, and it is hard even for the few, when they approach the copy, to discern darkly, through dim organs, the features of the original. Beauty, however, was then visible in her splendour, when, in happy company, ourselves attending Zeus

[1] Plato, Phædrus, 249, B.ff.

195

and others following some other divinity, we saw a spectacle of beatific vision and were initiated into the most blessed (as it may lawfully be called) of all revelations. . . . Let this, then, be our tribute to the power of memory, for whose sake I have spoken thus at length, as looking back with longing to the visions of that former life. Among them, as we have said, beauty shone ; and, since we came hither, we have seen the unrivalled clearness of her radiance through the clearest of the senses—sight, whose perceptions are keener than any others that come to us through our bodily organs."[1]

It is the first stages of this act of recollection, with all the checks, difficulties, sorrows, hopes and fears which attend it, that are expressed in " Mythistorima." We have seen its starting point, the contemporary world. But into this world, in spite of its vulgarity and its limitation, penetrate, as Plato divined, certain shoots and rays from the other, the lost world ; man can at fleeting moments glimpse the beautiful lineaments of an unearthly presence reflected in, parcelled out among the physical beauties of nature :

> Sleep has wrapped you, like a tree, with green leaves,
> you breathe, like a tree, in the quiet light,
> in the transparent spring have I seen your face :
> closed eyelids, eyelashes stroke the water.
> My fingers in the soft grass your fingers found,
> I held your pulse a moment,
> and I felt elsewhere your heart's pain.
>
> Under the plane-tree, close to water, among laurels
> sleep has displaced you and has morselled you out
> round me, close to me, not letting me touch you wholly,
> linked to your silence ;
> watching your shadow grow larger and grow smaller,
> lose itself in other shadows, in the other
> world which released you and held you back.

[66]

This understanding of Plato's, that the natural world of the senses is rooted in the supernatural world ; that the sight of beauty in

---

1 Plato, Phædrus, 250, C.ff. Trans. Cornford.

this world leads directly back to the world of ideas—this understanding has been preserved in the Greek East in a way that it has not been in the West.

But it is not only physical beauty which may awaken anamnesis, recollection, as Plato seems to have thought. There is much more. Seferis introduces his poem with a phrase of Rimbaud:

Si j'ai du gout ce n'est guère
Que pour la terre et les pierres.

There is another phrase of the same poet which might have served him equally well: "Dans tes environs affluera reveusement la curiosité d'anciennes foules et de luxes oisifs. Ta memoire et tes sens ne seront que la nourriture de ton impulsion créatrice."[1] Especially might this be so in Greece. Everywhere in Greece are memory and sense stimulated, stimulated by the abundant evidence of a break-through of the invisible world into the world of time and place. The spirit of man in its strange unpredictable course over the earth has taken up residence among the people of this peninsula not in one shape, but in many; not only in ancient Greece, but in Byzantine and modern Greece as well. It is in Greece perhaps more than in any other European country that one can become aware of the extraordinary variety of which this same spirit is capable when it embodies itself on earth: even the old sea-dwelling Nereus could scarcely equal the changes rung by the power which at one moment can appear as a Dionysus on the frieze of an ancient temple, the next as a Pantocrator in the dome of a Christian church, and then again as the dance of sailors in some Ægean sea-port. In few other places has so much conceived in the realm of ideas become actual. In few other places do the moulds which once envoys of the human spirit had filled with their vitality, give now, in their desertion, such feeling of loss and abandonment, such sense of a sunset of the gods:

We have not known them,
it was the deep hope that said
how we have known them from early childhood.
We saw them perhaps twice, and then they took to the
ships :

[1] Rimbaud, Les Illuminations: Veillées, IV.

o

cargoes of coal, cargoes of corn, and our friends
lost behind the ocean for ever.
Dawn finds us beside the tired lamp
drawing clumsily and with effort on the paper
sailing mermaids or shells ;
at twilight we go down to the river
because it shows us the way to the sea ;
and we spend the night in cellars that smell of tar.

Our friends have left us,
perhaps we have never seen them,
perhaps we met with them when sleep
still brought us close to the breathing wave.
Perhaps we search for them because we search for the
other life
beyond the statues. [54]

And in another part of the poem, Seferis returns to the theme, the fate of man in the face of such a history, such a process of birth and death and rebirth among ruins and relics of what were once full vessels of life:

Because we know so well this our destiny
circling round among broken stones, three or six
thousand years,
searching in wrecked buildings which were perhaps our
own home,
trying to remember dates and heroic deeds . . . [75]

It is no wonder that the burden of the memory of history sounds throughout Seferis' poetry. In a country like Greece, where at different epochs man has attempted and achieved so much only to see it destroyed and ruined with the passing of time, the oppression of history is sometimes overwhelming. What can a single individual, a link in an enormous chain, do that really makes the slightest difference ? Or even if he does attempt something, how trivial it will seem when compared with the great creations of those who have gone before him, and how the fate of those very creations reminds him of the fatuity of the attempt.

But precisely here, in this setting of despair, does an altogether different attitude to history clamour for recognition. All this ruin and wreckage, what does it signify ? Whence did it come ? Who wrought it ? Time itself, what does time signify ? As man casts his eye now on the pre-Homeric wall of some fortress, now on a Turkish minaret, now on a fragment of Corinthian pottery, now on the icon of a mediæval saint, now on a telegraph pole standing like some totem on a rocky headland, his normal conception of time seems somehow slightly ludicrous ; he begins in fact to lose his sense of time, he begins to feel that the man who built the wall three thousand years ago is as close to him as far as time is concerned as the man who served him with oranges this morning in the market. He begins, that is, to doubt whether time is more than something very superficial. And the ruins and wreckage of time, the broken column, the chipped mosaic, the tattered embroidery, all coexistent, all lying there before his eyes, seem to be not the expressions of different times, but the expressions of a reality which is ever present, which is now, and of which it is within his power to partake. He begins to see that he is not simply what he thought he was, a link in an endless chain, but that he possesses within himself a sort of microcosm in which the world of objective reality and all historical periods, exist in an ever present now. He is not what he seems, a fragment of a meaningless world. He is rather a world in his own right. There is a level of reality within him where there is no time, but from which time derives. If he could see history from the point of view of this level of reality it would then be no more than the past reflection of what is ever present ; he would, that is, have overcome the oppression of history by participation in a world of which history is but an external and transient manifestation. At the same time, all history's monuments and ruins, the discarded and broken receptacles of this world's expression, would be reminders of this world, stimulating, with even greater insistence than the physical beauties of nature, the act of recollection and creative understanding.

It is this attitude to history which, as a counterpart to the sense of its oppression, is implicit in " Mythistorima." Nature, rocks and trees, seas, broken marble, old sites, river and port haunted by legend and fable, bear silent testimony to the exis- tence of that other inner world from which they derive ; they are all signs, hieroglyphics in the language of this world, the sounds with which it spoke, words of its original Word. And as that world spoke in time through the creative activity of men of genius, through heroes, prophets, poets, saints, men of wisdom of the past, and as all these great ones have now been drawn back to that world whose existence they revealed to their fellow-men, that world can in some sense be called now the home of these ancestors, the kingdom of the dead. Thus we reach that seeming contradiction which lies at the heart of Seferis' poetry, that the kingdom of the dead is that true reality, the contemplation of which makes divinity divine ; and that realisation of that reality, on which depends man's knowledge of himself, is at the same time a process of dying, a journey to the dead.

This contradiction provides the dramatic tension of "Mythistorima." The hero of the poem looks round him and sees:

> Olive-trees with the wrinkles of our forefathers,
> rocks with the wisdom of our forefathers . . .
>
> [70]

He sees:

> Trees which breathe the black silence of the dead.
>
> [73]

Bound now like Andromeda to the rock of time and place, become part of the sweep of history, he asks:

> These stones that sink into the years, until where will
> they carry me ?
> [73]

He feels, as he sets out on this pilgrimage towards the other life, the kingdom of the dead, that:

> Death has unexplored roads
> and its own justice.
>
> [74]

As he struggles with his fear and reluctance to surrender the partial life he has known, to detach himself from the transient world of fleeting things, to die to them, so that they no longer hold him prisoner and so that he can bring to birth this other level of reality within him, he feels that:

> The ancient dead have left the circle and stand round
> and smile with a strange quietness.
>
> [74]

He laments that the wearisome condition of humanity involves such surrender:

*I have let a broad river pass between my fingers
without drinking a single drop.*

[71]

Moments of despair flood him as he faces that profound personal solitude in which alone can recollection take place and in which he sees again those scattered portions of himself which he must gather together:

*If I wished to be alone, sought
solitude, I did not seek such waiting,
portions of myself at the horizon,
these lines, these colours, this silence.*

[60]

He feels the long journey before him as a " bitter and unexplored sea " which " spreads out with boundless calm " [63], and he echoes the cry of Clytemnestra:

The sea, the sea, who can drain it dry ?

[73]

Finally, in a short section which deliberately recalls the 11th Book of the " Odyssey," where Odysseus, after parting from Circe, makes his *nekuia,* his journey to the dead, and slays the sheep over the trench—the trench of memory—so that by drinking of their blood the dead may speak with him, Seferis signals the departure of his hero (who is, after all, another Odysseus) from the world of flux and confusion, and asks that, just as he has not forgotten his dead ancestors, so later generations may not forget him. The dead need the living as the living need the dead:

*Here finish the works of the sea the works of love.
Those who sometime will live here where we finish
if the blood chances to darken their memory and overflow
let them not forget us, weak ones among the asphodels,
let them turn towards Erebos the heads of the victims :*

We who had nothing will teach them peace.

[77]

201

From one point of view, all Seferis' later poetry—and it includes some of his best work—is an elaboration and deepening of his understanding of themes and problems first grappled with or at least implicit in "The Cistern" and "Mythistorima." In considering this later work, I will not, as I have so far done, discuss the poetry according to its chronological sequence, but, regarding it as a whole, will look a little more closely at some of those themes and problems which recur again and again in individual poems. Of these themes and problems, four seem to to be of particular importance: the common man, woman, nature, and, finally, death.

The common man is he who, born into this world without, ostensibly, any particular wish on his part, never really wakes to a proper sense of his destiny, or, if he does wake to it, does not, through laziness, greed, or through a thousand and one other reasons, ever realise it. He makes his appearance in Seferis' poetry early on, and, as so many other aspects of this poetry, he is introduced by way of the "Odyssey." Odysseus is the pilgrim, the exile, he who wishes to return to his true home and to lead back, like the Old Testament patriarchs, his companions from captivity to the promised land. But in spite of all his efforts, Odysseus, who saves himself, cannot save them. They, through their own stupidity, and in spite of the warning they have received, kill and eat the cattle of the Sun, and in consequence suffer death as punishment, remain, that is to say, in Hades, bound "godless and satisfied" [18] to the wheel of the elements, never returning to their true home, never becoming what they might become. They are also those who wish to stay in the lotus-land of the senses, those who are turned to swine in the palace of Circe. The common man is one of these companions. He appears in Seferis' poetry sometimes as Elpenor, the youngest of the Odysseus group, the least brave and the least wise, who, woken from drunken sleep by shouts and footsteps on the morning of the hero's departure from Circe's isle, falls to his death from the balcony where he has been dying and descends to the House of Hades.

Yet there is another side to this common man which is also evident in Seferis' poetry. If, on the one hand, he is selfish, carnal, guilty of crimes against the gods and against his own nature, full of uncoordinated passion and perverse folly, blind, coarse and brutal, he is, on the other hand, the victim, he who struggles and suffers, loves and hates, rejoices and weeps his way through a life whose purposes he cannot see but whose pain, harshness, and degradation he knows only too well. He is one who tastes all the necessities and insults of life, but rarely tastes any of life's real fulfilments. That is his lot. Yet at the same time he is the " sinner " whom Christ so much preferred to the self-righteous, the grammarians, the wise in their own sight, not for any sentimental reason but because he felt that the very instability and spontaneity of the sinner, his closeness to the turbulent vitalities of nature, if it often made his life destructive and cruel, yet made it also unexpectedly full of unselfconscious and childlike gestures and sacrifice. A person who is vital, even in the most earthly sense, and even if he knows nothing at all of the spirit, is yet potentially closer to the spirit than the thinker or the moralist who has lost contact with what is primitive and earthly in himself. If he fails to live up to the great challenge of a unique individual destiny and so can never become a saint or a hero, he can often share instinctively the passion and purpose of a saint's or hero's life in a way that those who have lost contact with earth's primal forces seldom can. In this way, his ignorance of the spirit is of more value than much of the so-called wisdom of the educated or scientific mind, just as Socrates' ignorance was of more value than all the teaching of the sophists.

The common man, then, appears under both these aspects in Seferis' poetry. On the one hand, it is he who through his stupidity does not respect the cattle of the Sun, does not respect " the light of each day that God gives him,"[1] and who because of this not only forfeits his own chances of return home but also makes more difficult the return of everyone else. He prefers the pigsty of contentment to the more demanding roads of the spirit. He is the weak sentimentalist who is always weeping for old loves, or dreaming voluptuous dreams of loves which he hopes to taste, " like those which torment us so on summer beaches with gramophones " [181]. He becomes " a machine of fleshly pleasure that now has lost all meaning " [181]. In the end, he suffers the fate he has already chosen, dissolves back into the flux of things,

[1] Seferis, A Letter on the " Thrush," *op. cit.*, p. 505.

neither able to face the sun nor able to face man [230]. He is a puzzle and a tribulation:

> *I do not understand these people, I do not understand*
> *   them,*
> *sometimes they imitate death and then again*
> *they shine with the small life of a glow-worm*
> *with a gesture of limited despair*
> *squeezed between two wrinkles*
> *between two stained café tables*
> *they kill each other they get smaller*
> *stick like postage stamps on glass*
> *people of another tribe.*
> *We walked together, shared bread and sleep*
> *tasted the same bitterness of departure*
> *built with what stones we had our houses*
> *set out in ships were exiled returned*
> *found our women waiting*
> *they scarcely knew us; no one knew us.*
> *And now the companions wear statues, wear the naked*
> *empty chairs of autumn, and now*
> *they kill their own people. I do not understand them.*
>
> [142-143]

At the same time, this man is the unfortunate one, often prey of injustice which he does not seem to deserve and which has its origin elsewhere. He is one of the Argonauts, who endures the perils, fatigues, disgusts, hardship and boredom of the journey, who never understands what the journey is about, but whose loyalty and obedience make the journey possible:

> *They were good lads, the companions, did not complain*
> *either of heat or of thirst or of cold,*
> *they had the bearing of trees and waves*
> *which accept the wind and rain,*
> *accept night and the sun*
> *changeless within change.*
> *They were good lads, whole days*
> *sweating at the oar with lowered eyes*
> *breathing in rhythm*
> *their blood reddening submissive skin . . .*
>
> [52]

Only they never see the end of the journey. They too sink back into the elements, scattered. This is, Seferis seems to repeat, the lot of the common man, of him who never frees himself from the great wheel of necessity. Yet it is precisely for this reason that he deserves sympathy as much as condemnation. He is at the mercy of forces which drive him to acts whose consequences he does not understand. If his energies break out in ways that are destructive only, this is as likely as not because those in a better position set in their own lives no example of creative purpose to which he can dedicate his life. The man who sees, who does understand, and who does not indulge in hypocrisy or egotism, is bound to have a relationship of particular pathos with his people. He is bound to be aware of their folly, their stubborn selfishness, their blind greed which allows them to destroy what is most precious and sacred in life without the least sense of what they are doing. Then, too, he is bound to see them, even in their worst moments, or, rather, especially in their worst moments, as victims, vulnerable, pathetic, terribly deluded but terribly helpless creatures ; cogs in a machine wound up to kill, but still capable of suffering:

> Easily man is rubbed out in war :
> man is soft, a bundle of grass,
> lips and fingers that hunger for a white breast,
> eyes that half close in the dazzle of daylight,
> feet that would run, however tired,
> to the least whisper of profit.
> Man is soft and thirsty like grass,
> insatiate like grass, his nerves expanding roots ;
> when harvest comes
> he prefers the scythe to whistle in the other field ;
> when harvest comes
> some cry out to exorcise the daimon,
> some get tangled in possessions, others make speeches.
> But what will they profit you—exorcisms,
> possessions, speeches—when the living are absent ?
> Is man of another order ?
> Is it this that confers life ?
> A time to sow, a time to reap.
>   [217-218]

Between the pole of his anger and the pole of his compassion does the awakened man oscillate. He is the voice of judgment, but in the heart from which he judges is the longing to forgive, the longing to guide his people out of the darkness in which they wander. In supreme cases, he is Moses pleading with God's wrath for the tribes of Israel, he is Christ lamenting over Jerusalem, he is the Bodhisattva who seeks Nirvana not for himself, but that he may go back into the world to help those who suffer in it.

Yet it is in relation to this theme of the common man that something must be said of what would seem to indicate a certain failure of nerve implicit in the understanding of life Seferis communicates in his poetry. This comes out in relationship to fate and to the destructive forces of life. As in other cases, it is again by reference to the " Odyssey " that it can be pointed to. Odysseus, as was said, saves himself, but does not save anyone else. His companions one by one are killed, drowned, and scattered back into the elements. Odysseus, by dint of superior cunning, gets through, and reaches Ithaca, the lost home. He cheats fate of her prey. But what is this fate he has cheated but which his companions, who killed the Sun's cattle, did not cheat? As far as Odysseus is concerned, it is an impersonal power, God or gods, which he is in no way responsible for and which he can in no way change or control. The attitude he takes up in the face of it is an attitude of passive endurance and resignation. He submits to it, because it is external to him, has its all-powerful origin and intention in an " elsewhere " which has nothing to do with him, and thus to endure and resign himself to what it sends is the only course open to him.

This attitude has three inter-related consequences, all of which threaten man's creative life. The first is an act of exteriorisation which permits man, in crediting fate with supernatural purpose and volition altogether beyond the range of human influence, to indulge in a feeling of irresponsibility for what happens to himself and to other people. The second is that the regarding of fate and the suffering it brings as something extra-human and not the consequence of man's acts of omission and commission, induces in man a sort of hypnotised and entranced state, as of a bird before a snake, in which he does nothing but lament in a way that is not without a certain voluptuous attractiveness the enormity of suffering and of his own helplessness before what are made to appear unalterable facts of life. Thirdly, this entranced, almost idolatrous state before the spectacle of the suffering that fate brings, combined with a feeling of helplessness and irresponsibility, prevents man from recognising that the "destructive element" which causes such havoc, is not merely negative and "evil," but is another aspect of the same force on which all creative life depends.

It is an attitude similar to the one I have been describing that seems implicit in the understanding which Seferis' poetry communicates, and that indicates the failure of nerve of which I spoke. It can be recognised in several places, in the heavy note of weariness common to much of the poetry: in the feeling of powerless resignation and at the same time assumed irresponsibility which seems to be expressed in such lines as the following:

> *How have we fallen, friend, into this pit of fear?*
> *It was not your fate, neither was it my own,*
> *never have we sold or bought such things;*
> *who is it that orders and kills behind us?*
>
> [198]

Or, in a later poem:

> *Wet autumn in this depression*
> *turns bad the wound of each one of us,*
> *or what you might call nemesis, fate . . .*
>
> [217]

It appears again more directly in Seferis' characterisation of Socrates as a man who preferred to have injustice done to him rather than do injustice.[1] Quite apart from whether this is a just estimation in this particular case, as a general attitude it can only lead once again to apathy and resignation. For any act of creation involves a measure of destruction and therefore from one point of view of injustice, as someone like Yeats, for instance, well understood:

> *Did that play of mine send out*
> *Certain men the English shot?*
> *Did words of mine put too great strain*
> *On that woman's reeling brain?*

[1] Seferis, A Letter on the "Thrush," *op. cit.*, p. 505.

207

Could my spoken words have checked
That whereby a house lay wrecked?
And all seems evil until I
Sleepless would lie down and die.[1]

Yet it is precisely this lying down and dying, this refusing to act even though it involves injustice and suffering, that the responsible man must not do:

That were to shirk
The spiritual intellect's great work,
And shirk in vain. There is no release
In a bodkin or disease,
Nor can there be work so great
As that which cleans man's dirty slate.[1]

It is also to shirk that great work if one retreats as a consequence of one's attitude to fate before the tension involved in accepting the paradox that if one is always concerned not to commit injustice, the chances are that one will not do any justice either —a paradox whose importance Blake realised so well that he went as far as to say that active evil is better than passive good.[2] Yet sometimes Seferis does seem to be content with such a retreat, a retreat which comes from a sense of powerlessness before fate and not from a Brahmin-like superiority to fate. He echoes with his own emphasis Socrates' speech to the judges:

And if you condemn me to drink poison, I shall thank you.
Your law will be my law : where can I go
wandering through strange lands, a rolling stone?
I should rather die.
Only God can say who will prosper.

[229]

There must be no mistake. Seferis' attitude is not an ivory-tower attitude, against which he has spoken with considerable vehemence.[3] It is, if anything, a passivity and resignation before supposed laws and prescriptions governing the universe — the necessity, ananke, of certain ancient Greek philosophers[4]—whose

[1] W. B. Yeats, Collected Poems, London, 1952, pp. 393-394.
[2] Blake, Complete Poetry and Prose, Nonesuch Lib., 1941, p. 185.
[3] Seferis, Essays, Cairo, 1944, p. 108.
[4] E. G. Aristotle, Met. 1015 a, 32 ; Epictetus, Dissert., 11, 2.

GEORGE SEFERIS

authority is not only non-human, but superhuman in the sense
that while there is purpose in it, this purpose can never be subject
to human influence and so can only be obeyed and submitted
to and endured as a soldier must submit to and obey and endure
the orders of a superior rank. " I think," writes Seferis, " of that
mechanism of justice which demonstrates this interchange of
Hubris and Ate and which may not only be a moral law but even
a physical law. A hundred years before (Aeschylus), the Milesian
Anaximander believed that things pay with destruction the injustice they do when they transgress the order of time. And later
Heracleitos: " The sun will not transgress his measures; otherwise the Furies, ministers of Justice, will find him out."[1] And a
" mechanism of justice " which is a " physical law " is surely just
that impersonal device which allows one to wash one's hands
with assumed innocence before the crowd; which allows one to
take up the Odyssean attitude to fate of which I have spoken.

Perhaps what I am trying to say here can be expressed in
another way. The attitude of recollection is above all one of
passive receptivity—" be still and know "; it is one of extreme
attention and humility before the " facts " of the interior world.
If this attitude, positive from that point of view, is taken up also
before the " facts " of the external world, then it becomes negative
and crippling. The greatest have always managed to confer a
positive sense upon even what appear to be the most " evil " and
" non-spiritual " processes of life, and in so doing have established a personal and positive relationship with them. They have
been able to see that fate is not simply an exterior and absolute
power in the universe, but is a direct consequence, a reflection
of man's own condition. The world is a direct consequence of
what man has been and is. The force which destroys Odysseus'
companions is another aspect of that which makes possible his
return to Ithaca. Each is involved in what happens to all, what
happens to all is what happens to each. It may even be that such
a thing as personal salvation on the lines of Odysseus, and, it
might be added, as it has been envisaged in the Christian era,
is not possible; either we are all ultimately saved or no one is.
Be that as it may, the attitude which leads one to see in fate and
the destructive forces of life only the workings of an impersonal

[1] Seferis, A Letter on the " Thrush," *op. cit.,* p. 505.

209

and superhuman power and so to a sense of helplessness, irresponsibility and passive endurance, is a negative one. It is, of
course, also an artistically effective one, for our contemplating its
expression in a work of art allows us to give to our own feelings
of resignation, " suffering " and incapacity, a sort of reflected
glamour which is not, as I said, without a certain attractiveness.
Seferis has, one hopes, many years of creative life still to come.
One supreme task at least still awaits him, and that is to integrate,
in a more positive sense than it seems he has yet been able to,
the " destructive element " to his total understanding of life.

In writing as I have been of Seferis' poetry, it is difficult not
to give the impression that I am dealing with abstract ideas and
attitudes and not with an experience of life. To isolate themes
and problems as I have done may be helpful if it leads to a
deeper understanding and appreciation of the poetry, and the
critic who does not take upon himself the responsibility of saying
what a poet's communication is, will tend to become a grammarian among critics. On the other hand, a critic who does
nothing but this may treat something as a work of art simply
because he has been able to find a meaning in it and has forgotten
to ask whether the artist has been able to translate this meaning
adequately into the material of his art. To the best of his ability,
a critic should always be testing the one aspect of his task against
the other, without at the same time confusing them. This process
of testing may well go on in the critic's workshop before he begins
to write. It is for this reason that when he does begin to write,
and to discuss ideas and significances, it often seems to the reader
as if he had left out of account the nature and the value of the
poetry. It is important to remember this when we consider the
figure of the woman in Seferis' poetry. We are not setting out
to discover what opinions Seferis has about women. We are trying
to perceive what part woman has in that experience of life of
which the poetry is the expression.

It is in " Song of Love " that the figure of the woman makes
its first important appearance in Seferis' poetry. This poem was
written before " The Cistern," and, as far as technique is concerned, belongs to the same order and suffers from many of the
same faults ; it aspires, that is, to be a " pure poetry," and is not,
as his later poetry is, sufficiently actualised. Its theme is the

recollection of an experience of physical love and the significance of that experience, its place in the wider setting of man's individual destiny. It is from the point of view of this wider setting that the poem opens. The poet, the narrator, is outside the experience ; he is looking at the experience with the eyes of an understanding which has perhaps been given to him only because he has suffered the experience itself. The woman is not simply the physical creature whose love brought such strange shifts to birth within him ; she is also the emblem of fate, of that personal fate which like the daimon of Socrates stands behind the life of each one of us. It is this fate which seeks to enter into our lives, to wound us into an awareness of what we are, and to reveal to us our destiny. Her instrument and incarnation is the physical woman whom she sends as, so to speak, a priestess of the mysteries into our lives. The sudden appearance of the woman is at the same time the rising of fate's wheel ; it is the sudden introduction of a new element into us which transforms all creation, brings it to life in a way in which it never was before, and reduces the world to a marvellous facility, to " a simple vibration " [33].

The poet now turns to recall the history of this particular love with this particular woman who entered into his life, filled it with such intoxication, and then sunk out of it again, strange bearer of supernatural tidings which the passing of time threatens to obscure, to cover with prosaic ordinariness :

Secrets of the sea are forgotten on the shore
darkness of the depth is forgotten in the foam . . .
[33]

Only in memory can that intoxication be brought to life again, that moment when he first touched " the tree with its apples " and the world changed into an idyllic paradise. For the passing of time itself, merciless and indifferent, has brought all that great glory to an " ash and a dizziness." At the moment when two lives seemed about to attain some happiness and completion beyond the bounds of time, fate showed her other face, that of destruction, and brought to a halt what she had in the first place set in motion.

But in the memory, in the " fullness of silence," the " sleepless presence " wakes, the image of the lost human creature, the beloved woman, raises her head, words which fired the blood are spoken again, rich hair drops down in profuse sensuality. Then the eyes lower; she seems lying in calm and gentleness, embalmed, and she speaks of that love which is now past; how it was as if, with the flowering of their two bodies, flocks of pigeons came down and the stars were a human touch on the breast. The complaint of the world only now and then forced itself in on their happiness; the twin-branched word of passion ruled alone—the passion of lover and beloved united in one flesh—and release came from the violent "rattle of the wind," the world's hysteria. Then the "sleepless presence" falls back into the silence, and in the mirror of the fleeting world this love slowly vanishes and is lost in "the lull of a new embrace." From it may be born with time "the statue," the work of art which rises from the distillation of memory. But the bodies themselves will have dissolved "into sea, into wind, into sun, into rain." For such is the fate of splendours which nature gives us: the wheel turns, and in the place of happiness opens the wound of lament:

> Where is the two-edged day that transformed everything?
> Is there no river full for us?
> Is there no sky to drop dew
> for the soul lulled and fed by the lotus?
> [37]

Only in memory does the rhythm of that revelation brought through the physical love of woman persist, a distant vibration far up in the stretches of night.

Yet it is precisely here, Seferis would seem to suggest, that this same physical love achieves its meaning. The woman, the embodiment of fate, is an initiator, a priestess of the mysteries. She is the Ariadne whose love allows the hero to come face to face with his individual destiny, even if in obedience to that destiny he will later abandon her. For it is through contact with her, in moments of sexual passion, that the normal everyday world is overcome, time is cut in two, and man has glimpses into a world whose presence he has not before even suspected. Through his physical experience of love with woman, man becomes aware of a new level of reality; her beauty calls back into consciousness his latent memory of a deeper beauty. But here is the fatal element in such love. For while on the one hand man becomes aware of a richer life, yet on the other hand his experience of it is limited to the brief moments of sexual union and in any case is dependent upon a mortal creature whose companionship sooner or later he is bound to lose. Hence he is vulnerable to a degree which threatens to make the possession of his new awareness a torture and a mockery. Is it possible that those moments of illumination, that are his at times of love and that confer on his life such heightened beauty, can so easily and so eternally be taken from him ? Is the whole meaning of love in which man does seem to partake of a more generous existence, really exhausted in what is after all no more than the privilege of the most earth-bound animal ? Or is there not, even in that vibration which those moments leave in the memory, a significance of greater import ? Is it not that this love is a summons to man to recognise that the possibilities of his life are greater than he thought, and that this was the knowledge that woman was sent to give him ? She is the means through which he wakes to a sense of his own true nature. By rousing in man moments of unworldly bliss, she in fact reminds him of a lost other world that lies buried in the depths of himself. Once he has grasped this, then he will also understand that the key to his salvation lies in his own hands ; he must recover through his own efforts that lost other world of which he is now aware, so that his experience of it is not limited to brief moments nor dependent upon another mortal creature. And here we are back where we first started our discussion of Seferis' poetry: it is through his experience of the woman that man not only becomes aware of another world within him, but also receives the command to recover that world, to undertake that pilgrimage of recollection, recollection in a more than natural sense now, of which I said Seferis' poetry is a record. For it was after the experience expressed in "Song of Love" that Seferis wrote "The Cistern," that invocation and evocation of a hidden indwelling form at the heart of life, of a mysterious presence, of a Holy Mother.

Thus the woman unites in herself two aspects in Seferis' poetry. On the one hand, she is the sensual earthly creature, the daughter of Eve, Aphrodite Pandemos, in union with whom man achieves an awareness of life and of himself of which before he was ignorant, he gazes for brief moments upon the stars and

P

feels the world as a simple vibration. But this experience itself may, through its very transience, bring only bitterness and dis-enchantment. Only if it is grasped in its deeper sense, as a revel-ation of an obscured world within him, the recovery of which constitutes his true destiny, does the second aspect of woman become evident: the image and earthly counterpart of the eternal feminine, Aphrodite Urania, the Holy Mother who is the real object of man's love, the true figure of that destiny which entered his life at birth—

> *Figure of dark-shawled destiny over a child's cradle*
> *inexplicable smile and lowered eyelids and breast white*
> * like milk—*
> [197]

and which follows him, however he may obscure it, through all his years.

These then, are the two aspects of the part woman plays in the experience of life which Seferis' poetry conveys. The poet fuses them in an epigrammatic HaiKai:

> *Naked woman*
> *the pomegranate which broke was*
> *full of stars.*
> [100]

Yet here again is the twist of ambiguity and contradiction that gives Seferis' poetry much of its dramatic tension. For if man seeks to follow the destiny of which the first, the earthly sensual woman, has made him aware, then it is precisely this same woman who may be the great obstacle to his progress. For she may then become a Circe whose whole boudoir of enchantment is thrown open in an effort to hold back the hero whose real task demands that he leave her and begin his journey to the bodiless kingdom of the dead.

The experience of nature which Seferis' poetry expresses presents us with another of those contradictions so difficult, if not impossible, to explain rationally. How, for instance, can the world known by the senses, the visible world, be both changing and perishable, and yet at the same time be part of an unchang-ing, incorruptible reality? For this is how it seems to be revealed to us in Seferis' poetry. On the one hand, nature is a blind, destructive, and altogether godless thing, without meaning or goal, alien and indifferent to man and to man's destiny, an endless succession of circles whose total addition comes to nothing. She is " the powerful east wind which maddens us on winter nights " [49] ; it is her greed which devours the Argonauts, the " good lads," who strove so faithfully with the hero in his quest for the golden fleece ; she is the south wind which " strops upon our nerve a razor " [56] ; she is the inexhaustible, bitter sea whose malignancy Odysseus fought for so many years ; she is the " insatiable earth " [201], the " embroidered net " [206] in which man is tangled and from which he struggles to free himself ; she is even the nameless horror which " drips into day, drips into sleep " [219]. In short, she is the fatum, whose purposeless and unremitting course, the " yellow current " of birth, growth, decay, and death, is the despair of the poet who, as on some ancient site he contemplates the ruin she has made of what once was a " living existence," feels the impossibility of any love or of any life which is not eternally doomed :

> *And the poet loiters looking at the stones and asks himself*
> *Do they exist*
> *between these destroyed lines, the edges, the points, the*
> *hollows, the curves*
> *do they exist*
> *here where the passing of rain, wind and ruin conflict*
> *do they exist, the face's movement, the shape of tenderness*
> *of those who so strangely have shrunk within our life*
> *of those who are shadows of waves and thoughts with the*
> *boundlessness of the ocean —*
> *or perhaps no, nothing is left but the burden*
> *ache of the burden of a living existence*
> *where we now unsubstantial wait bending*
> *like boughs of the terrible willow-tree piled up in the*
> *continuity of despair*
> *while slowly the yellow current draws down reeds rooted*
> *up from the mud*
> *image of a form petrified with the finality of an eternal*
> *bitterness . . .*
>   [191]

On the other hand, this same godless destructive power is a temple of living presences; it is through her forms that man achieves occasional and sudden glimpses into a hidden world which fill his life with meaning and grace. At these times that duality between the invisible and the visible disappears, and the visible becomes the actual embodiment of the invisible and part of its timeless, unchanging existence. Seferis' poetry is full of these sudden glimpses, these sudden acts of perception which seem to tear the veil apart and reveal nature as the very landscape of our own inner being:

Now how at last with that light those mountains content me
with skin wrinkled like the elephant's belly
when his eyes shrink with age.
Now how these poplars content me, they are not many
raising their shoulders into the sun.
The tall hill-dwellers and the short valley-dwellers
summer with the sickle and winter with the axe
the same again and again, the same movements
on the same bodies . . .

[161]

Or in a poem entitled " Epiphany, 1937 ":

I climb the mountains; dark ravines; the snow-covered
plain, snow-covered plain to the horizon, nothing
does time in a dumb ruined chapel ask nor
hands stretched in appeal, nor the roads.
I have preserved my life whispered in boundless silence
I no longer know how to speak or to think; whispers
like the breath of the cypress trees that night
like the human voice of the night sea on pebbles
like the memory of your voice saying " happiness."
I close the eyes seeking the secret meeting-place of the
*   waters*
beneath the ice the sea's smile the closed wells
groping with my veins for those veins which escape me
there where the water-flowers end and that man
who walks blindly across the snows of silence.
I have preserved my life, with him, seeking the water
*   which touches you*
heavy drops on green leaves, on your face

216

in the empty garden, drops in the motionless reservoir
finding a swan dead in its white wings,
living trees and your eyes staring.

[145-146]

Or in another sustained passage:

And we travelled between island-shores bare like strange
fish-bone on the sand
and the whole sky was a big pigeon's wing with a rhythm
of silence, empty white,
and the dolphins beneath the coloured water darkened
quickly like the soul's movements,
like movements of imagination and the hands of men who
fumble and kill each other in sleep
in the huge rind of sleep which wraps us uncut, common
to all of us, our common grave
with shining microscopic crystals broken by the moving of
snakes.
And yet all was white because the great sleep is white and
the great death —
calm peace alone in a boundless silence.
And the cackling of the guinea-hen at dawn and the cock
which crowed jumping into a deep well
and fire on the mountain-side raising handfuls of smoke
and leaves of autumn
and the ship with its forked shoulder-blades more tender
than the embrace of our first love
were things isolated beyond even the poem
which remained when with its final word you fell heavily
ignorant of anything further among the white eyeballs of
the blind . . .

[185-186]

These passages, and many others like them, go beyond a mere description of nature. It is as if the poet has found a new method of speech, not any longer that of words, but that of plastic images. As Seferis himself has said, when speaking of Greek poets, the disembodied word is something " which surpasses our powers."[1]

How is it, then, that nature in Seferis' poetry, as in Solomos'

[1] Seferis, Letter to an Englishman on Eliot, Anglo-Greek Rev., Vol. 4, No. 1, Jan.-Feb., 1949.

poetry, is presented as an external object, indifferent if not hostile to man in his struggle for realisation, and at the same time as the very landscape of our inner being, the soul's living garment ? The clue to the understanding of this seeming contradiction would seem to be found in the poet's understanding of man himself. Paradox that it may sound, what nature is would seem to depend on what man is. Seferis would seem to agree with Heracleitos that " The eyes and ears are bad witnesses for men who have barbarian souls,"[1] for he seems to imply that the more man purifies his inner nature, the more he will purify his perception of outer nature. Nature is in fact a kind of reflex, a kind of reflection of man's inner world. As man, through his own process of self-realisation, uncovers ever-deeper layers of reality within himself, so at the same time does he uncover ever-deeper layers of reality in nature. If he achieves total realisation, there will in fact be a new heaven and a new earth. It is on man's own personal degree of realisation and self-knowledge that everything in the end depends.

Thus we return to the point at which we left the " pilgrim of recollection " at the end of " Mythistorima," at the moment when, on his journey towards life, he sets out for the dead ; we take up again, that is, the most important and most recurrent theme of Seferis' poetry, that of death. What does this journey to the dead, this insistence on the theme of death, signify ? Obviously it is not simply a morbid preoccupation with physical death, though the awareness of physical death may well be part of this other dying. Again it is Plato who may put us on the right track, when he says that those who study philosophy correctly study nothing but dying and being dead.[2] What is signified by such dying and death is a process of detachment from the false, superficial selfhood, that which makes the eyes and ears bad witnesses, in order to recover possession of the deeper self when all can be seen in its proper light. It is as if man, looking into a mirror, mistook the image of himself in it for his real self, a kind of Narcissus' intoxication. That, Seferis seems to imply, is what we all do ; we take for real our mirror-selves and forget our true selves ; we die to our true selves and

---

[1] Heracleitos, Fra. 107 in Diels, Die Fragm. der Vorsokr., *op. cit.*
[2] Plato, Phædo, 67, D.E.

" live " as our mirror-selves. Our task is to reverse the process and die to our mirror-selves to live as our true selves. " Each Man is in his Spectre's power," wrote Blake:

> Each Man is in his Spectre's power
> Until the arrival of that hour
> When his Humanity awake
> And cast his own Spectre into the Lake.[1]

As we saw, man, in his Humanity, to use Blake's term, lives on that plane of reality which in some sort corresponds to the kingdom of the dead, for it is on this plane, that of universal truth, that all the revelations which reach us through the lives and creative works of men of genius have their timeless and undying origin. Man's process of realisation is at once a dying to his mirror-self, his spectre, and a waking to this realm of origin, his true humanity. In that death man begins to recollect those things, the memory of which he had lost in the present life. It is precisely this dying that is man's life:

> But each earns his death, his own death, which belongs to
> no one else,
> and this game is life.
> [176]

It is also precisely this dying that man is so reluctant to undertake; he prefers his mirror-self, his spectre of illusion, to the ever-present but obscured truths of his humanity. It is important to remember that this humanity, man's knowledge of his true nature, is something which can be possessed here and now. Seferis is not positing some beyond-the-tomb beautitude. It is vision and understanding in this life that is within man's grasp if only he would make the adjustments in himself necessary to perceive them.

What are these adjustments ? " The soul, if she wishes to know herself, must look at a soul." Man, that is, must strip himself bare of all the accretions of time and place with which his inner being is smothered, even of those romantic regrets, so powerful in Greece, for:

> ces époques nues
> Dont Phoebus se plaisait à dorer les statues.[2]

---

[1] Blake, op. cit., p. 108.   [2] Baudelaire, Les Fleurs du Mal, 5.

Such regrets obstruct vision, prevent the clear look into the dark
waters of the inner world; they must be forgotten, dismissed:

> Bend if you can to the dark sea forgetting
> the flute's sound on naked feet
> which trod your sleep in the other, the submerged life.
>
> [81]

Man must free himself "from the faithless time, and sink" [82].
He must penetrate into the deeper strata of his being, into those
foundations of himself where voices of the "other time," the
timeless time, speak:

> Voices from stone from sleep
> deeper here where the world darkens
> memory of struggle rooted in rhythm
> which beat earth with feet
> forgotten.
> Bodies sunk into the foundations
> of the other time, naked.
>
> [84]

In the end, he must go beyond time altogether, beyond history,
must descend to "the land that is no-where,"[1] to the "substance-
less image that existed before the Ancestor[2]:

> And the King of Asine whom we seek for two years now
> unknown, forgotten by everyone, even by Homer
> only one word in the Iliad, and that uncertain
> flung here like a gold funeral mask.
> You touched it, do you recall its sound? hollow in the light
> like the dry jar in the dug earth;
> the same sound as our oars make in the sea.
> The King of Asine an emptiness under the mask
> everywhere with us everywhere with us, under one name:
> "Asinin te . . . Asinin te . . ."
>   and his children statues
> and his desires a fluttering of birds and the wind

---

[1] Cited on p. 59 of Wilhelm, R., and Jung, C. G., The Secret of the
Golden Flower, London, 1945.
[2] The Way and its Power, trans. Waley, London, 1942, p. 146.

in the spaces of his thought and his ships
anchored in a vanished port :
under the mask an emptiness.
[189-190]

Here at last is the realisation of that freedom from time, that penetration into the depths of detachment which from the point of view of all spectre-life and time-thought can only be seen as non-existence, emptiness, but which are really the ground of existence itself, the nameless actuality of which Seferis first spoke in " The Cistern," the kingdom of the dead which is at the same time the land of the living. It is now, and now only, that soul can look into soul, man know himself and what is divine in himself, his humanity awake, and a new sky and a new earth appear.

Thus it is that death is not something opposed to life. On the contrary, life is inseparable from death ; it at once affirms death and is consummated by death. In the midst of life we are in death and in the midst of death we are in life. " Aye on the shores of darkness there is light," as Keats expressed it.[1] One must die to be, or, rather, one must die to become. Life can only be fulfilled in accepting this contradiction. True existence begins, one might say, at the point where everything coincides, life and death, inner and outer, subject and object. It is like the river :

The long river which comes down from big lakes closed
deep in Africa,
which once was God and later became a route and a giver
and a judge and a delta ;
which, as the ancient wise-men taught, is never the same,
yet is always the same body, the same bed, the same Sign,
the same orientation . . .
[204-205]

It is :

This meaning which goes forward between plants and
grasses
between animals which graze and drink and men who sow
and harvest

[1] " Sonnet to Homer," p. 312, Oxford Ed. of Standard Authors, 1951.

between big tombs and small dwellings of the dead.
This current which pursues its course and is not so different
    from the blood of man
from man's eyes when without fear in his heart he looks
    straight ahead
not anxious about trivialities or even about important
    matters;
when he looks straight ahead like the tramp who measures
    his road by the stars . . .

[205]

It is in this reconciliation of opposites that man achieves his destiny, gathering together the scattered portions of his being in complete and undivided integrity.

All these themes and problems, the whole of this "pilgrimage of the soul," are recapitulated and consummated in the last poem Seferis has so far published, "Thrush." "Thrush" was the name of a ship sunk during the 1939-45 war off the island of Poros, where the poet was staying when he wrote the poem. The hero of the work, the protagonist in whom the drama unfolds, is, Seferis tells us in a published letter on the poem,[1] a kind of Odysseus. After many adventures and misfortunes, after the cyclops, after the restless Æolean isle, home of the winds, after the Laestrygones who harpooned his men like fish, Odysseus arrives at the palace of Circe. "It is the first luxury he finds: the warm bath, careful attention, rich food, the high bed and the body of a beautiful woman. It is soft, this house: it turns his companions not already lost into swine. Odysseus enjoys the voluptuousness; to what point and how he enjoys it we don't know, because he has other things in mind: his own home. Let us call his own home 'the light.'"[2]

In this atmosphere, then, Odysseus day dreams. He muses on the strange personality of houses, how they have their own life which somehow corresponds to human life, and like man are full of memories and desires. This particular house of Circe brings into mind a scene of old women murmuring with quiet

[1] Letter on the "Thrush," *op. cit.*
[2] *Ibid.*, p. 501.

222

voices as they dress someone in robes of black and white, of death and marriage—someone who comes to say farewell:

> *Sometimes, close to the sea, in bare rooms*
> *with an iron bed and nothing of my own*
> *watching the evening spider, I think to myself*
> *that someone prepares to come, that they adorn him*
> *with white and with black robes, jewels of many colours*
> *and round him dignified women murmur—*
> *grey hair and dark shawls—*
> *that he prepares to come to say farewell to me . . .*
>
> [224]

It is the image of Elpenor, who is to appear later in the poem. Here, though, he has something of an aspect of a ritual figure, of an Adonis whose death is the prelude to the secret marriage, to the putting on of a new and more splendid robe.

Now, interrupting this reverie, Circe, emblem of sensual pleasure, of the instinct and desire of the senses, passes before the eyes of Odysseus. She, wrapped in concern for her own immediate sensual gratification, has no regard for those invisible presences of another world, the dead who sleep "under the stairs" [224] of the sensory world and whose influence now begins to stir in the mind of the hero, reminding him that it is time for him to set out on his journey to their kingdom. With the stirring of this new desire to depart for his true home, the light, the house of Circe begins to oppress the hero. He becomes restless. Yet, as we saw when discussing the figure of woman in Seferis' poetry, it is the woman, Circe herself, who rouses the hero to this longing to relinquish the sensory world and realise his deeper nature. Seferis comments on this significance that in the "Odyssey," Odysseus sets out for the other world from Circe's isle: "Sometimes these old texts hide limitless understanding. Take Circe: the senses of the body, our sensuality, send us to the other world, to the dead, to show us the way to return home. And, truly, what we call eroticism does have bearing, as many things show, on the longing and struggle of man for perfect liberation, which some call return to a lost Paradise and others union with God."[1] It is at this point, with the longing for departure roused in the hero, that the first part of the poem closes.

[1] *Ibid.*, p. 504.

The second part of the poem is largely a conversation between Elpenor, the lazy, sensual common man, and Circe. They appear beneath the window of the hero:

I saw him yesterday standing at the door
beneath my window; somewhere about
seven o'clock it was; a woman was with him.
He had the look of Elpenor, a little before he fell
and smashed himself, but he was not drunk.
He spoke very rapidly, and she
gazed distractedly towards the gramophones;
sometimes she interrupted him to say a word
and then she looked impatiently
there where they were frying fish: like a cat.
He whispered with a cigarette stub between his lips.

[225]

Elpenor tries to speak to Circe of the love of bodies. He talks of the statues—an image Seferis often uses for the body—which " sway in the moonlight sometimes like the reed between living fruits " [225]; of the night which " opened, blue pomegranate, dark breast, and filled you with stars " [225]. By such indirect suggestions he hopes to excite Circe, to persuade her to love. Here the presence of Elpenor in some sense suggests the romantic dream of the false paradise, that of sensual enchantment and bliss, when:

L'homme et la femme en leur agilité
Jouissaient sans mensonge et sans anxiété,
Et, le ciel amoureux leur caressant l'échine,
Exerçaient la santé de leur noble machine.[1]

He is the voice playing on the body's fears of the passing of its beauty and urging it not to waste the few years it has for pleasure:

Now therefore, while the youthful hew
Sits on thy skin like morning dew,
And while thy willing Soul transpires
At every pore with instant Fires,
Now let us sport us while we may . . .[2]

[1] Baudelaire, *op. cit.*
[2] Marvell, " To His Coy Mistress," p. 27, The Poems and Letters of Andrew Marvell, Oxford, 1927, Vol. 1.

Circe, however, her mind filled with Odysseus and sick at the thought that he is about to leave her, has no time for the second-rate Elpenor. She cuts him short. The statues, she tells him, are in the museum, and she turns her back on him. Elpenor, rebutted, becomes vicious. His next words are no longer an invitation to love. They speak instead of the other side of that eroticism which Circe embodies, its devouring inhuman greed and cruelty, its rottenness. Again as Marvell puts it:

> Like an Enchantress here thou show'st,
> Vexing thy restless Lover's Ghost;
> And, by a Light obscure, dost rave
> Over his entrails, in the Cave;
> Divining thence, with horrid Care,
> How long thou shalt continue fair;
> And (when inform'd) them throw'st away,
> To be the greedy Vultur's prey.[1]

Here Circe, who understands perhaps the drift of his words and knows their truth, dismisses Elpenor altogether, and goes down to the beach from which Odysseus has set sail. The second part of the poem ends with a song which comes over the wireless on the beach, such a song as Circe might " sing at her loom after the departure of Odysseus, to beguile her grief."[2]

These two first parts of the poem, written in an almost prosaic language, are, it must be admitted, not very satisfactory. One is in an allegoric world whose burden has only been made more lugubrious by the author's lengthy explanations of what it is about. But in any case, these parts are only introductory, leading into the third and most important part of the poem, where the poetry recaptures the vitality that they lack. The third part opens with the voice of Elpenor, heard now for the last time as he surrenders the green branch of the senses:

> This branch which has cooled my forehead
> at hours when noon fevered the veins
> will flower in other hands. Take it, I give it you . . .
>
> [229]

The hero hears the voice as he gazes at the sea trying to make

---

[1] Marvell, op. cit., p. 30, " The Gallery."
[2] Seferis, A Letter on the " Thrush," op. cit., p. 504.

out the hull of a ship which has been sunk there a few years before, the " Thrush." It is the black ship with which Odysseus makes his journey to the dead, it is that memory by means of which man travels to his inner depths, it is those inner depths themselves, the silent indwelling presence at the heart of things whose influence reaches up even to the surface of life:

> The masts
> broken, wave crookedly in the depths, like tentacles
> or the memory of dreams, showing its hull—
> dull mouth of some huge dead sea-monster
> sunk in the water . . .
>
> [229]

All round an utter calm spreads ; the earth is still, the sea is still, the air is still, it is that total quiet in which the soul, at rest with the body and with the world about, can behold the other soul, can hear the voices of the dead, of the long sleepers, the mother's voice, that of old friends, of old heroes, speaking into the silence, asking for that drop of blood to drink which will allow them to communicate with this new hero, this Odysseus:

> And other voices slowly in their turn
> followed : low thirsty whispers
> coming out of the other side of the sun, the dark side :
> it seemed they sought a drop of blood to drink ;
> they were known, but I could not distinguish them.
> And the voice of an old man came . . .
>
> [229]

It is the voice of Teiresias: " It is the return sweeter than honey you seek, Odysseus ; it will be hard, as the god wishes." But the voice of Teiresias gives place to that of Socrates, the just man, who, speaking of his own death—" And if you condemn me to drink poison, I thank you "—encourages further this living suppliant to dare that final bound which separates him from union with the source of life and with the universe. And it is significant that for this final act, the figure of the hero himself changes and becomes no longer that of an Odysseus, but that of the blind Œdipus, the Œdipus of the closing scene of Œdipus Coloneus.

The poem now reaches its climax, the revelation of " the light." By way of introduction to it—for it is not easy to grasp the significance it concentrates—I will quote from an unpublished diary kept by the poet during the time when the poem was in gestation:

JUNE, SUNDAY—KINETTA WOOD

"Ce que nous sommes, Dieu seul pourra le completer."[1] Impossible—since it means nothing—for me to use the word "beauty" or the word "nature" when speaking of the face of Attica.

Dialogue between man (myself, o altra cosa) and man (a god) —this incessant exchange between sea, light, colour, and air.

The mountains, one between the other, are bodies embracing each other, overflowing the one into the other, they advance and they complete you. This astonishing thing *happens*. The same with the sea, the same with the light.

Impossible to speak of this revelation more clearly. From now on it does not matter whether you are a person or not, or: the person is not any longer *you*, the person is *there*. If you can, you complete it. If you can, you perform a holy task.

Expansion of the soul into this other world. A terrible abyss in front of you until you experience, like a murder, the contraction of the soul. How to cross this abyss.

Unbearable painful silence.
Black and angelic Attic day.

TUESDAY

. . . The sea, the mountains dancing without movement, I find them also in those waving tunics (of the statues then being unburied after the war in the Archæological Museum of Athens), marble water around breasts and sides of those headless fragments. And this means nothing and I know that all my life I shall never be able to express what I want to say, these many days now—the union of nature with the simple human body . . .

MONDAY

. . . There is a drama of blood which summer plays between the light and the sea, here, around us. It is not a drama of the

[1] Cf. Hölderlin: "Was hier wir sind, kann dort ein Gott ergänzen."

sense, it is something very much deeper than known desire. . . . There is a drama of blood much more organic (body and soul) which he will perceive who perceives that behind the grey and gold woof of the Attic summer exists the *terrible black* . . ."

What Seferis is trying to describe here is a visionary experience of considerable complexity. It seems that at the moment of vision, the soul, or man's inner being, expands in an embrace which infolds all Nature. Only Nature is no longer merely that Nature of which our senses tell us. Nature is now a theophany, *Natura naturans*, the living *body* of the god, of the divine Man, whom man, the individual, must complete if he can, just as the god will also complete him. There is a mutual infolding in which the one completes the other. The contraction of man back to his individual selfhood, the disunity of the individual selfhood and the Other, is like a murder, the sudden destruction of both partners. But in the vision itself, the human body is recognised as part of the body of the divine Man, as part of this whole creation which is the body of the divine Man ; the tunic of the statue—again Seferis is using the statue as the image of the human body—is a part also of mountain and sea and light:

> *The doric tunic*
> *which your fingers touched and it swayed like the mountains*
> *is a marble in the light, but the head is in the dark.*
>
> [230]

All is an aspect of a single reality, of this divine Man of whom what is visible is the body, but whose head, whose ground and source that is, is hidden and invisible, the " terrible black." The whole Man, visible and invisible, is the divine Humanity.

At this point, it is worth while to quote some lines of Blake which describe a vision in many ways similar to that of Seferis. Blake's vision also takes place by the sea, and it is also a vision of the light in which everything is perceived as a divine Man, who, as Seferis also experienced, begins to infold him, purging away all that is dross in him:

> *Over Sea, over Land*
> *My Eyes did Expand*
> *Into regions of air*
> *Away from all Care,*

Into regions of fire
Remote from Desire;
The Light of the Morning
Heaven's Mountains adorning;
In particles bright
The jewels of Light
Distinct shone and clear.
Amaz'd and in fear
I each particle gazed,
Astonish'd, Amazed;
For each was a Man
Human-form'd . . .

Then, as the eyes of vision expand still further, all these human-formed particles appear as a single unity, as one Man:

My Eyes more and more
Like a Sea without shore
Continue Expanding,
The Heavens commanding,
Till the Jewels of Light,
Heavenly Men beaming bright,
Appear'd as One Man,
Who complacent began
My limbs to infold
In his beams of bright gold;
Like dross purg'd away
All my mire and my clay.
Soft consum'd in delight
In his bosom Sun bright
I remain'd . . .[1]

Yet it is not in the sun but behind the sun that Seferis sees the source and ground of this Humanity, in the kingdom of the dead where human life is not destroyed but is consummated and reborn. There is the deep and dazzling matrix of all, the abyss of life, the Divine Darkness that " is impervious to all illumination and hidden from all knowledge."[2] There is the fulfiller and container of all paths, the Great Sea into which all mortals

[1] Blake, *op. cit.*, p. 846-847.
[2] Pseudo-Dionysius, in Ep. ad Caium Monach.

Q

plunge as it were from the bowsprit of the world at death (the coin between the teeth of the dead person being Death's fee, and the white lekythoi, oil-flasks, those placed in the grave for that far journey):

> *And those who dive from the bowsprit*
> *go like spindles still twisting*
> *naked bodies sinking into the black light*
> *with a coin between the teeth, still swimming*
> *while the sun with golden stitches sews*
> *sails and wet wood and colours of the sea;*
> *and still slant-wise fall*
> *to pebbles of the deep*
> *the white lekythoi.*
>
> [230-231]

There, in the deep, in the blackest of the black, is the mysterious and silent presence, the Great Mother of Rebirth, Creatrix, of whom Seferis had first spoken in "The Cistern." In this final vision of the light which is at once angelic and black, in this reconciliation which embraces both the living and the dead, the visible and the invisible, man completes his journey; he crosses over, like Œdipus when the god called him, that gulf between his individual and his divine nature; his selfhood, the tyrant within him, which had kept him separate both from his deeper self, and, as a consequence, from his sense of his participation in the whole of life, is overcome, and, like Aphrodite rising from the sea, his consciousness opens to a new and more splendid world:

> *Sing, little Antigone, sing, sing . . .*
> *I do not speak to you of things past, I speak of love;*
> *dress your hair with the sun's thorn,*
> *dark girl;*
> *the heart of the Scorpion is set,*
> *the tyrant fled from within man,*
> *and all the sea's daughters, Nereids, Græae,*
> *hasten to the rising-one's irradiance:*
> *whoever has never loved, will love,*
> *in the light.*
>
> [231-232]

The revelation is given. Odysseus-Oedipus, the traveller-wanderer, returns to his home, to that recollected world of light where he knows himself and his true nature, and where a new sky and a new earth open out before him in that " perfect liberation which some call return to a lost Paradise and others union with God ":

> *And you are*
> *in a big house with many windows open*
> *running from room to room, not knowing from where to*
>   *look out first,*
> *because the pine-trees will vanish and the reflected*
>   *mountains and the twittering of birds,*
> *the sea will empty, broken glass, from north to south*
> *your eyes will empty of the light of day—*
> *how the cicadas suddenly and all together stop.*
>
> [232]

VI. The Poetry and the Myth

WE have now considered the work of five of the most
important poets of modern Greece, and have distinguished what seem to be the main features of the experience and understanding of life it communicates. The question
that arises at this point is: what, if anything, have these poets
in common ? Is it possible to discern behind their particular
qualities any shared characteristics ? Or at least, since the poetry
of Cavafis lies, for reasons which are obvious, outside the main
stream to which that of the four other poets belongs, is it possible
to discern any shared characteristics in the case of these four
other poets ? Such an inquiry has two aspects. The first concerns
the nature and type of the poetry, the way the poet operates ;
the second concerns what is said in the poetry, the imaginative
pattern it reveals. It is from the point of view of these two
aspects that the work of the four poets must now be considered
if we are to discover what, in spite of its obvious variety, it yet
has in common.

In the opening chapter of this book I said, with reference
to Solomos' later poetry and to his own attitude to his work,
something about the nature of what may be called traditional
art. Such art, it was said, is not the product of aimless "inspiration." On the contrary, it is an "imitation" of a reality which
can be known not by observation or discursive reasoning, but
only by contemplation. It is not "naturalistic." It has its origin
in a supersensual world whose forms the artist has come to understand. The artist's expression of an imitable form is born of his
wisdom, just as the forms themselves, in the Platonic sense, are
born of universal Wisdom. If images, visibilia, of natural origin
enter into the artist's work, this does not mean that thereby he
is a "naturalistic" artist, or that they are essential to his art.
They are simply the material in which the forms, or ideas, are
represented. It is with the experience of these latter that the
artistic operation begins. Only when the form, the idea, of the

233

thing to be made is known, does the artist then set about its making. The idea of the work must first be conceived within him, and it will be from this supra-individual life of the artist that the work itself will derive its vitality. Contemplation must precede the act of creation.

By contemplation what is implied is the raising of the consciousness from observation to vision, from the outward present to the inward presence. Obviously, the degree to which this can be done will depend on the capacity of the individual artist. It is the difference in the capacity of individual artists to respond to the universal truths which largely accounts for the variety of styles even within a traditional culture. It is this individual variation of styles which allows us to date and place a work if we so wish. But the artist himself is not concerned with such stylistic sequences and discriminations. Style, his way of expression, is the accident, not the essence of his art. It is only when interest shifts from essence to accident, from what is and was to be expressed to the individual idiosyncrasies of expression, that we begin to concern ourselves with differences of style and the attribution of works to a particular artist or to a particular time and place. But such concerns, as well as an impertinent curiosity about the artist's private life, only occur with the collapse of a traditional society, and the replacement of its values by that kind of exaggerated individualism which typifies, for instance, the "humanist" culture of the last few centuries.

For such a break with a traditional society took place, where the West is concerned, at the time of the so-called Renaissance. It was at this time that interest began to shift from the inner to the outer world, from the universal to the individual. This shift of interest is reflected in the course of art. With the Renaissance, art as the expression of private and individual thoughts and feelings began to take the place of art as the expression of the universal verities. We can put this another way, and say that the mental image to which the artist works, changes. He no longer thinks of himself as the servant of the Great Realities, to use Solomos' phrase, but only as a private individual with his own ideas and emotions to express. He is no longer concerned to represent in his work what eternally exists, really and unchangeably, but only what is presented to him by his own immediate and natural environment, or by his memory of it.

234

At the same time, art loses its symbolic and mythological nature. Myth is the natural language of the supra-individual world. Only in terms of those symbols and images that constitute a myth is it possible to give expression, not to that which is transient, but to that which abides through all change. Only in these terms can the inner reality of man's life be mirrored. It is important to stress this point. We have developed a tendency to treat myth in historical terms, and to forget that the reality which myth renders intelligible, and of which it partakes, is not something which varies from generation to generation, from age to age, but is what is constant behind all temporal and phenomenal events. Myth therefore is never *only* historical, and what we imply when we treat it as such is that we have lost the capacity to experience for ourselves that reality which it once and for ever embodies. The atrophy of this capacity to respond to the mythological content of great art is simply another of the consequences of that shift of interest from the inner to the outer, from vision to observation, from what always is to what fugitively passes, which indicates the nature of the break which took place in the intellectual life of Western Europe at the time of the Renaissance. Concern for what is said has given place to an æsthetic appreciation of the way of saying it, or to a preoccupation with who said it, or with the individual style in which it is said ; for the study and analysis of individuality has acquired an importance both for the artist and for the critic quite unknown to those cultures in which the merely individual and separate self is regarded as an anomaly from which deliverance is sought.

For a number of reasons which need not concern us here, Greece did not suffer in the same way that break we have just described. She had, that is, never lost her traditional roots. These roots, as we saw when discussing Sikelianos' poetry, went back through Byzantium to the great metaphysical tradition of the ancient world, in its Orphic and Pythagorean form. Of this tradition, the Greek people's tradition was a survival, fragmentary but genuine. This is not to say that Christian Byzantium played no part in the formation of the cultural life of modern Greece. On the contrary, it played a central part. Rather is it to say that in the Christian myth of Byzantine Greece were enshrined in the main the same principles as those of the Orphic and Pythagorean tradition. Only the moral bias of Christianity, the intrusion into

235

its mythology of a dualistic ethic, for which, indeed, as Nietzsche pointed out, the philosophers of classical and post-classical Greece prepared the way, divided the two traditions. And it was the qualities of thought and feeling of this traditional background that lay, at least until recently, behind the cultural development of modern Greece.

How far this is true ; how far, that is, the possession of this background has given to Greek art of the last few centuries a character closer to that which I have described as traditional than to that of the " humanist " art of the modern West, can be seen not only in the art of the simple people or of earlier masters like El Greco, but also in the work of the four poets we are now considering. A poem like Solomos' " The Free Besieged " is, in conception and so far as it is realised, a mythological work. The poet is concerned to present, through the figures of his poem, the lineaments of a supernatural drama in which individual men and women are involved. His standpoint is therefore not that of his own private thoughts and feelings, but that of supra-individual truth to which he must give expression. He is the servant of principles to which he has conformed his understanding not necessarily because he wants to, but because they are a part of a supernal wisdom which exists quite independently of his likes and dislikes, and he will fail in his duty as a poet if he does not do so. For his function as a poet, as he conceived it, is to present in his poetry an imaginative pattern through which his readers may realise the true nature of life. It is to present this pattern in such a way that its contemplation will restore to the reader an awareness of the obscured truths of his humanity. The purpose of the work is therefore strictly practical. The work is not meant only to be enjoyed ; it is meant also to proclaim an understanding. It is not meant only to proclaim an understanding; it is meant also to provide the means through which that understanding can be realised. It is an initiatory drama, a shadowing forth in images and symbols of perennial issues. That Solomos should have chosen to represent these issues in terms of a contemporary historical event is much to his credit. The poet's great achievement is to make us realise the primordial realities not as static concepts but as living actualities. It is to interpret our immediate temporal environment to us in such a way that we see it not just as a confusion of unrelated events, but as part of

a larger drama in which each action and each man and woman
has a significant rôle. From one point of view, the primordial
realities are always the same. But the world of temporal events
is in continual flux. To reveal the relationship between the one
and the other is the proper task of the poet.

The mythological nature of Palamas' work is not perhaps so
evident, especially if we are to understand by myth something
which corresponds not merely to the poet's own subjective
world, but also to an abiding reality which exists whether the
poet or anyone else is aware of it or not. If, as it seems, Palamas,
at least in the years in which he was writing his main works,
had no knowledge of such a reality, even doubted its existence
altogether, it is difficult to see how his work can be said to be
of the same type as that of Solomos. Yet it is precisely in the case
of Palamas that is revealed most clearly the extent to which an
artist's participation in a living tradition will determine the nature
of the art which he produces.

We saw that where there is a tradition the focus of interest
tends to be on the inner rather than on the outer world. Experience that comes from within is valued more highly than external
" facts." Inner presence, indeed, is felt to include outer present.
For the traditional artist, the ideas, of which his work is to be
the copy, although supra-individual, must yet, before he is able
to realise them in his work, be experienced by him. He must make
them a part of his own subjective world. He must, by contemplation, so deepen his consciousness that it conforms to the eternal
pattern of which the work is to be the likeness. In other words,
the kingdom of heaven is within. In the depths of the individual's
own subjective world the eternal ideas are revealed. It is from
this point of view that poets are most universal when they are
most profoundly subjective. When they turn their attention outward, on to the shifting scenes of the temporal world and their
own reactions to them, they become less, not more, universal.
It follows therefore that if a poet works within a tradition whose
influence induces him to value more highly his own inner and
subjective experience, than the " facts " of the external world
and his own reactions to them, then his poetry is likely to be
nearer to the kind of work I have been describing as typical of
traditional societies, than it is to other kinds ; and the further
the poet deepens his experience of his interior world, the more

likely is his work to possess the features of a traditional work, for it will be conceived under similar conditions, and hence reflect many of the same qualities. And this will be so in spite of the fact that the poet may not attribute the same ultimate significance to what he experiences.

Something like this we can say happened in the case of Palamas. So strong were the predispositions which he had, so to speak, inherited from his background and tradition, that they were effective in his poetry even in spite of the other influences with which he sought to modify, if not altogether to overlay them. Thus, Palamas' " Great Visions " are imaginings of what constitutes the poet's deepest and most personal experience, of his most intimate subjective life. But as it is within the depths of subjective life that the eternal ideas, the forms of divine wisdom, reveal themselves, it follows that what Palamas has to express will be permeated by the vitality of these ideas or forms. It is not coincidence that in areas widely separated both in time and space, and between which there can be no question of direct transmission or influence, occur works of art that embody ideas and forms of an almost, if not completely, identical nature. It is that these ideas, these forms, are archetypal. They exist, unchangeably and principially, in the depths of life itself. They are what underlie all temporal and phenomenal manifestation. Thus, they will occur and recur in works of art whenever and wherever the artist has had the creative capacity to attain to that level of consciousness, to penetrate to that depth of subjective experience, at which they become the determining forces of his life. At that level of consciousness, what man experiences will always be the same. It is only as he falls below it that his experience will begin to differ from that of other men. Thus, it is no coincidence also that the culture of the post-Renaissance West is characterised by a diversity and fickleness of styles and movements such as possibly no other culture has known. With the focus of attention increasingly directed not towards those levels of experience at which what all men experience is the same, but towards those areas where what is experienced is determined by that psychophysical nature in which all men differ, it could not be otherwise. Where Palamas' " Great Visions " are concerned, we are in fact aware of the intrusion of the poet's own nature to a degree which reduces the pure mythological quality of the

238

work. We are aware too much that the poet is himself involved, as an individual, in the central figures and episodes of the myth. At the same time and as a consequence, the myth itself often seems an invention in the sense that it represents only subjective experience and nothing more—does not, that is, correspond to that level of consciousness at which subjective experience meets and becomes one with the archetypal experience of human life, and thus ceases to be only individual and becomes universal as well. Where the two do meet, as, we shall see, in the central experience that the myth relates, Palamas is fulfilling the rôle of mystagogue and prophet which he so ardently desired to fulfil.

That the poetry of Sikelianos is of a mythological nature cannot perhaps be made more clear than it has already been made. His whole conception of his rôle as a poet and of the function of poetry, was a harking back to an understanding of them such as had been recognised among the Brahmins, among the mantic classes of ancient Gaul, by the seers and poets of ancient Ireland, in early Thrace, and also in the Greece of Pindar and Aeschylus. The poet is a messenger between the super-natural and the natural world. His art is a kind of knowledge, not a way of feeling. The artistic operation begins in the intuition of a divine reality at moments of inspired vision. The poet must prepare himself for his task by periods of withdrawal and segre-gation, and devotion to a contemplative life. How far Sikelianos fulfilled this rôle of a poet we have already seen. Even his early poetry, such as " The Visionary," is not either narrative or des-criptive in the sense usually understood by these words ; or, at least, if it is, it is descriptive of, a narration of, inner experience as it appears when translated into natural images. In fact, such terms as these cannot really be used at all, for what we have to do with even in this early poetry is a mode of understanding to which they do not apply, for this mode is rooted in actual experi-ence of which the terms of description, the natural images, are themselves an integral part. There is, in other words, a dynamic relationship in which man's own life is felt to participate in the life of nature, natural phenomena are felt to participate in human experience. This relationship is, indeed, not primary, but some-thing that is itself the consequence of a deeper realisation, that the ultimate subjective ground of individual human life and the source of life in all its various and successive manifestations, are not different; that the inner immortal self and the great cosmic power are one and the same; and that what happens in the life without is at the same time what happens in the life within. It is this realisation, implicit in " The Visionary," and the consequences that derive from it, as well as the perversions by which it is obscured, that are the subject of Sikelianos' subsequent poetry. Within nature, in natural forces, in the lives of individual men and women, Sikelianos recognised the activity of the gods. He became increasingly aware that all history is the changing configuration of spiritual forces. Thus, all history became for him symbolic, all historical events the reflection, the shadowing forth, of divine activity. And his later works were more and more concerned to show what configuration lay behind the history of his own time; to ask what errors of human action and understanding issued in what consequences; to reveal in what shape, in what mode, the gods are at work among us, and how they may be propitiated.

With the poetry of Seferis, we are again without question in a world in which the attention is turned towards the inner centre of life, away from its tumultuous flow. We may recall the opening line of Seferis' early poem, " The Cistern ": " Here, in the earth, is a cistern rooted," leading on into the poet's attempt to express his intuition of an obscure, unmanifested intelligence at the root of life. In this poem, it is true, the symbols are somewhat static; only in later poems are they given the movement and interplay essential to the flowering of myth. Or we may recall the note which Seferis appended to his first important work, " Mythistorima," and in which he indicates as clearly as he can his mythopoeic intention—he is describing why he chose the title: " Myth, because I have used in a fairly obvious way a certain mythology; History, because I have tried to express, with some connection, a situation as independent of myself as the figures of a myth-history." Thus, the central figure of " Mythistorima," its protagonist, is, as I pointed out when discussing this poem, not merely an individual belonging to a particular time and place; he is, rather, an archetypal man living out a universal human destiny in the particular historical context provided by the contemporary world. This destiny, Seferis would seem to claim, is always the same. What differs is the historical context in which it must be realised. Every generation needs its

poet to mirror for it in imaginative terms the living of this universal destiny within the particular historical situation in which
it finds itself. Thus mirrored, each generation can become aware
of it in relationship to its own individual life. The poet's task is,
we might say, twofold. He has not only to reveal to us the
great underlying fabric of the universe, its unalterable principles.
He has also to reveal to us the relationship of these principles
to the dizzying process of becoming in which we are involved.
He has not only to tell us in what is human destiny fulfilled. He
must also give us some example of how we may fulfil it. He must
not only be the visionary seer wrapt in contemplation of invisible
essences. He must also be the hierophant initiating us into the
sacred mysteries. What has to be mirrored in his poetry is always
one and the same thing. It is always the same ritual drama. If the
way in which it is mirrored varies, this is because the historical
contexts in which it has to be realised and lived, themselves
change. In settled, traditional societies, where there is little
change in environment, the way of expression may vary little
over centuries. In societies in which the environment changes
rapidly, as in the modern world, the poet's task of presenting the
same universal drama in immediate and living terms, and hence
of giving significance to the contemporary scene, confronts him
with difficulties unknown in more stable ages. Seferis, it is true,
has not so far fulfilled the two aspects of the poet's task as
Solomos and Sikelianos, for instance, fulfilled them. But a consciousness of working within a tradition where this understanding
of the poet's task is still alive, is reflected throughout his poetry,
and gives it the quality which relates it directly to that of his
predecessors.

It would seem, then, that the work of these four poets is of
the same type, and springs from an understanding of the poet's
function that is common to all of them. The poetry is, above all,
mythological. It is concerned less with the small data of sensory
observation or the memory of natural experience, than with the
inner nature of life ; less with individual vagaries of thought and
feeling than with perennial issues. In order to make intelligible
the inner nature of life as he has conceived it, the poet employs
images and symbols. These are not an " imitation " of nature, or,
as in allegories, mere transcriptions of abstract notions into a
picture language which is itself nothing but an abstraction from

objects of the sense. They are, on the contrary, copies, or like-
nesses, of that inner nature of life which the poet has conceived.
They both " half reveal and half conceal " the truths which the
poet seeks to communicate. They are reflections of these truths.
They make it possible for us to see, not indeed in its essence,
but " as in a glass, darkly," what would otherwise be lost in total
ignorance. They are fusions of the universal in the particular,
of the invisible in the visible. In other words, the poet's visibilia,
though they may be taken from his immediate environment, are
not intended to evoke mere individual and psychological associations. They are intended to reveal to us the eternal through
the temporal. The poet, through his use of myth and symbol,
seeks to give expression to certain archetypal patterns of experience and to certain universal truths in terms of the particular
time and place in which he finds himself. From this point of view,
the poetry has something of the function of a ritual drama ; and
the poet regards himself less as an individual expressing himself,
than as a mystagogue, a psychopompos, whose concern is through
his poetry to communicate an awareness of an underlying pattern
in life, the knowledge of which will help his readers towards
personal fulfilment. Such a poetry and such an understanding of
the poet's function are normal in any traditional society. That
they could arise in modern Greece is a measure of the extent to
which that country still had contact with something of a traditional nature.

We come now to a second and more difficult question. We
have seen that as far as the type of work, as far as the mental
image to which the artist works, are concerned, there are similarities between these four poets. They belong together. What we
have now to distinguish is whether there are similarities between
them, not only with regard to the way they operate, but also with
regard to what is said. In fact, as I hope I have made clear, it
would be surprising if there were not such similarities. A mythological poetry presupposes a certain definite orientation on the
part of the poet. It presupposes that his attention is directed more
towards those regions of experience where what is experienced
is the same for all men at all times and at all places, than it is
towards those regions where what is experienced differs for each

man at each time and at each place. As has been said, how these archetypal experiences are represented in the work of the poet will depend both on the historical context in which the poet is working, and on the poet's individual capacity to conform his understanding to them. But, if my thesis is correct, we should in the case of these four poets be able to discern behind the differences of style, and in spite of the idiosyncracies of the poets themselves, the same recurring imaginative pattern, the same ritual drama, reinterpreted afresh in their work. And here it must be repeated that, from the point of view adopted in this study, any such recurring pattern that we do discern is not to be explained merely in historical terms. It is not merely the result of living within a particular religious or cultural environment in which certain beliefs or ways of thought and feeling predominate. What lies behind myth, the reality of which myth partakes and which it helps to make intelligible to us, is something which always exists. It is the world of the everpresent and primordial realities, which it is the artist's concern to reveal to us in the living material of his art.

What is the pattern that occurs in Solomos' work? Already, in his early poems, we were able to distinguish the outlines of a myth that informs the whole of his later poetry. The individual, in his or her natural state, is a " fallen " creature. He or she is in the sway of passions which, if left unpurified, corrupt and in the end destroy altogether the human victim. They obscure, so that it is no longer vital and radiant, the principle of divinity in man. They obscure his knowledge of what he really is. In his natural state, this man is caught up in the world's flow, by forces of evil, which lead him to commit crimes of whose real nature he is often unaware. But he is not doomed to remain prisoner of this world or of these forces. He may, if he has the courage and the perseverence, break through them. There are divine powers in whose realisation he may find release. If he breaks through the entanglements in which as an individual he is caught, if he penetrates into the naked ground of the spirit, he will experience the touch of divinity and wake to a new life. The way of realisation is the way of sacrifice, of self-annihilation. Stripped bare of all that binds him to the world of time and place, he discovers his true nature, he knows himself. " The Free Besieged " is a paradigmatic statement of this self-divesting. Only with the conquest of the final fear, that of individual death, is self-knowledge given, is the liberation sought for actually achieved.

Here we must digress to prevent a possible misunderstanding. We must be careful not to assume that when poets like Solomos, or like the other three with whom we are concerned, posit or imply the existence of a level of reality other than that which can be seen and touched, they necessarily mean that there is another world existing alongside or parallel to this visible, tangible world, one that is just as "objective" and "factual" as this world, only in another dimension. One is here coming up against the limits of rational description. For it may be that it is quite impossible to *think* of the temporal and the eternal worlds except as two distinct worlds, both equally objective, both possessing their own sets of facts, one true in one world, the other true in the other. But it is often just this kind of conception that the poet wishes to destroy. That is why he leaves behind the categories of rational description and has resort to myth. For while it may be quite impossible to *think* of the temporal and eternal as other than two opposed but equally objective worlds, myth is able to transcend the limitations of rational categories, and to reveal to us the actual participation of the temporal in the eternal, their simultaneity not in terms of objective facts, but in terms of actual experience. While we remain at the level of consciousness on which purely rational categories have the last word, we may be bound to experience the temporal world as one thing, and to think of the eternal world, if we think of it at all, as another thing. But if we raise the level of our consciousness, so that we see from a point of view higher than that accessible to the reason, then the temporal world may appear to us in quite another light, and we may experience it in quite another way than we are able to when we allow ourselves to be dominated by rational categories. We may then experience the interpenetration of what from the lower level of consciousness appear to us as irreconcilable opposites. This experience, being supra-rational, cannot be described in terms of reason. It can only be represented in terms of myth. And we will, I think, come closer to understanding what poets like Solomos, or Palamas, or Sikelianos, or Seferis, mean when they posit or imply the existence of a supra-rational world, if we conceive it not as just another objective world existing in another dimension, but as this present world experienced not from the point of view of our normal consciousness, but from the point of view of a level of consciousness obscured for us by the purely rational categories by which for the most part we allow ourselves to be dominated. The " fall " which is implicit in the myth which these poets unfold for us would, therefore, be the obscuring of this higher level of consciousness, and our confinement in a lower level where how we see is dictated by the reason. It is this reason, for instance, which creates the illusion of our individuality—it is not coincidence that the " age of reason " of the last few centuries is also that of individualism. And the liberation these poets speak of would be a process of self-knowing through which we raise our consciousness above the categories of reason—and hence above the illusion of our individual and separate existence—and once more discover the true nature of life. That, through this rediscovery, our consciousness actually realises its divine nature and becomes one with a higher power, is something that these poets would seem to claim.

For, if we return to an examination of Solomos' myth, we find that at its heart is the imagining of a divine presence, of a feminine, maternal power, who seems to possess all the qualities of an all-seeing, eternal Wisdom. She would seem to be the source of that life which man through his " fall " loses. When the individual loses contact with this divine Wisdom, he is no longer capable of perceiving his true nature, but is led astray among the world of appearances, which he mistakes for the only reality. At the same time, through this loss, the forces of the lower world take possession of the individual, and pull him this way and that in a maze of error and vice. It may, indeed, be wrong to think of these forces as " evil," and not as themselves original divine energies compelled to act destructively and indiscriminately because, through man's " fall," they are severed from their controlling principle. Be that as it may, the " original sin " for Solomos would seem to be the eclipsing of man's true self-knowing nature by his lower nature, identified with the passions, which now becomes dominant in him, and, lacking its controlling principle, works his destruction. This lower nature Solomos also seems to regard as feminine. At its worst, it becomes the woman of Zakynthos. But at all times it is the temptress in man, the Eve-element, which seek to keep him enchained to that world of

245

R

materiality and external appearances to which alone his normal consciousness can respond.

It might be worth while at this point to try to reconstruct briefly the imaginative pattern we find in Solomos' work, in terms of Christian myth. In the beginning—which we must understand as meaning " in principle," in the ultimate source which is actually rather than temporally prior to all things—man possesses a full and self-knowing life. He enjoys the true nature of everything, from the point of view of the ideas after which all that is created, is created. He enjoys the unity of all things and their intrinsic beauty. Being at one with the source of all that is, everything is part of his own nature, there is nothing which is outside himself or in whose existence he does not participate.

Man—Adam—now falls from this paradisaical state ; he loses, that is, his full original life. He is tempted by Eve, by the passionate side of his nature which until now has been as it were a handmaid to his spiritual nature. Falling under the spell of this lower nature, he falls from the centre to the circumference. He cannot any longer realise the unity of all things ; he can only see their multiplicity. He cannot experience his oneness with everything ; he can only think of himself as a separate and independent identity among thousands of other equally separate and independent identities. He has lost the knowledge of what he really is. He mistakes the external, material aspect of things, that aspect of them which can be seen and touched, for their only aspect. At the same time, his now uncoordinated passions drive him to crime and bestiality. Love is deformed into lust, creation into destruction. He is a prisoner, besieged by violent, alien forces in a wretched and suffering world.

It is now a question of the fallen man regaining the lost full and self-knowing life which was once his. This recovery is represented in Christian myth by the birth of the divine Word, the Logos, through Mary. We can only find a parallel to this in the imaginative pattern of Solomos' poetry if we are prepared to recognise in Mary a symbol of an eternal feminine, of a " donna-Divinità," Sophia, whose celestial ray or Word lies concealed in a darkness enveloped by greater darkness ; and if, further, we are prepared to equate this ray or Word with the spiritual consciousness that man possesses " in the beginning." Then it will be by a forsaking of his ordinary self and by entering

into this dark ground of existence that the divine Word which
this ground conceals is born within man. He recovers his true
nature, which is at the same time a knowledge of what he really
is. This initiation is, in Christian myth, mirrored in Christ's
passion, his death on the cross, his entombment, and his resurrection; and although the cross as such, or any specific symbol
which may be said to replace it, does not appear in Solomos'
poetry, "The Free Besieged" does nevertheless represent much
the same action as that which Christ performed through his
passion: the freeing of man from all the ties that bind him to his
ordinary and imprisoned self, and, through this *Via Negativa,*
his entering, as Christ into the tomb, into a state of total detachment when the divine Word is again born within him; when,
that is, he recovers that full, liberated, and self-knowing life,
which was originally his:

> *From depth to depth he fell until there was no other :*
> *Thence he issued invincible . . .*

And:

> *Light flashed and the young man knew himself.*

His lost consciousness is regained, and he begins a new, resurrected life at one with the eternal Wisdom to which all moves
and in whose will is peace.

It would be unwise to push this assimilation of the imaginative pattern in Solomos' poetry to Christian myth too far, or to
claim that the interpretation which it has meant giving to the
phases of the Christian drama are necessarily orthodox. Nevertheless, it has made it possible to present a fairly coherent picture
of the phases of Solomos' pattern, and of what is signified by
them; and this, as we shall see, will be useful in tracing to what
extent the same pattern recurs in the work of the other two poets.

For, first, in the work of Palamas, although the poet lacks the
clear grasp of his myth which Solomos possessed, and although
he seems to affirm the divine only as a vast process of Becoming,
and to exclude Being from his view of things altogether, yet it is
much the same pattern that does recur. What has altered now
is the point of view from which the pattern is unfolded. As I
pointed out above, we are very much aware in the case of

Palamas that the poet himself is involved, as an individual, in a way that Solomos is not, in the central figures and episodes of the myth. The focus of attention therefore tends to be the struggles and trials of the individual in a world in which the "fall" has already taken place. We are given the picture of someone enslaved to his passions, cut off from any vital contact with a higher principle or with his fellow men, entirely ego-centred. At the same time, this individual is aware that his present state is the result of some catastrophe, some deformation of his nature: "It is something like sin, and like a fall, like a descent, like exile, loss of some paradise that he would think his life was destined to dwell in originally, a displacing on to a now barren and joyless earth. A secret affliction devours him. Remorse. Something which prevents him from ever treading firmly. A terrible powerlessness." And the drama which unfolds in Palamas' poetry is the result of the individual's longing and search to escape from his ego-pathic condition, to put an end to that tormented state which is the consequence of his "fall," and to find again that complete, refulgent life which he has somehow lost.

As in the poetry of Solomos, even, in fact, to a greater degree, woman plays a central rôle in Palamas' poetry. Moreover, in Palamas' poetry, the emphasis is more on the fleshly, carnal aspects of woman. This is to be expected. We are in the world of the "fall." Man's spiritual nature is eclipsed by his passionate nature. He is under the spell of the Eve-element. The passions, lacking any controlling principle, pull the individual towards their own fulfilment, they drag him down into that world of materiality and physical lust in which, severed as they are from that principle, they are compelled to act. But now we encounter a phase in the unfolding drama of Palamas' poetry for which there does not seem to be any exact parallel in that of Solomos' poetry. It is woman, the sensual creature, that leads the individual to liberation. We might even say that, in Palamas' myth, woman represents the cross. She has a redemptive function. Through her the individual enters into a kind of pre-natal state from which his ordinary, waking consciousness, that of his selfhood, separates him. He returns to the womb of existence, a state of darkness. He suffers a kind of death, an entombment. He descends into the underworld, into Hades, divested entirely of his normal self:

And your Soul, accursed City,
will not find rest ;
the ladder of evil it will
step by step descend,
and wherever it goes, wherever it stops,
into a worse body will it enter . . .

Until the god of love
has mercy on you,
and dawn breaks,
and deliverance summons you,
O Soul tormented by crime !
And you will hear the deliverer's voice,
you will shed the dress of evil,
and again controlled and light
you will move like the grass, like the bird,
like the breast of woman, like the wave,
and not having beneath another step
to fall lower
down the ladder of evil, —
for the ascent again to which he summons you
you will feel there blossom on you
the wings,
your great original wings !

It is the same pattern that we found in Solomos' poetry. Through this Negative Path, the *Via Negativa*, man enters the dark ground of the spirit and experiences the waking of a new life. Again, in Palamas, this dark ground is symbolised as a feminine power. In "Ascraios," she is Persephone. She is the source from which the new life is born. She confers a new insight. As in the case of Solomos, it is important to emphasise this point, that the new life experienced after the "awakening" is not that of another world remote from this world, or even a state of mystical ecstasy. It is far rather the attainment of a new level of consciousness. The old level of consciousness was that which could only think in terms of opposites, subject and object, self and not-self, ideal world and empirical world. The new level of consciousness transcends these dualities. It makes it possible to see all processes that take place in time as expressions of a single reality. It experiences the ideal world not as something set apart from the empirical world but as the very heart of it. As I said when discussing his work, Palamas went so far in his affirmation of the divinity of the perpetual stream of things, their perpetual flux, that he proclaimed a kind of pantheism. The idea of the universe as constant motion and unceasing change was always before him, a stream sustained in its flow by ever new waters. So preoccupied was he with this aspect of existence, that he seems to have failed, at least at the time of his writing of the " Great Visions," to have discerned any eternal basis, a unique original principle, behind it. Or, rather, since one must posit a principle of unity somewhere, if not at the base or in the essential nature of things, at least in their action, the principle he discerned behind it was not one of identity, of unchangeable existence, but only one of constant determination—Fate, or War—which kept everything bound to an endless chain of becoming. From this point of view, he seems to stand, as was remarked, at the opposite pole to someone like Solomos, for whom the world of flux, of becoming, seems to be largely without value and negative, and who affirms to a corresponding degree the world of eternal Being. But it may be a mistake to stress these differences too much. They may only be the consequence of trying to explain what is experienced, whereas the experience itself is much the same in both cases. That it may be so, we could perhaps conclude from the fact that the attainment of that level of consciousness at which the experience becomes possible at all, requires, as both poets evince, that we pass through a kind of death and resurrection which liberates us from our former and frustrating self.

Sikelianos would seem to evince the same condition : " The only method is death " ; and by this death he means that going beyond individuality and achievement of an all-seeing consciousness which the two other poets indicate. Man in his original state was universal. At one with the source of all that is, he radiated the inner quality of the whole of life. He was beyond all dualities, beyond such divisions as self and not-self, good and evil. He embraced male and female in his own nature, he was androgynous. Behind man's creation and the creation of the rest of the world is a cosmogonical process. In the beginning was a darkness shrouded in darkness, a primal undifferentiated abyss, the Orphic Night. This fathomless abyss of potentialities is at the root of God and of all existence. From it develops the self-conscious being of the One, which gives it existence by impressing its forms or Ideas on it. The whole world is formed by the union of being and the unformed non-being, the " Chaos " or primordial Ocean which is the source of all. The first product of being, of the self-conscious One, is the cosmic rhythm, the purposeful will which is the heart of the Divinity. Creation is the act of a purposeful will and intelligence. In the work of creation the unity of the One is polarised into two complementaries, mythically presented as the Sky and the Earth, male and female. Through the intercourse of these two elements, the masculine spirit and the feminine substance, are generated living things. All living things thus partake, are indeed the offspring, of the divine nature in its integrity. In their original state they mirror the divine nature in its integrity. Man, one such living thing but by no means exceptionally privileged, reflects in his original state the whole cosmic order ; he is universal.

From this original state man falls. His fall is not primarily of the moral order. It is an obfuscation of his intelligence. He begins to think that he is himself the source of life and light, and not their expression, their offspring. He sets himself up on a seat of false glory, his own mind divorced from its roots in the universal order. He thinks of himself as a separate and independent individual. His fall is one from unity into division. At the same time it involves the whole of creation in a fall from unity into division. It divorces it from its unifying principle. It imprisons it in the false and partial existence to which man has condemned himself.

Sikelianos represents this fall as the loss by man of contact with that transcendent and universal wisdom which he symbolises as a feminine power, as a Divine Mother, on whose sustenance depends the vitality of man's life and the truth of his understanding. Woman, or, rather, the feminine, again is at the centre of Sikelianos' imaginative world. But now the emphasis is not, as in the case of Palamas, so much on the fleshly, carnal aspects of woman, as on the supernatural aspects, on the eternal feminine. Man through his fall loses contact with this eternal feminine. He separates himself from Earth. Visible woman, the human creature, is at once evidence of his own divided state, and a reminder of his loss : she reawakes his recollection of it. The recovery of his integral and original nature demands the recovery of the lost transcendent Intelligence. The "original sin" which had as its consequence this loss was a loss of consciousness. Man ceased to realise his universal stature, himself as organ and expression of life, and began to think of himself as an independent centre of life, a separate identity. He began to think of himself as an individual. Intellectual errors create their own corresponding events. Through thinking himself to be an independent centre of life, man closed himself up in the categories of individuality. He mistook the psychophysical aspects of his nature which compose his individuality, for the whole of his nature. He became the prisoner of his psychophysical self. The recovery of his universal nature demands, then, the surpassing of the limits of individuality. It demands the surpassing of all those states which the individual mistakenly identifies with his life. From the point of view of individuality, there must be a kind of death. The living soul must be stripped free of all manifested states, of all that belongs to time and place. It must go out of its created and uncreated nature. Man must penetrate into the preontological abyss of his nature. He must descend into Hades. For in that abyss, in Hades, he attains that state of total undifferentiated potentiality in which the forms of divine Wisdom can again fill his being:

> *Ah, not even the Sulamite lay thus*
> *to give warmth to David's frozen limbs*
> *within the bed . . . as You close to me*
> *when my heart sunk down to Hades!*

Once this state has been realised ; once man has "died" to the falsities and limitations of his individual self, then the light of perfected consciousness breaks in upon him ; he realises his original and universal nature ; he is resurrected to that unity which through his fall he lost, and he radiates once more the inner quality of the whole of life.

In the case of Seferis, much the same pattern as we have found in the work of the three other poets is repeated. Indeed, in Seferis' poetry, it is perhaps more evident, more direct. From his early poem, "The Cistern," in which the poet seems to posit behind the flux of things the existence of an obscure, unmanifested intelligence, a nameless actuality behind the multifarious and fragmentary appearances of the temporal world, an indwelling presence, until the last part of "Thrush" where the compelling illumination born of this presence breaks in upon the poet's own consciousness and fills it with radiance, there is a gradual line of development. We watch the slow stages by which the protagonist of Seferis' myth, his archetypal man, moves forward towards the fulfilment of his human destiny, towards "that perfect liberation which some call return to a lost Paradise and others union with God." We see him first, bound to the wheel of becoming, swept round in the endless flow of things, yet aware that somewhere, behind all this, within all this, is that principle of identity, that mysterious Other, whose realisation is the purpose of his life. We see him gradually gather together his powers, turn away from the outside flux, in order to plunge into his own interior depths and there recover contact with the obscured source of his existence. And this journey into his own depths Seferis likens to a kind of dying. It is again the *Via Negativa*, a going beyond oneself, a detachment from all attachment, an emptying of oneself, a *nekuia*, a descent into the underworld, an entry into the naked ground beneath all the visible masks of existence, beneath even the memory of what has once known visible existence:

> And the King of Asine whom we seek for two years now
> unknown, forgotten by everyone, even by Homer
> only one word in the Iliad, and that uncertain
> flung here like a gold funeral mask.
> You touched it, do you recall its sound? hollow in the light
> like the dry jar in the dug earth;
> the same sound as our oars make in the sea.
> The King of Asine an emptiness under the mask
> everywhere with us everywhere with us, under one name:
> "Asinin te . . . Asinin te . . ."
> and his children statues
> and his desires a fluttering of birds and the wind
> in the spaces of his thought and his ships
> anchored in a vanished port:
> under the mask an emptiness.

Only at this point of emptiness and detachment is the revelation given, does the light of a new consciousness break in upon the darkened mind, and does man, knowing himself through what is divine in him, begin a full and liberated existence.

And again, in Seferis' myth, the figure of woman occupies a central position. I spoke of this sufficiently in the study on Seferis' poetry not to have to do more than briefly recall what was said there. Woman unites in herself, as she does also in Palamas' myth, two aspects. On the one hand, she is the daughter of Eve, Aphrodite Pandemos, under whose spell man falls through the loss of his spiritual nature. Yet in union with her, in moments of physical love, he experiences an intoxication which before he has not known. Time seems suspended, cut in two. His normal, every-day consciousness is displaced, he gazes upon the stars and is ravished by an unsuspected delight. But this experience, through its tantalising brevity, brings only disillusion and despair. Or it may bring only disillusion and despair. For there is a possibility —and in this, Seferis would seem to imply, lies the significance of such physical love—that the experience physical love gives will remind man of something he was in danger of forgetting: that life can be other than his normal consciousness allows him to realise; that there are realms of experience which everyday life obscures; and that these realms exist nowhere else but in himself, in the unexplored depths of his own being. Once he has grasped this; once he has become aware that within him is a world of experience which custom, habit, routine, has overlaid, and that this was the knowledge which woman was sent to give him, then can begin that pilgrimage of recollection, the stages of which constitute the recurring pattern I have attempted to describe. Thus, if woman is from one point of view the visible sign of man's declension into a world in which his true nature is eclipsed, she is from another point of view an initiator, a priestess of the mysteries, through whom he becomes aware that he possesses this nature. If she is the cross on which this true nature is cruci-fied, she is also the cross from which, casting off his selfhood, he descends into the dark, pre-natal abyss of his inner world to find once more the source of his lost life. If she is the daughter of Eve, she is also the image of a greater power, of a Magna Mater who is at the same time the Mater Dei.

Thus, then, we return to the mysterious presence that so haunts the imagination of these poets, to this Divine Nature, Sophia, Creatrix, this transcendent Intelligence beyond all ordinary knowledge and only revealed when all its veils are stripped. This it is that unites and completes the scattered and partial forms of created and uncreated worlds. This is the source of our true and original life, that which in the most intimate part of ourselves we are, and what we do not realise until we " give up the ghost," and, like the Prodigal Son, come alive again. It is this process of " coming alive again," of rebirth, and all that it involves, that is, if anything, the central theme of the poets we have been considering, it is this that is mirrored in the recurring imaginative pattern of the poetry. Yet there is one aspect of it which I have not remarked, and which for these poets is perhaps the most poignant aspect of all. For what is implicit in their myth is that while we refuse to recognise our true nature, what we also deny is precisely the original life that dwells in the depths of each of us ; and it is this life, no less than our own, that cannot be realised except and unless we, through that sacrifice of which these poets speak, deliver it from bondage.

Highgate, 1954.

Index of Proper Names *

* Proper names occurring only in poems, or in their titles, are not included.